Green Lawfare

Simon Cottle
General Editor

Vol. 30

Claire Konkes

Green Lawfare

The Strategic Use of Law in Mediatized Environmental Conflict

PETER LANG
New York - Berlin - Bruxelles - Chennai - Lausanne - Oxford

Library of Congress Cataloging-in-Publication Data

Names: Konkes, Claire, author.
Title: Green lawfare / Claire Konkes.
Description: New York: Peter Lang, 2024. | Series: Global crises and the media, 1947-2587 | Includes bibliographical references and index.
Identifiers: LCCN 2024004145 | ISBN 9781433196447 (paperback) | ISBN 9781433196478 (hardback) | ISBN 9781433196423 (ebook) | ISBN 9781433196430 (epub)
Subjects: LCSH: Lawfare. | Environmental law. | Environmental law, International. | Climatic changes–Law and legislation. | Government liability.
Classification: LCC K3585. K66 2024 | DDC 344.04/6–dc23/eng/20240129
LC record available at https://lccn.loc.gov/2024004145
DOI 10.3726/b21774

Bibliographic information published by the Deutsche Nationalbibliothek.
The German National Library lists this publication in the German National Bibliography; detailed bibliographic data is available on the Internet at http://dnb.d-nb.de.

Cover design by Peter Lang Group AG

ISSN 1947-2587 (print)
ISBN 9781433196447 (paperback)
ISBN 9781433196478 (hardback)
ISBN 9781433196423 (ebook)
ISBN 9781433196430 (epub)
DOI 10.3726/b21774

Published by Peter Lang Publishing Inc., New York, USA
info@peterlang.com—www.peterlang.com

This publication has been peer reviewed.

For my parents, Jean and George Konkes, in whose memory I still find love and good advice.

CONTENTS

LIST OF CASES

Ashgar Leghari v. Federation of Pakistan. Case No: W.P. No. 25501/2015.
Australasian Centre for Corporate Responsibility v. Santos Limited NSD858/2021 (Federal Court of Australia).
Chevron Corporation and Texaco Petroleum Corporation v. Ecuador (II), PCA Case No. 2009-23.
Commonwealth v. Exxon Mobil Corp., 489 Mass. 724.
Commonwealth v. Tasmania (1983) 158 CLR 1 (July 1, 1983).
Duarte Agostinho and Others v. Portugal and 32 Other States (2020) 39371/20.
Eco Oro Minerals Corp. v. Republic of Colombia (ICSID Case No. ARB/16/41).
Energy Transfer Equity, L.P. v. Greenpeace International, 1:17-cv-00173.
Future Generations v. Colombia (STC 4360-2018).
Gloucester Resources Limited v. Minister for Planning (2019) NSWLEC 7.
Greenpeace, Inc. v. The Dow Chemical Co., Case No. 13-CV-685 (D.C. C.A., Aug. 21, 2014).
Greenpeace Australia Ltd v. Redbank Power Co. [1994] 86 LGERA 143.
Greenpeace France, Amis de la Terre France, Notre Affaire à Tous v. TotalEnergies SE, TotalEnergies Electricité, Gaz France, Court of Paris (France).
Gunns Ltd v. Marr [2005] VSC 251.
Held v. Montana, No. CDV-2020-307 (1st Dist. Ct. Mont., August 14, 2023).
Juliana v. United States, 947 F.3d 1159.
Luciano Lliuya v. RWE AG, 2 O 285/15 (Essen Oberlandesgericht 2015)
Mackay Conservation Group v. Commonwealth of Australia (Federal Court of Australia, NSD33/2015).

Massachusetts v. EPA, 549 U.S. 497 (2007).

McDonald's Corporation v. Steel & Morris [1997] EWHC 366 (QB).

M.C. *Mehta v. Union of India* (AIR 1987 SC 1086).

Milieudefensie and others v. Royal Dutch Shell plc ECLI:NL:RBDHA:2021:5339.

Mineral Sands Resources (Pty) Ltd and Others v. Reddell and Others (CCT 66/21) [2022] ZACC 37 (November 14, 2022).

Municipalities of Puerto Rico v. Exxon Mobil Corp. et al., 3:22-cv-01550 (D.P.R.).

Pabai Pabai & Anor v. Commonwealth of Australia (Federal Court of Australia Proceedings).

Rockhopper Exploration Plc, Rockhopper Italia S.p.A. and Rockhopper Mediterranean Ltd v. Italian Republic, ICSID Case No. ARB/17/14.

Sharma and others v. Minister for the Environment (2022). Federal Court of Australia, VID 389, April 22 (Australia).

Sierra Club v. Morton, 405 U.S. 727 (1972).

The State of the Netherlands v. Urgenda Foundation Supreme Court of the Netherlands (December 20, 2019).

TransCanada Corporation and TransCanada PipeLines Limited v. United States of America (I) (ICSID Case No. ARB/16/21).

Urgenda Foundation v. The Netherlands [2015] HAZA C/09/00456689 (June 24, 2015).

ACKNOWLEDGMENT OF COUNTRY

Most of this book was written in the foothills of kunanyi, the mountain that looks over nipaluna. The mountain is also known as Mount Wellington, named after an Englishman, as is the capital city of Hobart. The islands of lutruwita, are more commonly known as Tasmania, after a Dutchman. Most of the place names in lutruwita, an archipelago of islands, were brought over from Britain and Europe, alongside the religious, economic, and political cultures imposed on the land and its peoples with devastating consequences.

The shifting island weather wraps kunanyi lightly in chiffon mists or, when it is colder, cloaks her in thick cloud or glittering snow. When kunanyi was first proposed as the preferred name for the mountain, the shape of the syllables felt awkward and unfamiliar to many of us. But soon enough, three syllables *koo-narn-yee* rolled from our tongues. We got used to saying the word, reading kunanyi on signs, and thinking of our mountain as part of a much older human story. Names are important because they convey meaning and signal connection. Restoring old names acknowledges longer histories. Recognizing the other knowledges, values, worldviews and practices that shape our island home not only acknowledges the past but also provides a richer palette from which to imagine our futures.

ACKNOWLEDGMENTS

The idea for this book began in 2016 and has been helped along the way by the generosity and enthusiasm of many good people.

I am grateful to the editor of this series, Simon Cottle, who gave a thoughtful nod to the idea of green lawfare over a beer at Preachers one night and later commissioned this book. I have had the pleasure of working with the team at Peter Lang, especially Elizabeth Howard and Naviya Palani.

I have the good fortune to work with Libby Lester of Monash University whose contribution to environmental communication and commitment to generous and courageous scholarship have greatly influenced my work. Thank you, Libby, for your friendship, bemusement, and wisdom over many years and for your commitment to lutruwita.

My collaboration with Kerrie Foxwell-Norton of Griffith University continues to deepen my thinking. Our work on the Great Barrier Reef can be found throughout these pages. In particular: Foxwell-Norton, Kerrie, and Claire Konkes. 2019. "The Great Barrier Reef: News Media, Policy and the
n." *International Communication Gazette* 81 (3): 211–34;
rrie and Claire Konkes. 2021. "Climate change and the
Environmental protest, climate science, and new/s media"
and Journalism edited by Henrik Bødker and Hanna E.

Morris, pp. 103-120. London and New York: Routledge; and, Konkes, Claire, and Kerrie Foxwell-Norton. 2021. "Science Communication and Mediatised Environmental Conflict: A Cautionary Tale." *Public Understanding of Science* 30 (4): 470–83. Thanks also to Cynthia Nixon, whose doctoral work on the mediatization of public interest litigation has informed my ideas, particularly: Konkes, Claire, Cynthia Nixon, Libby Lester, and Kathleen Williams. 2021. "Coal versus Coral: Australian Climate Change Politics Sees the Great Barrier Reef in Court." *Queensland Review* 28 (2): 132–46; and Nixon, Cynthia, Claire Konkes, Libby Lester, and Kathleen Williams. 2021. "Mediated Visibility and Public Environmental Litigation: The Interplay between Inside and Outside Court during Environmental Conflict in Australia." *Laws* 10 (2): 35.

Scholarship is enriched by the company of people who support and challenge us in equal measure and I am grateful to Brett Hutchins, of Monash University, Pieter Maeseele of the University of Antwerp, Mikkel Eskjær of Aalborg University and Sy Taffel of Massey University for their company, advice, and critical engagement.

Thank you to my colleagues and students at the University of Tasmania for your curiosity and enthusiasm. I am particularly grateful to the following for their support, book loans and reading suggestions, and collegial provocations that have shaped and inspired my work: Israel Adeseko, Bill Dodd, Kianna Gallagher, Oren Gerassi, Lisa Gershwin, Linda Hunt, Meg Keating, Jamie Kirkpatrick, Alana Mann, Ben Richardson, Denise Robinson, Bliss Sandhu, Andy Terhell, Kate Warner, Rob White and Kathleen Williams. A special acknowledgement goes to the University's librarians for their patience and persistence. Librarians, too rarely mentioned in acknowledgments, are essential cogs in the team effort of scholarship. Thanks, too, to Alexander Tiberius Bayley for helping with preparing the manuscript.

Big gratitude to Stephenie Cahalan, Jocelyn Nettlefold, Katherine Scholes, Cath Hughes, Rupert and Nettie Davies, Maria Duggan, Andy Welling, Jim Connah, and Sarah Walker for your friendship and often wickedly funny observations about media, politics, and environmental matters.

This project took a little longer than planned. A huge thanks to my family on both the Bayley and Konkes sides, especially Chris Konkes and Heidi Konkes, for your encouragement and understanding. To my little family, Sam, Beatrix and Alex, your love, kindness and sense of adventure inspires and nurtures me and makes everything possible. Thank you.

LIST OF ABBREVIATIONS

ECT	Energy Charter Treaty
EPBC	Environment Protection and Biodiversity Conservation Act 1999 (Australia)
ICC	International Criminal Court
IPCC	Intergovernmental Panel on Climate Change
ISDS	Investor-state dispute settlement
NAFTA	North America Free Trade Agreement
NEPA	National Environmental Policy Act (U.S.)
NGO	Non-governmental organization
RICO	Racketeer Influenced and Corrupt Organizations Act (U.S.)
SLAPP	Strategic Lawsuit/Litigation Against Public Participation
UNDP	United Nations Development Programme
UNEP	United Nations Environment Programme

UNESCO	United Nations Educational, Scientific and Cultural Organization
UNFCCC	United Nations Framework Convention on Climate Change

· 1 ·

GREEN LAWFARE

The phrase "green lawfare" surfaced in Australian news media in 2015 after the Federal Court set aside the approval of a massive coal mine proposed by the Indian energy giant, Adani *(Mackay v. Australia)*. A local environmental organization, the Mackay Conservation Group, had successfully argued that then Environment Minister, Greg Hunt, had not taken into consideration the vulnerable status of two reptiles during the approval process. The court agreed. Most Australians had never heard of the yakka skink (*Egernia rugosa*) or the ornamental snake (*Denisonia maculata*), who are neither charismatic nor large, but now these two vulnerable species were "standing in the way" of Australia's largest coal mine. The response from the Australian Government was unequivocal: first, it attacked the court for getting the decision wrong; then the NGO and their legal team for conducting "green lawfare" and "vigilante litigation"; and finally, they attacked the nation's key environmental laws, vowing to remove the provisions in the *Environmental Protection and Biodiversity Conservation Act* that grants environmental advocates access to the courts. The MCG's legal challenge was part of a much larger campaign against the Adani project that involved protests, lawsuits and consumer boycott campaigns (Beresford 2018; Konkes 2018), but criticizing environmental groups for using the courts as "green lawfare" struck a note. As Cristy Clark

(2015) summed up: "The Adani case was settled after Hunt conceded he had failed to abide by the law—that he had rushed [his decision]. The judgment merely requires the government to abide by its own laws." The media-focused strategy by the government to politicize a legal decision and wind back environmental legislation struck me as a critical moment that revealed the power dynamics occurring at the junction of media, law and environmental conflict.

Australia is not alone in the politics of climate change taking a strategic turn toward the legal sphere. Since the signing of the United Nations Framework Convention on Climate Change in 1992 and the Kyoto Protocol in 1997, national and international laws dealing with climate change grew from just 60 in 1997 to more than 2,100 in 2021, and litigation has followed (Eilstrup-Sangiovanni and Sharman 2022, 88). We are now seeing landmark cases, such as *Netherlands v. Urgenda*, being undertaken to challenge the idea that climate change is a problem "too wicked" (Lazarus 2009) to solve. Here, the courts are being used to hold governments and corporations to account for putting political advantage and profits over human and ecological health.

Action on climate change is just one aspect of a wider movement to engage with the ecological crises the world faces. Having emerged alongside the social justice movements of the mid-twentieth century, particularly those in common law countries, environmental jurisprudence has evolved into a collection of "contagious" ideas, principles and approaches that stretch across state boundaries, legal cultures, judicial discourses, and international organizational practices (Affolder 2019). Today, every nation in the world has adopted at least one environmental law and most have established environmental ministries to oversee them (UNEP 2019). The challenge for those sharing these "contagious" ideas is not to lose sight of the local because it is through the lived experiences, histories and knowledges that good ideas can be translated by those most affected by the change they offer.

The strategic use of law and the public and political debates that ensue are forms of communicative action undertaken to achieve certain goals (Habermas 1984, 1987; see also, Deflem 2008). When communicative acts travel to wider audiences through news and other media, the public appetite for change is tested (Nixon et al. 2021). Headlines, such as "Is democracy threatened if companies can sue governments?" (Robinson 2015), "Human rights issue or 'green lawfare'? Citizens take to the courts to fight climate change" (Furnell 2021) and "Vigilante green groups destroying thousands of mining jobs" (Medhora and Robertson 2015) point to the salience of such actions for audiences across the political spectrum.

It would be naive to assume the evolution of environmental law is linear or progressive. Gains are the result of furious contests and progress-making "moments" that are "easily undone by powerful, short-term political and economic pressures" (Lazarus 2009, 1156). The retaliation against gains in environmental law includes companies harassing campaigners and journalists through litigation; draconian anti-protest laws to quell dissent; and transnational corporations suing governments for changing their policies in response to public demand for greater environmental protections.

While a brief skirmish in Australia's long-running environmental history, the so-called "green lawfare" debate was noted by many working at the intersections of media politics and environmental law (notably, Clark 2016; Cruger and Martin 2019; Jolley and Rickards 2019; Konkes 2018; Murphy and McGee 2018; Nixon et al. 2021; Pepper 2017; Woronov 2017). The debate pointed to the myriad battles occurring in politics, law and media that are contributing to local and global efforts to protect the natural systems that sustain all life on this planet. While used pejoratively by irate conservatives, the term "green lawfare" is a useful shorthand that encapsulates the strategic use of law by the networks of activists, government, industry and media that constitute the enactment of mediatized environmental conflict.

A focus on green lawfare

This book is about the strategic use of law, especially the courts, during environmental conflict. It is not about the evolution of the considerable body of environmental and international law governing the environment, which can be found elsewhere (e.g., Fisher 2017; Godden, Peel and McDonald 2019; Lazarus 2023; Lim 2019). Instead, this book is interested in how law, as a "field" constituted by epistemological traditions, defined institutions, and professionally defined practices (Bourdieu 1986), engages with other fields and networks to "provide stability in times of rapid change and uncertainty" (McDonald 2011, 283).

Environmental problems have always been about change, risk and uncertainty, with climate change no exception (Beck 1995, 2014; Giddens 1991). The theorization of green lawfare presented here follows the broad interdisciplinary approach of Lee Godden, Jacqueline Peel and Jan McDonald (2019, xxiii) that treats environmental law as more than a "tool for imposing liability or enforcing rules" and instead

> emphasizes the multi-faceted roles of law in the environmental area, which include articulating management objectives and agency responsibilities, enabling participation, ensuring government accountability, determining governance arrangements, creating institutions, providing a framework for regulatory approaches, protecting rights, ensuring compliance and sanctioning offenders.

This definition recognizes how environmental law is especially influenced by other disciplines (Philippopoulos-Mihalopoulos 2011, 15; see also Goodie 2011; Hilson 2022). As Richard Lazarus (2023, 4) observes, the emergence of environmental law over the past 50 years "has triggered a broader evolutionary process in the law" whose significance is not confined to environmental protection. Rather, he goes on to observe, "the teachings and values of environmentalism have infused one intersecting category of legal rules after another."

Environmental law is in a great state of flux. In an oft-cited article, Fisher (2013, 350) calls environmental law "hot law", which draws on economist Michael Callon's description of "hot" situations as moments when

> everything becomes controversial: the identification of intermediaries and overflows, the distribution of source and target agents, the way effects are measured. These controversies, which indicate the absence of a stabilised knowledge base, usually involve a wide variety of actors. The actual list of actors, as well as their identities will fluctuate in the course of a controversy itself and they will put forward mutually incompatible descriptions of future world states.

Fisher (2013, 350–351) argues that observing environmental law as "hot" recognizes that

> many environmental law issues are not just "controversial", but that the controversies are structural and foundational. There is difficulty in identifying source and target agents as there is a wide group of actors. There is a lack of a stabilised knowledge base. There are mutually incompatible understandings of the world.

The idea of environmental law as hot law is well-received, with Elise Scotford (2022, 381) noting that "the polycentric, uncertain and dynamic nature of many environmental problems" makes even defining the ideas and principles informing environmental law complex, not least because these ideas, and ideals, carry political and polemical force. The concept of green lawfare contributes to this idea of environmental law as "hot law" because it describes the actors and processes contributing to how environmental problems are imagined, constituted and communicated for different purposes that, in turn, informs not only the evolution of environmental law but also wider understandings and expectations of what law can do.

The idea of green lawfare engages with the emerging scholarship into the opportunities and processes that lead to legal mobilization by civil society groups (eg. Lehoucq and Taylor 2020; Peel and Osofsky 2020; Setzer 2022; Vanhala 2018, 2022) by emphasizing the role of media and communication, especially news and other media, in these processes (which are generally overlooked or ignored). Much can be learned by de-centering law from such analysis (Setzer and Vanhala 2019). If international law and constitutional law are indeed the "common communication tools of a globalized judicial front" (Colombo 2017) then understanding the networks through which communication flows is vital. The environmental movement was early to adopt international law because it provided a range of principles, such as the precautionary principle, that could be adopted and adapted to local contexts (Sands 1993), however, legal analysis is not enough to consider the legal opportunities and political contexts that enable developments in law or legal action or to determine the efficacy of such action (Peel and Osofsky 2020). More can be learned by understanding the spaces and flows of mediated communication (Castells 2011), where our understanding of the environment is continually reconstituted through mobilization, visibility and contest. Green lawfare goes beyond litigation to include the networks that use protest and other symbolic acts and the communicative logic that ensures even failed cases continue to inspire and influence. Such an approach takes care not to assume that globalized media are synonymous with Anglo-American networks, and instead explore the transnational, albeit mostly capitalist, networks of media and communication across Asia, Africa, Latin America, and the Middle East (Punathambekar and Mohan 2019). If communication is to be approached as a "constitutive practice, rather than as a matter of the transmission of messages" (Carvalho, van Wessel and Maeseele, 2017, 124), then the processes and practices through which environmental law is communicated is an important component in understanding how the legal frameworks constituting environmental governance are deliberated, enacted and maintained. It may be, as Brian Preston (2011) observes, difficult to quantify the extent to which media representations influence governmental decision-making, but the increasing use of legal action by environmental groups and others suggests a trend worthy of closer examination. Fortunately, a considerable body of work to date presents a solid theoretical foundation for such an investigation.

Green lawfare is about the strategic use of the law as communicative action, which locates communication media, especially news as an important constituent. We can no longer use "the media" as a useful shorthand for the news organizations that produce the newspapers and broadcast news from which we found "the news." While news journalism has been "the primary sense-making practice of modernity" (Hartley 1996, 12) and news headlines once served as a proxy for public opinion, the rapidly changing media landscape can no longer be described so simply (if indeed it ever could) as "the media". To keep referring to "the media" masks the profound changes to the networks of mediated communication, especially news (Couldry and Hepp 2017, 2). Adding to the increasingly complex networks of communication are social media platforms where people enact their social and political lives. While activists have long used alternative media to communicate and disseminate their messages (Forde 2017), the digital affordances of social media and the Internet more widely mean the communication strategies of local and transnational activist networks extend beyond reaching the gatekeepers of news organizations (Giddens 2015). In other words, news media organizations no longer dominate the constitution of mediatized democratic discourse. However, news media remains a key feature in the local, national and global debates about environmental problems and governance (Lester 2019), so should not be ignored. The phrase "news and other media" describes sources of news, which includes newspaper and broadcast news, and their online equivalents, but also social media, messaging apps, blogs, and streaming services where people are increasingly turning for their news and where "journalists and news media have to carve out their places if they want to connect with the public" (Newman et al. 2023, 5). In particular, environmental news is increasingly global news. As Simon Cottle (2019, 102) observes, global journalism is not simply foreign news, but "the professionally purposive, globally aware and critically engaged orientation and forms of journalism that report on, from or about faraway places" that is informing how we interpret various crises, such as climate change.

Theorizing Green Lawfare

From its nascent origins in environmental protests in the 1960s to the global movement today, the environmental movement has been the subject of broad study, which has included research into how news and other media inform our understanding of the nature of "the environment" and its problems (see, e.g., Anderson 2003; Cottle and Lester 2011; Hansen 2019; Lester 2010). While covered in more depth in Chapter Two, it is important to note here that the environmental movement has long understood the logic and processes of mediated visibility and has used various media to powerful effect. For now, several key concepts in media and communication are useful.

Firstly, the idea that news and other media can be regarded as constituting spheres of action, or arenas (Wolfsfeld 1997), in which battles for authority, definition and influence are fought by journalists and various other actors who actively engage with media to pursue their objectives. Secondly, the idea of media logic first described by David Altheide and Robert Snow (1979) to describe the processes, routines, and formal and informal rules that shape how news, particularly political news, is selected and produced. The idea of media logic usefully engages with how actors are increasingly adapting their communication practices to appeal to media, such as the timing and nature of announcements or providing spectacular images to attract media attention (Cushion 2019). It has been nearly 50 years since Altheide and Snow observed how the significance of media is boosted by the adoption of media logics by politicians, governments and others, but various affordances of digital media, particularly social media, to attract audiences demand that the nuanced observation of media logic continues. With social media no longer "new media", we are able to observe how social media logics are driving many of the ways in which content is not only shared but also produced and received. For instance, social media are proving to be not only a tool for organizing protests but also the platforms targeted for the communication of protest (Lester 2019).

The idea of mediatization tries to encapsulate the intrusion of media logic into other fields and daily life (Esser 2014,160). Mediatization has become "shorthand" to describe the changes in "communicative and social processes, and the social and practical forms built from them, which follow from our increasing reliance on technologically and institutionally based processes of mediation" (Couldry and Hepp 2017, 3–4). Mediatization describes the complex mix of practices, technologies, ownership, relationships and other influences that constitute media which has "played a more fundamental role in the shaping of modern societies" (Thompson 2020, 3). In short, mediatization describes not only what media "does" but, by embracing the mutability and instability of social relations in late modernity, describes how media technologies, platforms and engagement are transforming our social, cultural, and political lives (Cottle 2006; Hjarvard 2008; Hepp 2013; Strömbäck 2008). As communication media become more integrated into different practices and institutions that constitute society, media logic will continue to influence not only communication, but social organization. Mediatization describes how media, especially news media, goes beyond "mediating" the communication between the governed and the governing and instead "invokes the ubiquity and pervasiveness of media in the contemporary world [where] media are no doubt the most significant spaces where civic cultures can flourish—as well as be obstructed" (Dahlgren and Alvares 2013, 51).

An understanding of the processes of mediatization gives us a vantage point from which to observe the various struggles for visibility, definition, and influence that constitute our understanding of environmental problems. Simon Cottle's concept of "mediatized conflict" (2006) helpfully describes how various media extend conflict from its originating site—the battlegrounds of street protests, forest protests, office sit-ins, and so on—to wider audiences who then witness and sympathize or, better still, deliberate on how we should respond. Drawing on a wide range of recent social theory, especially the work of Anthony Giddens, Manuel Castells, and Ulrich Beck and the assemblage of work on globalization, post-traditionalism and social reflexivity, Cottle (2006, 9) writes that mediatization deliberately captures

> something of the more complex, active and performative ways that the media are used in conflicts today. The media ... are capable of enacting and performing conflicts as well as reporting and representing them; that is to say, they are actively "doing something" over and above disseminating ideas, images and information.

When applied to environmental conflict, the network of actors who constitute "the environment movement" have been particularly adept in their approach to using media to mobilize supporters and drive political pressure (Lester and Cottle 2009; Lester 2010). For this reason, Brett Hutchins and Libby Lester's "mediatized environmental conflict" (2015), following on Cottle's work, provides the foundation from which to build an understanding of the process and practices that inform "green lawfare."

Hutchins and Lester conceptualize mediatized environmental conflict as constituted in the interactions between four "spheres of action": activist strategies and campaigns; journalism practices and news reporting; formal politics and decision-making processes; and, industry activities and trade. They describe how each of these spheres is governed by institutional affordances and limitations, professional norms and practices, and commercial opportunities, and each has its own networks of media, political and economic power. Their identification of four spheres was developed by a nine-year examination of environmental conflict in Tasmania, Australia. In different contexts, other spheres of action—such as what Bourdieu (1986) called "the juridical sphere"—are likely emerge. Law may be situated in what Brett Hutchins and Libby Lester (2015) call the sphere of "formal politics and decision- making processes" but, drawing from Bourdieu, green lawfare conceptualizes law as an identifiable field that engages with other spheres (of fields) during mediatized environmental conflict. It imagines the legal sphere, like other spheres of action, as constituted by identifiable professionals and practices, and institutions and discourses, but also having a powerful influence on the social, political, economic and discursive practices it encounters. Indeed, Hutchins and Lester write: "The key to understanding mediatized environmental conflict [is to observe] those moments and spaces where two or more spheres of action interlock" (2015, 339), which can be both physical—such as at protest sites, newsrooms and courtrooms—but also mediated through news and other media. Others are using the framework of mediatized environmental conflict in a range of contexts, including the emergence of conflicts that pit different environmental considerations against each other, such as debates between nuclear energy and renewables (Eskjær and Horsbøl 2023), my earlier work on the Australian green lawfare debate (Konkes 2018), and Kerrie Foxwell-Norton and I (Foxwell-Norton and Konkes 2021, 2022; Konkes and Foxwell-Norton 2021) have explored the role of science as a sphere of action in mediatized environmental conflict in relation to Australia's Great Barrier Reef.

Choosing the term "green lawfare" is a conscious decision to reclaim the idea of lawfare as a fairly neutral description of the strategic use of law as part of wider campaigns. The first mention of "lawfare" has been traced back to two Australians, John Carlson and Neville Yeomans (1975, 3), who, in the spirit and idiom of the decade in which they wrote, envisaged lawfare replacing warfare so that "the duel is with words rather than swords." The idea resurfaced in an oft-cited speech by Charles Dunlap Jr. (2001) who described lawfare as "a method of warfare where law is used as a means of realizing a military objective" (2001, 4), but which he later defined as

> the strategy of using—or misusing—law as a substitute for traditional military means to achieve an operational objective. As such, I view law in this context much the same as a weapon. It is a means that can be used for good or bad purposes.

From here, the idea of lawfare found its home in international relations and public international law to describe the use, or misuse, of law to achieve wider objectives. As Siri Gloppen (2018, 6) notes, "lawfare is understood as the strategic use of rights, law and litigation by actors of different breeds to advance contested political and social goals" and, more recently, Jaume Castan Pinos and Mark Friis Hau (2023, 75) defined lawfare as "a multifaceted law-based instrument that can be used by a wide range of actors in both military as well as non-military contexts to pursue political objectives."

In its short life, lawfare has come to signify the importance of law in the conflicts of the twenty-first century (Gloppen 2008; Scharf and Andersen 2010), especially where the legal field is expanding into areas where governance structures appear weak (Carvalho, van Wessel and Maeseele 2017; Gloppen and St Clair 2012). Such weaknesses have come to light in revelations about the extent to which Britain's legal system is used, or misused, in the flow of information, capital and, ultimately, power by the world's financial elite (discussed more fully in Chapter 7). As one parliamentarian, David Davis, told the British Parliament in 2022:

> Lawfare is the misuse of legal systems and principles by extraordinarily rich individuals and organizations to destroy their critics and opponents. In many cases, our reporters face reputational and financial ruin in defending themselves from these malevolent cases; even if they win, the expense and impact are huge. The chilling effect on a free press is extraordinary. (Slattery 2022)

Lawfare remains an unstable concept. In 2022, the word was added to the Collins Dictionary to describe "the strategic use of legal proceedings to intimidate or hinder an opponent"; the Cambridge Dictionary kept the earlier association with modern warfare; and the Oxford Dictionary has no entry. Lawfare has also been repositioned as a pejorative, mostly by conservatives, to criticize the use of international law in claims against state and national security matters (Scharf and Andersen 2010). The use of "green lawfare" by conservatives critical of legal proceedings can be seen as an example of how communication strategies are shared through transnational networks and repurposed for local contexts (Castells 2009; Lester 2019). Its use as a pejorative by some should not diminish its usefulness as a term to conceptualize the connections between media and law during environmental conflict.

Catalina Vallejo and Siri Gloppen (2013) were the first to mention "green lawfare" in their analysis of how climate change litigation occurs at the intersections of socio-economic (red) and environmental (green) issues.

From this brief etymology, the idea of green lawfare emerges to describe the myriad ways that various actors engaged in mediatized environmental conflict involve the law as part of their communication strategies. The mediatization of environmental law, such as news coverage of judicial decisions, the public and political commentary around environmental law, the sharing of ideas across mediated networks, and the communication strategies deployed during conflict, are all moments holding the potential to shift power relations — for better or worse.

One way to study strategy is to observe the consequences and sites of engagement and impact. There are material, symbolic and political consequences to green lawfare (Konkes 2018). The consequences of legislation and legal action can be material: laws and litigation can stop people, projects and processes in their tracks, or at least delay them; even the threat of legal action has the power to hinder and delay projects, "chill" political speech, and influence decision-making and deliberations on policy. Like other forms of protest, legal action also has the symbolic power contained in its "capacity to make visible arenas of action that were previously hidden from view" (Thompson 2005, 39). Combined, the material consequences and symbolic power of legal action during environmental conflict carries political consequences. While legal action can be seen as an attempt to move issues of public interest out of the political forum and into the controlled communication arena of the courts (Canan and Pringle 1989), media and communication networks can ensure a contentious issue is returned reconstituted to the political sphere to be adopted, amended or repealed in response to the public pressure (Lazarus 2009; Preston 2016). In this sense, green lawfare is part of the wider communication processes informing the construction, interpretation, discussion and analysis of environmental problems including the actions put forward to solve them (Dryzek 2013).

Green lawfare provides a framework to observe the myriad ways law is deployed during environmental conflict, including the fast-evolving jurisprudence providing a global framework to target industry and trade; climate litigation demanding polluters and reluctant governments respond to calls for action on climate; strategic lawsuits used to harass and silence advocates; and, transnational trade deals designed to deter governments from responsive changes to policy. As with environmental conflict more generally, each of these instances of green lawfare compresses the local and the global, and the symbolic and the material, such as when: a global network of lawyers and activists focuses on a single case in a relatively obscure Australian court that proposes a bold new direction in climate law; the Sioux gather on sacred ground, but also in court, to protest a gas pipeline threatening the Standing Rock Sioux Reservation; and, an American attorney invites British celebrities to promote a class action being undertaken by the Ecuadorian tribespeople most impacted by the drilling for oil. While focusing on the role of media and communication in the construction of these conflicts, the conceptualization of green lawfare is unavoidably interdisciplinary. In their earlier work, Lester and Hutchins (2012) identified how the processes of mediatization can result in an absence of media content, or "strategic invisibility." Developing their idea in transnational contexts, Lester (2019, 9) went on to observe:

> major corporations, regional and national governments, international governance regimes, nongovernment organizations, community groups, industry associations and scientific institutions are all important actors in these new forms and means of engagement. Mediatization is as much about what is happening in other social institutions as in media.

Can green lawfare be conceived as a global phenomenon? What are the risks in the development of an international body of environmental law? Writing in Tasmania, a former British colony and still part of the Commonwealth, with a common law system and an international reputation for fierce environmental politics and protest, I am mindful of the provenance of my understanding of media and law. The international organizations and prestige journals of my field remain largely tethered to their North American and European origins (Volkmer and Sharif 2018, 3), maintaining a persistent hegemony of assumed universal values and aspirations (Waisbord 2022). Academic legal culture appears much the same (Twining 2009). The assumptions buried in the terms we use, like signposts carrying names from other places, reveal our ongoing allegiances to certain points of view. Common terms—"the environment," "activism," "the West," the "Global South"—are quick nods to shared meanings that come apart on closer examination. How does someone writing from a wealthy country, such as Australia, located in the far south of the Asia-Pacific, conceptualize "the Global South" (Connell 2020)? Is it better, given our wealth and allegiance to the Commonwealth, to envisage Australia as part of the Global North? Does that do away with the whole North-South divide altogether? In doing so, are we able to find ways to acknowledge the different knowledge traditions and worldviews of our country, and our neighbors in the Asia-Pacific (Foxwell-Norton 2018)? These questions are important. If we are to tackle global problems, then a global perspective must encompass different knowledges and viewpoints rather than remain wedded to the dominant theories and traditions of thought that are part of the problem. Perhaps we can borrow from Henry David Thoreau's suggestion that "what we call wildness is a civilization other than our own" to reconsider that too often the Global South is used to describe cultures, economies and societies that are "not like us". This bifurcation of the world, of us and them, of North and South, of colonizers and the colonized, fails to address the stultifying homogenization of humanity evoked in the grim generalizations that our species is fated to despoil the Earth and all life on it. Indeed, as Silvio Waisbord (2022) suggests, any intellectual shift away from the gravitational centers of scholarship is a deliberate political act. If scholars, particularly those from wealthy countries, cannot step far enough away from the comforts of their own traditions to explore and try to understand lesser-known worldviews and knowledge traditions, and then turn around and see the blind spots and ignorance of their own assumptions anew—then how can we, in good faith, ask others to change their minds, their practices, their allegiances?

In theorizing green lawfare, some argue that the weaponization of law is not only central to colonial and imperial projects, but continues to echo in the global networks that facilitate the global trade of services, commodities and people. During the British colonial enterprise, law was used as a "civilizing" force, which legitimized other forms of violence used to sublimate peoples, acquire and control land, and extract resources (Merry 1993) and the transfer of legal traditions, institutions, and practices from one society to another was largely done in service to capitalism (McAuslan 2015). With this colonial history in mind, any contemporary analysis of green lawfare needs to apply some criticality to calls for international governing bodies with global oversight. Who gets to decide who is in the room when treaties are negotiated? Whose understanding of science, law and economics decides what is possible? How do we understand ownership and property rights or sovereignty and stewardship within global governance frameworks? Is the science we are using to argue for an environmental rule of law limited to the "hyperscientism" of modern, Western science (Beck 1995, 40) or can we embrace other ways of knowing our world? Are our dominant apocalyptic narratives of the approaching future too universal in their telling (Rose, Wewerinke-Singh and Miranda 2019)? How do current global networks of law and finance "colonize the future" forcing young people to protest and campaign against events that are yet to happen (Bourgeois et al. 2022)? These questions locate green lawfare within a much wider project best described by Jeffrey Alexander (2006, 3) as "civil society" in which the struggle for social solidarity remains in constant contradiction and flux but is always oriented toward ideals of justice and the common good and antagonistic to those who use power as a weapon:

> The premise of the Civil Sphere is that societies are not governed by power alone and are not fueled only by the pursuit of self-interest. Feelings for others matter, and they are structured by the boundaries of solidarity. How solidarity is structured, how far it extends, what it's composed of—these are critical issues for every social order, and especially for orders that aim at the good life. Solidarity is possible because people are oriented not only to the here and now but to the ideal, to the transcendent, to what they hope will be the everlasting.

What social or political forces demand solidarity? What is the counterforce to those responding to the awareness of shared interests at local and global scales? Tyranny is used here, perhaps evoking Arendtian notions of corrupted power, to describe the actors and structures that resist the rule of law —which describes the systems in place that mandate accountability and responsibility to others over the excesses of self-interest. Tyranny, in this sense, is both ancient and contemporaneous. It is predatory, self-insulating and global in reach (Fraser 2008, 2023). The tyrannical impulse, not the nature of power itself, that wields law as a tool of injustice. By positioning tyranny as the counterforce to solidarity, green lawfare describes how law, and ideas about law, are evoked in speech and action to resist the tyrannies of organized self-interest at the heart of global environmental crises.

Order of Book

The purpose of this book is to provide a framework from which to observe and analyze the strategic use of law in mediatized environmental conflict. It draws from a range of literature from media and communication, jurisprudence, sociology, earth sciences, economics and philosophy to find the threads that contribute to various understandings of "the environment" and, more recently, our understanding of the various ecological crises, including climate change, pushing our world to a dangerous tipping point. Following Wolfsfeld's (1997, 4) observation that "the best way to learn the rules of combat is to watch the battle," classic and more recent case studies from across the globe are used to illustrate the various ways in which the legal system is embroiled in environmental conflict to influence political, economic and social outcomes. This book is ultimately about networks—sometimes messy and ad hoc, at other times well-organized and deliberate—and their strategic use of media and law to achieve wider objectives.

Traversing the development of environmental awareness through a media and communication lens, Chapter 2 presents the conceptual underpinnings of green lawfare by focusing on the deliberate strategies to bring mediated visibility to environmental problems that underpin much of the environmental movement.

Recognizing that the legal understanding of the environment is shaped by the law's interactions with a range of non-legal discourses and ideas (Goodie 2011), Chapter 3 observes the environment as an unorthodox legal object. It locates its early origins in the tension between liberty and responsibility in the foundations of the common law system and discusses how these tensions inform the key normative ideas of environmental law—including the commons, public interest, human rights, and environmental and climate justice—around the world.

Having established the role of news and other media in environmental conflict and outlined some of the key discourses, and their accompanying assumptions that thread through contemporary debates occurring at the intersections of law, media and environment, the book turns to classic and contemporary case studies to further develop the idea of green lawfare. Chapter 4 focuses on strategic litigation used by the early environmental movement that progressed the development of domestic environmental law. Drawing on classic case studies, particularly from Australia and the United States, this chapter highlights the role of news and other media in the communication of the material, symbolic and political consequences of these key moments in environmental law-making.

Having drawn from a history and the present to set the scene, the rest of the book casts an eye to the future. Chapter 5 focuses on recent litigation undertaken by young people and others plaintiffs. Drawing on landmark cases, this chapter discusses the rise of climate change litigation and the challenges and opportunities presented by this rapidly growing body of international environmental law to challenge and change government and corporate recalcitrance to meaningfully act on climate and other environmental and social problems.

Ecological and Earth systems science and scientists are increasingly influencing environmental law. Chapter 6 explores the communication of science in climate litigation, including the phrase "best available science." Focusing on the emerging field of attribution science as an example of how science communication is used strategically to progress climate action inside and outside of the courtroom, this chapter explores how science is shaping environmental law and the discourses of climate and environmental justice.

Having established the legal sphere as a key arena in the battles to protect forests and rivers, to tighten regulations on pollution and waste, and coordinate global action on climate, Chapter 7 engages with the retaliation to recent gains. It identifies the places and instances where law is strategically used to control and silence those working toward a more sustainable future. It looks at three areas: strategic lawsuits against public participation (or SLAPPs), which are used to harass and intimidate critics; the rise in draconian anti-protest legislation which signals a particular turn in the use of law to control activism, especially climate action; and, the use of arbitration in the international treaty systems, which is one of the major hurdles to meaningful action on climate change. Each of these areas encompasses large and distinctive areas of law, so the focus of this chapter is how various legal mechanisms can be weaponized by powerful interests. Overall, this chapter presents three relatively separate forms of green lawfare that carry the hallmarks of deliberate efforts to silence the voices of resistance to the excesses of power.

Chapter 8 provides a conclusion by returning to the questions raised in this chapter about the ways in which environmental law is represented, transformed and contested in communication media. Who are the actors engaged in the development of international environmental law and the global climate regime? How do news and other media provide visibility and interpretation to these "moments" and what are the communication strategies that led to them? How does our media-saturated world communicate the opportunities and consequences of environmental law being used to protect the environmental systems on which we all depend? Who is benefiting from the enactment of new environmental laws when global aspiration is translated into national law and policy?

This book is about connections rather than differences. Observing the interlocking activities of journalists, activists, scientists and government and industry actors during environmental conflicts that engage with law, we can see how environmental law is part of a much wider struggle to bring visibility to environmental problems. Interdisciplinary in approach, *Green Lawfare* provides readers with a useful theoretical framework, supported by empirical examples, from which to observe and better understand the mediatization of environmental law.

References

Affolder, Natasha. 2019. "Contagious Environmental Lawmaking." *Journal of Environmental Law* 31(2): 187–212.

Alexander, Jeffrey C. 2006. *The Civil Sphere*. Oxford and New York: Oxford University Press.

Anderson, Alison. 2003. *Media, Culture and the Environment*. London: Routledge.

Beck, Ulrich. 2014. *World at Risk*. Cambridge and Malden: Polity Press.

Beck, Ulrich, Anthony Giddens, and Scott Lash. 1994. *Reflexive Modernization: Politics, Tradition and Aesthetics in the Modern Social Order*. Stanford: Stanford University Press.

Beresford, Quentin. 2018. *Adani and the War over Coal*. Sydney: NewSouth.

Bourdieu, Pierre. 1986. "The Force of Law: Toward a Sociology of the Juridical Field." *The Hastings Law Journal* 38: 805–853.

Bourgeois, Robin, Geci Karuri-Sebina, and Kwamou Eva Feukeu. 2022. "The Future as a Public Good: Decolonising the Future through Anticipatory Participatory Action Research." *Foresight*. https://doi.org/10.1108/FS-11-2021-0225

Carson, David and Yeomans, Neville. 1975. "Whither Goeth the Law—Humanity or Barbarity." In *The Way Out: Radical Alternatives in Australia*, edited by Margaret Smith and David Crossley. Melbourne, Australia. http://www.laceweb.org.au/whi.htm (Accessed June 12, 2023).

Carvalho, Anabela, Margit van Wessel, and Pieter Maeseele. 2017. "Communication Practices and Political Engagement with Climate Change: A Research Agenda." *Environmental Communication* 11 (1): 122–135.

Castan Pinos, Jaume, and Mark Friis Hau. 2023. *Lawfare: New Trajectories in Law*. Oxford and New York: Routledge.

Castells, Manuel. 2009. *Communication Power*. Oxford and New York: Oxford University Press.

Clark, Cristy. 2015. "The Government versus the Environment:" *The Conversation*, August 18.

Clark, Cristy. 2016. "The Politics of Public Interest Environmental Litigation: Lawfare in Australia." *Australian Environment Review* 31 (7): 58–262.

Connell, Raewyn. 2020. *Southern Theory: The Global Dynamics of Knowledge in Social Science*. London: Routledge.

Cottle, Simon. 2006. *Mediatized Conflicts*. Maidenhead: Open University Press.

Cottle, Simon. 2013. "Environmental Conflict in a Global, Media Age: Beyond Dualisms." In *Environmental Conflict and the Media*, edited by Libby Lester and Brett Hutchins, 19–33. New York: Peter Lang.

Cottle, Simon, and Libby Lester, eds. 2011. *Transnational Protests and the Media*. Global Crises and the Media. New York: Peter Lang.

Couldry, Nick, and Andreas Hepp. 2017. *The Mediated Construction of Reality*. Cambridge and Malden: Polity Press.

Dahlgren, Peter, and Claudia Alvares. 2013. "Political Participation in an Age of Mediatisation: Towards a New Research Agenda." *Javnost—The Public* 20 (2): 47–65.

Deflem, Mathieu. 2008. "Law in Habermas's Theory of Communicative Action." *Universitas* 116: 267–285.

Dryzek, John S. 2013. *The Politics of the Earth: Environmental Discourses*. 3rd ed. Oxford: Oxford University Press.

Dunlap, Charles J. Jr. 2001. "Law and Military Interventions: Preserving Humanitarian Values in 21st Conflicts." Presented at the Humanitarian Challenges in Military Intervention Conference, Carr Center for Human Rights Policy Kennedy School of Government, Harvard University Washington, DC, November 29. https://people.duke.edu/~pfeaver/dunlap.pdf (Accessed May 5, 2023).

Dunlap, Charles, J. 2008. "Lawfare Today: A Perspective." *Yale Journal of International Affairs* Winter: 146–154.

Fisher, Elizabeth. 2013. "Environmental Law as 'Hot' Law." *Journal of Environmental Law* 25 (3): 347–358.

Fisher, Elizabeth. 2017. *Environmental Law: A Very Short Introduction*. Oxford: Oxford University Press.

Foxwell-Norton, Kerrie. 2018. *Environmental Communication and Critical Coastal Policy Communities, Culture and Nature*. Oxford and New York: Routledge.

Foxwell-Norton, Kerrie, and Claire Konkes. 2019. "The Great Barrier Reef: News Media, Policy and the Politics of Protection." *International Communication Gazette* 81 (3): 211–234.

———. 2022. "Is the Great Barrier Reef Dead? Satire, Death and Environmental Communication." *Media International Australia* 184 (1): 106–121.

Fraser, Nancy. 2008. *Scales of Justice: Reimagining Political Space in a Globalizing World*. New York: Polity Press.

Fraser, Nancy. 2023. *Cannibal Capitalism: How Our System Is Devouring Democracy, Care, and the Planet - and What We Can Do about It*. New York: Verso.

Furnell, Antony. 2021. "Human Rights Issue or 'Green Lawfare'? Citizens Take to the Courts to Fight Climate Change." *ABC RN*, July 27, 2021. https://www.abc.net.au/news/2021-07-27/climate-change-human-rights-legal-challenge/100310206 (Accessed August 22, 2022).

Gloppen, Siri. 2018. *Conceptualizing Lawfare: A Typology & Theoretical Framework*. Working Paper, Centre on Law and Social Transformation, University of Bergen.

Goodie, Jo. 2011. "The Ecological Narrative of Risk and the Emergence of Toxic Tort Litigation." In *Law and Ecology: New Environmental Foundations*, edited by Andreas Philippopoulos-Mihalopoulos, 65–82. London: Routledge.

Habermas, Jürgen. 1984. *The Theory of Communicative Action, Volume 1, Reason and the Rationalization of Society*. Boston: Beacon.

———. 1987. *The Theory of Communicative Action, Volume 2, Lifeworld and System: A Critique of Functionalist Reason*. Boston: Beacon.

Hansen, Anders. 2019. *Environment, Media and Communication*. 2nd ed. Oxford and New York: Routledge.

Hilson, Chris. 2022. "The Role of Narrative in Environmental Law: The Nature of Tales and Tales of Nature." *Journal of Environmental Law* 34 (1): 1–24.

Hutchins, Brett, and Libby Lester. 2015. "Theorizing the Enactment of Mediatized Environmental Conflict." *International Communication Gazette* 77 (4): 337–358.

Jolley, Connor, and Lauren Rickards. 2020. "Contesting Coal and Climate Change Using Scale: Emergent Topologies in the Adani Mine Controversy." *Geographical Research* 58 (1): 6–23.

Konkes, Claire. 2018. "Green Lawfare: Environmental Public Interest Litigation and Mediatized Environmental Conflict." *Environmental Communication* 12 (2): 191–203.

Konkes, Claire, and Kerrie Foxwell-Norton. 2021. "Science Communication and Mediatised Environmental Conflict: A Cautionary Tale." *Public Understanding of Science* 30 (4): 470–483.

Konkes, Claire, Cynthia Nixon, Libby Lester, and Kathleen Williams. 2021. "Coal versus Coral: Australian Climate Change Politics Sees the Great Barrier Reef in Court." *Queensland Review* 28 (2): 132–146.

Lazarus, Richard. 2009. "Super Wicked Problems and Climate Change: Restraining the Present to Liberate the Future." *Cornell Law Review* 94 (5): 1153–1234.

———. 2023. *The Making of Environmental Law*. 2nd ed. Chicago: University of Chicago Press.

Lehoucq, Emilio, and Whitney K. Taylor. 2020. "Conceptualizing Legal Mobilization: How Should We Understand the Deployment of Legal Strategies?" *Law & Social Inquiry* 45 (1): 166–93. https://doi.org/10.1017/lsi.2019.59.

Lester, Libby. 2010. *Media and Environment: Conflict, Politics and the News*. Cambridge and Malden: Polity Press.

———. 2019. *Global Trade and Mediatised Environmental Protest: The View from Here*. Cham: Springer International.

———. 2020. "Media and the Environment." In *The Media & Communications in Australia*, edited by Stuart Cunningham and Sue Turnbull, 4th ed., 321–326. London and New York: Routledge.

Lester, Libby, and Simon Cottle. 2009. "Visualizing Climate Change: Television News and Ecological Citizenship." *International Journal of Communication* 3: 920–936.

Lim, Michelle, ed. 2019. *Charting Environmental Law Futures in the Anthropocene*. Singapore: Springer.

McAuslan, Patrick. 2015. "Property and Empire: From Colonialism to Globalization and Back." *Social & Legal Studies* 24 (3): 339–357.

Medhora, Shalailah, and Joshua Robertson. 2015. "George Brandis: Vigilante Green Groups Destroying Thousands of Mining Jobs." *The Guardian*, August 17. https://www.theguardian.com/environment/2015/aug/17/george-brandis-vigilante-green-groups-destroying-thousands-of-mining-jobs (Accessed October 6, 2022).

Merry, Sally Engle. 1991. "Law and Colonialism." *Law & Society Review* 4: 889–922.

Murphy, Brendon, and Jeffrey McGee. 2018. "Lawfare, Standing and Environmental Discourse: A Phronetic Analysis." *University of Tasmania Law Review* 37 (2): 131–168.

Newman, Nic, Richard Fletcher, Kirsten Eddy, Craig T Robertson, and Rasmus Kleis Nielsen. 2023. *Reuters Institute Digital News Report 2023*. Oxford: Reuters Institute for the Study of Journalism.

Nixon, Cynthia, Claire Konkes, Libby Lester, and Kathleen Williams. 2021. "Mediated Visibility and Public Environmental Litigation: The Interplay between Inside and Outside

Court during Environmental Conflict in Australia." *Laws* 10 (2): https://www.mdpi.com/2075-471X/10/2/35

Peel, Jacqueline, and Hari M. Osofsky. 2020. "Climate Change Litigation." *Annual Review of Law and Social Science* 16 (1): 21–38. https://doi.org/10.1146/annurev-lawsocsci-022420-122936.

Pepper, Rachel. 2017. "Ms Onus and Mr Neal: Agitators in an Age of 'Green Lawfare.'" *AIAL Forum* 90: 52–64.

Philippopoulos-Mihalopoulos, Andreas. 2017. "Critical Environmental Law as Method in the Anthropocene." In *Research Methods in Environmental Law*, edited by Andreas Philippopoulos-Mihalopoulos and Victoria Brooks. Cheltenham: Edward Elgar.

Preston, Brian J. 2011. "The Influence of Climate Change Litigation on Governments and the Private Sector." *Climate Law* 2 (4): 485–513.

———. 2016. "The Contribution of the Courts in Tackling Climate Change." *Journal of Environmental Law* 28 (1): 11–17.

Punathambekar, Aswin, and Sriram Mohan, eds. 2019. *Global Digital Cultures: Perspectives from South Asia.* Ann Arbor: University of Michigan Press.

Robinson, Michael. 2015. "Is Democracy Threatened If Companies Can Sue Countries?" BBC, March 31, 2015. https://www.bbc.com/news/business-32116587 (Accessed July 17, 2022).

Sands, Philippe, ed. 1993. *Greening International Law.* International Law and Sustainable Development Series 1. London: Earthscan Publications.

Scharf, Michael, and Elizabeth Andersen. 2010. "Is Lawfare Worth Defining? Report of the Cleveland Experts Meeting—September 11, 2010". *Case Western Reserve Journal of International Law* 43 (1 & 2): 11–28.

Scotford, Eloise. 2022. "The Status of Environmental Principles in Environmental Law." In *Research Handbooks in Environmental Law*, edited by Douglas Fisher, 2nd ed., 381–405. Cheltenham: Edward Elgar.

Setzer, Joana. 2022. "The Impacts of High-Profile Litigation against Major Fossil Fuel Companies." In *Litigating the Climate Emergency*, edited by César Rodríguez-Garavito, 1st ed., 206–20. Cambridge University Press. https://doi.org/10.1017/9781009106214.013.

Slattery, Jon. 2022. "Press Freedom 2022: The Good & the Bad." *InPublishing*, August 2, 2022. https://www.inpublishing.co.uk/articles/press-freedom-2022-the-good-and-the-bad-21005 (Accessed August 23, 2023).

Thompson, John B. 2020. "Mediated Interaction in the Digital Age." *Theory, Culture & Society* 37 (1): 3–28.

Twining, William. 2009. *General Jurisprudence: Understanding Law from a Global Perspective.* Cambridge: Cambridge University Press.

United Nations Environment Programme. 2017. Status of Climate Change Litigation: A Global Review. United Nations Environment Programme Columbia University, Sabin Center for Climate Change Law. http://wedocs.unep.org/handle/20.500.11822/20767 (Accessed June 23, 2023).

Vallejo, Catalina, and Siri Gloppen. 2013. "Red-Green Lawfare? Climate Change Narratives in Courtrooms." In *Climate Talk*, edited by Jackie Dugard, Asuncion Lera St. Clair, and Siri Gloppen. Claremont: Juta Law.

Vanhala, Lisa. 2018. "Is Legal Mobilization for the Birds? Legal Opportunity Structures and Environmental Nongovernmental Organizations in the United Kingdom, France, Finland, and Italy." *Comparative Political Studies* 51 (3): 380–412. https://doi.org/10.1177/0010414017710257.

Vanhala, Lisa. 2022. "Environmental Legal Mobilization." *Annual Review of Law and Social Science* 18 (1): 101–17. https://doi.org/10.1146/annurev-lawsocsci-050520-104423.

Volkmer, Ingrid, and Kasim Sharif. 2018. *Risk Journalism between Transnational Politics and Climate Change*. Cham: Springer International.

Waisbord, Silvio. 2022. "What Is Next for De-Westernizing Communication Studies?" *Journal of Multicultural Discourses* 17 (1): 26–33.

Wolfsfeld, Gadi. 1997. *Media and Political Conflict: News from the Middle East*. Cambridge: Cambridge University Press.

Woronov, Terry. 2019. "Waging Lawfare: Law, Environment and Depoliticization in Neoliberal Australia." *Capitalism Nature Socialism* 30 (3): 110–128.

Cases

Mackay Conservation Group v. Commonwealth of Australia (Federal Court of Australia, NSD33/2015).

The State of the Netherlands v. Urgenda Foundation Supreme Court of the Netherlands (December 20, 2019).

· 2 ·

COMMUNICATING THE EARTH

In December 1994, a group of Greenpeace activists climbed one of the tall smokestacks at the Yallourn W Power Station in Australia's southeast and unfurled a long, narrow banner. The words "STOP COAL POWER" tumbled down the chimney. A helicopter circled nearby and below, a few workers and police had gathered. Harnessed and attached to the safety rail at the top of the chimney with my three companions, I scanned the high blue sky and wondered if communicating climate change as an environmental message was even possible. By the mid-1990s, environmental groups had well-established communication strategies that drew on the visual spectacularisms of nature and the passion of political protest, but I wondered then how we could draw the same concern for the intangible atmosphere that could be achieved for forests and whales. Months earlier, we had dropped a banner in Melbourne's central business district. After these actions, we would turn to the television news to measure our success, which ultimately rested on getting the right media attention to stimulate public interest and political debate. Of course, there are other ways to grab media attention, such as green lawfare.

That year, Greenpeace embarked on Australia's first climate case, *Greenpeace v. Redbank*, which challenged the approval of a new coal-fired power station on the grounds that the emissions from the station would contribute to the greenhouse effect. The court ultimately ruled against Greenpeace, finding Australia's obligations under international and domestic law did not prohibit the building of a new power station (Pepper 2017). Although unsuccessful, the case became the model for decades of "first wave" climate litigation that challenged planning and environmental legislation until, eventually, climate change was increasingly factored into new project approvals (Osofsky and Peel 2013). Action on the coal industry that year, which included the spectacularisms of mediated protest and less visible efforts in the courts, was part of a much larger social movement that since the 1960s has synthesized ecological science, ethical thinking and protest politics into what is now widely known as "the environment movement" (Lester 2010; Worster 1994). Broadly speaking, the environment movement aims to bring an ecological perspective to every aspect of human activity from the choices individuals make through to the economic and political systems that govern us. To explore this central element of green lawfare, this chapter begins with a brief history of the environmental movement with a particular focus on the role of news and other media before turning to contemporary examples of efforts to address the unfolding global crises of biodiversity loss and climate change.

A Brief History of the Environmental Movement

The various claims to the origins of the modern environmental movement suggest it sprung from many tributaries, including: the 1945 bombings of Hiroshima and Nagasaki that signaled the beginning of the nuclear age; the post-war transformation of the English and European countryside; the 1962 publication of Rachel Carson's *Silent Spring*; the 1968 "Earthrise" photograph taken from the Apollo 8 spacecraft; and the first "Earth Day" in 1970. Each of these moments occurred at the convergence of several defining features of the mid-twentieth century, including rapid developments in science, the rise of global mass media, and the various waves of civil rights movements. This section briefly covers the early features of the environmental movement, including the intersections of protest and media, environmental discourses and the communication of risk, and the politics of changing the world.

It all begins with ecology, a science that emerged as a discipline in the late nineteenth century as a response to geologists' growing appreciation of deep time, measured in epochs rather than centuries, and Charles Darwin's theory of evolution (Worster 1994). Reaching back in time, early ecologists began to trace and record the interconnection between living and non-living entities, including humanity, and found nature's dynamic systems vulnerable to human activity, particularly when technology was harnessed to economic enterprise (Goodie 2011; Worster 1994). The powerful cultural narrative that mastery over nature—including damming rivers, poisoning insects, and dumping waste in the waterways and skies—was beneficial to human society was reframed to be as threatening to human life and well-being as war and a new narrative began to emerge that called for greater protection of the environment. The American biologist, Rachel Carson, and her book *Silent Spring* (1962) epitomizes the strategic synthesis of science and mediated communication undertaken to influence politics and policy. Written for general audiences, *Silent Spring* described a world without insects and birdsong which, of course, presages ecological collapse. The United States chemical industry fought against its publication, threatening legal action against Carson and her publishers (which is a classic example of green lawfare) and started a public scare campaign about a world of pestilence and disease that would occur without their products. These tactics only amplified the publicity surrounding the book, which ultimately resulted in a national pesticide policy and the launch of the United States Environmental Protection Agency in 1970 (Banks 2003, 222).

The early environment movement was emerging, but science and scientists alone could not build the momentum for social change. The works of philosophers, naturalists and conservationists who had long looked at the countryside with concern provided the necessary ethical perspective. A favorite was Aldo Leopold's *A Sand County Almanac* ([1949] 1989) which chronicled the ecological tragedy of industrialization and described a "land ethic" based on the idea that

> [a]ll ethics so far evolved rest upon a single premise: that the individual is a member of a community of interdependent parts. The land ethic simply enlarges the boundaries of the community to include soils, waters, plants and animals, or collectively the land. (Leopold [1949] 1989, 203–204)

Similarly, a new audience found Henry David Thoreau's essay *On the Duty of Civil Disobedience* ([1849] 1983). While Thoreau was defending his objection to slavery as the moral duty to break unjust laws, his stance was reinterpreted by Edward Abbey in his novel *The Monkeywrench Gang* (1975) to justify environmental activism, including the destruction of machinery and infrastructure, as both a moral duty and a political right. Early environmentalists elsewhere drew on more local sources of inspiration. For instance, the Chipko movement, which formed to protect the forests in the Chamoli hills of Himalayan India in 1973, found inspiration and ideas from Mahatma Gandhi's legacy of protecting local cultures from colonial domination through non-violent direct action (Pathak 2021). As discussed in Chapter Three, the environmental movement found echoes and inspiration in ancient and indigenous ethics that positioned a duty of environmental care to be a matter of public health, social justice and the sacred. For now, however, we will focus on the modern environmental movement to observe how ideas and knowledge are translated into political action, which includes exploring the networks of communication that constitute the spaces and places where ideas are shared, fought, and accepted— or defeated.

The Intersections of Protest and Media

What role does communication media play in negotiating the rifts and ruptures in our understanding of the environment? Since its early days, the environmental movement has had "little choice" but to engage with news media "as the key structuring intermediary in the conduct of public affairs" (Hutchins and Lester 2006, 437). Successful environmental campaigns are notable for engaging with news media's appetite for the spectacular and the symbolic, as well as the novel affordances of new media technologies. In the 1960s, developments in underwater color photography were adopted to reveal the wonders of coral reefs and the deep ocean, in the 1970s hand-held cameras were used to show the violence of whaling and seal-hunting, and, more recently, drones have been sent into the forest canopy to show a single tree as a complex community of lifeforms.

In addition to having an aptitude for new media technology, successful environmental campaigns adapted to the demands of "media logic" (Altheide and Snow 1979), a term that describes the assumptions and processes of institutional cultures, individuals, and information technologies and media platforms that informs media production. Beyond the logistics of production, media logic describes how ingrained and largely unquestioned professional norms result in practices, such as the preference for the dramatic and sensational. Media logic includes the idea of news values, a term that describes the unspoken but "relatively consistent criteria" by which news is selected from the myriad events of any given day (Allan 2004, 63), such as "the power elite" and "celebrity" (Harcup and O'Neill 2001, 278–279) and "conflict" and "the unusual" (Ricketson 2004, 9–12). While the unspoken criteria of news values explain the selection of issues for coverage, understanding the logic of media framing is another important tool for communicators (McCombs et al. 1997; Reese et al. 2001). News framing describes the deliberate selection and presentation of specific aspects of an event or issue that unavoidably begins the moment journalists select a story or begin to make sense of an event (Cappella and Jamieson 1997; Gitlin 1980) using a logic "composed of little tacit theories about what exists, what happens, and what matters" (Gitlin 1980, 6). The idea of problem frames is particularly useful in the context of how media frames social and environmental problems because problem framing constructs a story through identifying that "something is wrong" before attributing blame, and prescribing a "correction" or "repair agent" (Altheide 1997, 655).

Media logic, including concepts such as new values and framing, remains a useful approach for understanding the choices social actors make when engaging with news and other media. Like all social movements, the environmental movement engages with a wide range of media for many purposes, including using media to mobilize and expand their constituencies and to gain political legitimacy (Gamson and Wolfsfeld 1993). As well as engaging with legacy news media, environmental actors have long used independent media networks—sending photocopied newsletters, handbooks, and videos via postal services before the Internet presented faster, cheaper alternatives. Environmental protesters continue to find new ways of creating spectacle to grab the attention of news and other media (Anderson 2014; Pezzullo 2021) and to maintain and build global networks of communities of concern (Anderson and Lester 2020; Hansen 2015). For instance, climate activists have taken to using the shock of throwing paint and soup on priceless artworks and blocking major transport routes to grab people's attention. Many of these global actions are organized under the Global Civil Resistance Network, whose website describes the network as "a group of connected projects engaged in a mad dash to try to save humanity" (Noakes 2022). As activist Harley Brewer told the *Saturday Paper*, "we essentially help each other out and work in concert, you know, sharing information about what's worked, sharing best practice, et cetera, to try and bring this international thing to happen" (Noakes 2022). While relatively disparate, these activists are using digital media to not only share ideas … out to spread images of disruption to global audiences to foster … ities of concern.

As noted earlier, and further developed in Chapter Three, the environmental movement describes a diverse and global social movement united in its resistance to incursions into nature and human culture by exploitative and destructive practices. While climate change, pollution and biodiversity loss are identified as the key issues facing the planet, action on climate change appears to be separated from wider environmental topics in academic, policy, activist and media discourses and quarantined from the wider projects of social transformation associated with the environment movement. Is the distinction to ensure the urgency of reducing greenhouse gas emissions remains central to climate messages? Does the term "environmental" carry too many ideological or political connotations? Does this separation quarantine action on climate from the wider projects of social transformation associated with the environment movement? Does distinguishing climate and environment simply ensure the urgency of reducing greenhouse gas emissions remains central to climate messaging? If this is the case, does the focus on reducing greenhouse gas emissions privilege scientific approaches, such as carbon sequestration and other technological fixes while ignoring other solutions? If indeed we should focus on climate change, who decides what problems are prioritized as action on climate and what might be deemed of less importance (Painter 2021)? What are the risks of not giving equal consideration to the other ecological crises before us, such as plastic pollution and species extinction, access to fresh water and clean air, and the increasing pervasiveness of the industrial footprint across the Earth? Perhaps "climate change" has become a new catch-all for the myriad ecological crises the world faces? If this is the case, and sometimes it does seem this way, is all journalism— food and agriculture, politics, economics, even sport— now climate journalism (Collingridge et al. 2021)? What does such a shift signal to what we expect from news and those who produce it? Studies have found climate change journalists, who typically follow the scientific consensus on climate change, also tend to report favorably on climate activism (Wonneberger 2024) and are less likely to present so-called objective or balanced reporting, in favor of interpretative reporting (Brüggemann and Engesser 2017). Whether these shifts can be seen in other forms of reporting, remains less understood. For instance, the well-documented relationship between the fossil fuel industry and politics suggests climate journalism should include investigations into corporate tax avoidance, government accountability, and the structural biases in our institutions and systems that hinder climate action (Lucas 2021). While Ulrich Beck (2010) argued that the shift from environmental communication to climate communication suggested orientation of environmental awareness toward social inequality at a global scale, the extent to which news media coverage of climate is extending to questions of equity or governance is less understood. Certainly, the consensus on climate change is increasingly sedimenting as a master narrative (Brüggemann and Engesser 2017).

However we look at it, environmental communication, which includes climate communication and journalism, faces the challenge of translating and interpreting matters at the confluence of scientific knowledge and political, economic, and social action. As such, effective environmental communication extends beyond conveying scientific knowledge to engaging with the activities and actors who are pushing humanity closer to the edge of extinction (Cottle 2023).

Environmental Discourses

Ideas about what constitutes the environment and its problems are shaped and reshaped by the grand narratives and discourses of politics, religion, ecology, and economics, as well as personal values and beliefs. The meaning of the term "discourse" varies, but is used here to describe the "systems of meaning" (Howarth 2009, 311) and the "ensemble of ideas, concepts and categories" (Hajer 1993, 45) we use to interpret our world. In this sense, legal discourses are "among the most evident, tangible, and institutionalized forms of socio-ethnological communication" (Humphreys 1985, 242). More than just describing how we "talk about things," the term conceptualizes the communicative processes we use to understand the world in ways that inform our actions and cultural practices and that often appear to be the natural way of doing things (Curran and Hesmondhalgh 2019; Dryzek 2021, 33). The discourses used to construct our ideas about the "environment" and "environmental problems" are continually constituted through communication and communicative action. For some, the natural world is a force to be harnessed and only made valuable through extraction; for others it is little more than an aesthetic backdrop to the grander drama of human relations; for others still, it is the sacred cosmos that connects all of time and creation. A wide range of environmental discourses constitute "the politics of the Earth" (Dryzek 2013) and include anti- environmental communication, such as climate skepticism and other nihilisms, greenwashing and litigation, because these discourses also describe a worldview that relates to the natural world (Dinan and Miller 2022).

Following Cottle's (2006) observation that media are always "doing something," mapping the passages of environmental discourses through media is one way to chart the flow of shared concepts and ideas that, in turn, inform our understanding of the world beyond humanity's preoccupations. Such mapping includes observing the contests over the definition and construction of meaning (Carvalho 2008; Entman 1993). Indeed, environmental conflict, including disputes that engage in green lawfare, are often contests over ideas and definitions from both environmental and anti-environmental messaging. For this reason, within various environmental discourses, we can find a spectrum of worldviews including those that promote an ecocentric perspective, which locates humanity within the web of life, and those maintaining anthropocentric worldviews, which separates and elevates humanity from the natural world (Hay 2002). Mapping such discursive struggle enables us to engage with the actors, institutions, and social processes that constitute the contests for political and economic power that underpin most environmental conflicts. Michel Foucault (1980) famously linked discourse to power relations by tracing the links between discourse and the processes, procedures, and institutions where truth, knowledge and belief are produced, sustained, and contested. By understanding discourse as not just a matter of speech acts, but also communicative processes that inform social and political action, we can begin to understand how struggles for hegemonic power within the elite and by those seeking to counter hegemonic power shape our world (Fairclough 1995). A classic example of how shared meaning informs action is in the communication of uncertainty and risk.

The Communication of Risk

The emphasis on ecology, and science more generally, in environmental communication is an uneasy one, with a general agreement that while science played a key role in the first wave of environmental thought, environment communication goes well beyond (Anderson and Lester 2020; Cottle 2023). This tension is not easily resolved. While environmental discourse is often hostile to modern science—especially the entrapment of science in the processes of industrialization—actors in environmental conflict frequently rely on science-based claims to provide not only information but a sense of authoritative objectivity (Scoones 1999, 488). Never more so than in the communication of risk. Many, if not most, environmental threats and problems are difficult to "see" because they include invisible elements, such

Following Cottle's (2006) observation that media are always "doing something," mapping the passages of environmental discourses through media is one way to chart the flow of shared concepts and ideas that, in turn, inform our understanding of the world beyond humanity's preoccupations. Such mapping includes observing the contests over the definition and construction of meaning (Carvalho 2008; Entman 1993). Indeed, environmental conflict, including disputes that engage in green lawfare, are often contests over ideas and definitions from both environmental and anti-environmental messaging. For this reason, within various environmental discourses, we can find a spectrum of worldviews including those that promote an ecocentric perspective, which locates humanity within the web of life, and those maintaining anthropocentric worldviews, which separates and elevates humanity from the natural world (Hay 2002). Mapping such discursive struggle enables us to engage with the actors, institutions, and social processes that constitute the contests for political and economic power that underpin most environmental conflicts. Michel Foucault (1980) famously linked discourse to power relations by tracing the links between discourse and the processes, procedures, and institutions where truth, knowledge and belief are produced, sustained, and contested. By understanding discourse as not just a matter of speech acts, but also communicative processes that inform social and political action, we can begin to understand how struggles for hegemonic power within the elite and by those seeking to counter hegemonic power shape our world (Fairclough 1995). A classic example of how shared meaning informs action is in the communication of uncertainty and risk.

The Communication of Risk

The emphasis on ecology, and science more generally, in environmental communication is an uneasy one, with a general agreement that while science played a key role in the first wave of environmental thought, environment communication goes well beyond (Anderson and Lester 2020; Cottle 2023). This tension is not easily resolved. While environmental discourse is often hostile to modern science—especially the entrapment of science in the processes of industrialization—actors in environmental conflict frequently rely on science-based claims to provide not only information but a sense of authoritative objectivity (Scoones 1999, 488). Never more so than in the communication of risk. Many, if not most, environmental threats and problems are difficult to "see" because they include invisible elements, such orientation of environmental awareness toward social inequality at a global scale, the extent to which news media coverage of climate is extending to questions of equity or governance is less understood. Certainly, the consensus on climate change is increasingly sedimenting as a master narrative (Brüggemann and Engesser 2017).

However we look at it, environmental communication, which includes climate communication and journalism, faces the challenge of translating and interpreting matters at the confluence of scientific knowledge and political, economic, and social action. As such, effective environmental communication extends beyond conveying scientific knowledge to engaging with the activities and actors who are pushing humanity closer to the edge of extinction (Cottle 2023).

Environmental Discourses

Ideas about what constitutes the environment and its problems are shaped and reshaped by the grand narratives and discourses of politics, religion, ecology, and economics, as well as personal values and beliefs. The meaning of the term "discourse" varies, but is used here to describe the "systems of meaning" (Howarth 2009, 311) and the "ensemble of ideas, concepts and categories" (Hajer 1993, 45) we use to interpret our world. In this sense, legal discourses are "among the most evident, tangible, and institutionalized forms of socio-ethnological communication" (Humphreys 1985, 242). More than just describing how we "talk about things," the term conceptualizes the communicative processes we use to understand the world in ways that inform our actions and cultural practices and that often appear to be the natural way of doing things (Curran and Hesmondhalgh 2019; Dryzek 2021, 33). The discourses used to construct our ideas about the "environment" and "environmental problems" are continually constituted through communication and communicative action. For some, the natural world is a force to be harnessed and only made valuable through extraction; for others it is little more than an aesthetic backdrop to the grander drama of human relations; for others still, it is the sacred cosmos that connects all of time and creation. A wide range of environmental discourses constitute "the politics of the Earth" (Dryzek 2013) and include anti- environmental communication, such as climate skepticism and other nihilisms, greenwashing and litigation, because these discourses also describe a worldview that relates to the natural world (Dinan and Miller 2022).

as one of the first international organizations working with wildlife conservation (Sachedina 2010) and Chile's first environmental organization, the *Comité Nacional Pro Defensa de la Flora y Fauna* (National Committee for the Defense of Flora and Fauna) was established in 1968 (CODEFF n.d.), which was the same year as the first protest to protect Australia's Great Barrier Reef (Foxwell-Norton and Konkes 2019) and, as noted earlier, the 1973 Chipko movement in the Indian Himalayas drew on Gandhian principles of non-violence (Pathak 2021; see also Pezzullo 2021). Some argue that the environment movement has older roots, such as the founding of the Coal Smoke Abatement Society in 1871 as a very early response to Britain's rapid industrialization (Thorsheim 2006). The same goes for the origin stories of environmental law. In 1972, Christopher Stone famously unsettled the American legal sphere when he asked if trees should have legal standing but, around the same time, the Chilean writer Godofredo Stutzin was also writing in Spanish about the rights of nature, which went on to have a stronger influence in Latin America than Stone's work which was so influential in the Anglosphere (Tănăsescu 2013).

The environmental movement is global and diverse, but in the discussion so far has been largely defined as a movement emerging from the scientific traditions established during the Enlightenment, including ecology, which are not the only knowledge systems concerned with the relationship between human culture and the natural systems that sustain life. Understanding the processes and negotiations between various kinds of knowledge, including scientific, lay, local and indigenous knowledges, provides an important lens on the evolution of a truly global ecocentric perspective informing contemporary expressions of environmentalism (Scoones 1999, 495). Much work remains to be done on how ecological perspectives are transferred from one location and context to another. To date, environmental ethics have largely been defined by actors in wealthier nations and then introduced into poorer communities with "deeply ambiguous results" (Scoones 1999, 489) that have been likened by some to being akin to colonialism (Agarwal and Narain 2019; Takahashi 2023; Thaker 2022). While the environmental movement remains "the principal site of resistance to global capital and the domination of social life by economic interests" (Castells 2004, 182) we must ensure environmental discourses, including international environmental law, can meet this challenge to the benefit of all (Anderson and Lester 2020, viii).

Stories of Our Times

Observing the flow of discourse through mediated communication brings insights into how actors construct the dominant discourses through which we understand the environment and its problems (Carvalho 2008). Discourses inform our sense of shared places, moments, and ideas that help us to not only ask "how did we get here?" but also to decide what we should do next (Lester 2019). The dominance of two ideas in global environmental discourse illustrates the practical, political, and ethical challenges to the question about what we should do next. The first is the idea of the Anthropocene as a scientific term that has passed into political rhetoric and, secondly, is the motif of the Apocalypse in climate communication.

From Ecology to the Anthropocene

In the early days of ecological science, natural systems were theorized and modeled as a kind of equilibrium, but this mechanistic understanding began to shift in the 1970s as modeling found unexpected chaos and uncertainty. As Donald Worster (1994, 412) writes, by reaching back into deep geological time, ecologists increasingly understood that ecosystems were not fixed, but rather were:

> shifting patterns in the endless flux, always new, always different. Ecosystems emerged out of the evolutionary turmoil in the grasslands or coral seas just as human kingdoms, empires, and civilizations arose out of the constant turmoil in people's lives, and then they fell apart. Like eddies appearing in a turbulent stream, such complex systems did not last forever, but while they lasted, they showed an astonishing capacity for dynamic cohesion, stability, and order.

The turmoil of complex systems and the impermanence of all life on Earth is captured in the idea of the Anthropocene. While the precise date of the commencement of the Anthropocene, or its categorization as an epoch, remains a subject of intense scientific debate (Witze 2024), the term works as "a powerful intellectual bridge" and "paradigm shift in the Western philosophy of science" (Cottle 2023, 7). In short, the concept of the Anthropocene, unanchored from its usefulness as a geological idea, has come to encapsulate what we know of the complexity of Earth systems and the devastating impact of human culture on those systems.

The concept of the Anthropocene was first described by biologist Eugene Stoermer in the 1980s but did not become widely known until Stoermer revisited the idea in an article with meteorologist and atmospheric chemist Paul Crutzen (Crutzen and Stoermer 2000). In describing the Anthropocene, the authors pointed to the role of media and communication in meeting the challenge, arguing that

> a worldwide accepted strategy leading to the sustainability of ecosystems against human-induced stresses will be one of the great future tasks of mankind, requiring intensive research efforts and wise application of the knowledge thus acquired in the noösphere, better known as knowledge or information society. (Crutzen and Stoermer 2000, 18)

In a later article, Crutzen (2002) reoriented the mission to emphasize the role of science as directing, rather than informing, decision making, writing that

> a daunting task lies ahead for scientists and engineers to guide society towards environmentally sustainable management during the era of the Anthropocene. This will require appropriate human behavior at all scales, and may well involve internationally accepted, large-scale geo-engineering projects, for instance, to "optimize" climate. (Crutzen 2002, 23)

The drift in discourse from science informing decision-making to having a mandate to make decisions gathered momentum with the idea of planetary boundaries that emerged a decade or so later.

The idea of planetary boundaries defines the thresholds or "safe operating space for humanity" (Rockström et al. 2009a). Johan Rockström's team established nine "tipping points": climate change, stratospheric ozone depletion, land system change, global freshwater use, biodiversity loss, ocean acidification, interference with phosphorus and nitrogen cycles, atmospheric aerosol loading, and chemical pollution. Importantly, these thresholds are interdependent, meaning a change in one of the key processes is likely to lead to shifts in others. In another article, Rockström and a list of distinguished scientists, including Paul Crutzen and James Hansen, argued that the Anthropocene presented "a new approach to global sustainability" that found "as long as the thresholds are not crossed, humanity has the freedom to pursue long-term social and economic development" (Rockström et al. 2009, 475). Overall, the introduction of planetary boundaries to the idea of Anthropocene presented a "rupture" that shifted the Anthropocene from being a description of humanity's impact on the Earth to one that defined humanity as a threat to itself and all life on Earth (Kim 2022, 5).

The planetary boundaries framework found significant interest in academic, policy and social advocacy circles (Dryzek 2021; Fernández and Malwé 2019; Webster and Mai 2020) with key debates relating to questions about who sets the limits, on what basis and for whom. In particular, are questions as to the merit of limits being set by a small group of scientists mostly located in the natural sciences and in the institutions of Europe and Northern America (Kim and Kotzé 2020). In particular, the idea that planetary boundaries science should inform global climate governance remains "conspicuously silent about the structurally embedded causes of Earth system transformation" which then side-lines how cause, fault and remedy can be understood (Kim and Kotzé 2020, 5). Indeed, while action on climate appears to have been decoupled from the ideological connotations of the environmental movement, the discourses of the Anthropocene can be seen to shift from being a scientific theory to a case for radical social change coming from a small but powerful group of actors. In other words, the depoliticization of action on climate change can be seen as an explicitly political project.

Promoted, even "pushed aggressively" (Dryzek 2021, 39), by sections of the scientific community, the planetary boundaries concept has slowly been adopted into international governance frameworks. Having been removed from the final draft declaration of the 2012 UN Conference on Sustainable Development (Rio+20) and left out of the 2015 Sustainable Development Goals, "planetary boundaries" are mentioned throughout the IPCC's Sixth Assessment Report (IPCC 2022). Alongside this gradual adoption is a renewal of criticisms that democracy is not up to the task of climate action following the perceived failures of the United Nations Climate Conferences, especially the 2009 Copenhagen summit, followed by the 2010 Cancún and 2011 Durban summits (Stehr 2013, 57). Even if democracy is up to the task, in order to "construct a democratic imaginary wherein political agency is possible for citizens, as well as the non-human environment and future generations, the Anthropocene has to be reconstructed not only as an epoch but also as a new scale of democratic governance" (Mert 2019, 142). In other words, traveling with the scientific discourses of the Anthropocene and planetary boundaries framework is a sub-set of political discourse that deserves some attention.

Governing the Anthropocene

Criticisms from the scientific community over the failings of democracy predate our knowledge of anthropogenic climate change. Malthusianism prophecies of civilizational collapse resurface in debates over overpopulation, natural resource exhaustion, and other environmental problems (Shahar 2015; Stehr 2013). These debates stir up old questions about whether the public can be trusted, or is even needed, in matters of importance. Arguing against the idealized notion that every person wants, deserves or should be expected to participate in civic matters, Walter Lippmann ([1927] 1993) famously began his manifesto on the "phantom public" with a particular kind of disdain (1927, 188–189):

> A false ideal of democracy can lead only to disillusionment and to meddlesome tyranny. If democracy cannot direct affairs, then a philosophy which expects it to direct them will encourage the people to attempt the impossible; they will fail, but that will interfere outrageously with the productive liberties of the individual. The public must be put in its place … so that each of us may live free of the trampling and the roar of a bewildered herd.

Without engaging with questions of power and hegemony, Lippmann ([1927] 1993, 189–190) goes on to argue for leaving decisions to the experts with "the least possible interference from ignorant and meddlesome outsiders."[1] Decades on, his impatience with the "phantom public" can be found in calls for science to have a greater role in governance especially around population growth and social decline. For instance, Garrett Hardin (1985, 473) insisted that a central dogma of ecology includes the rule that "population growth ultimately makes democracy impossible"[2] with the disaster best avoided "through a frank policy

1 This position was challenged by John Dewey (1927) who, in reply to Lippmann, defended the ability of everyday people to solve their problems. Far from seeing the public as ignorant and meddlesome, Dewey reasoned that "the man who wears the shoe knows best that it pinches and where it pinches, even if the expert shoemaker is the best judge of how the trouble is to be remedied" (Dewey 1927, 207). This exchange, known as the Lippmann–Dewey debate, strikes at the heart of perceptions of apathy and civic disengagement and questions of public involvement in complex matters of policy.

2 Interestingly, Hardin (1985) also argues that democracy is impossible because an expanding population would burden a well-defined communication network by an ever-increasing size that would lead to "information-overload, which leads to misunderstandings, social pathologies, and (ultimately) the acceptance of a totalitarian regime as the least of the evils available to an overpopulated political unit."

of 'mutual coercion, mutually agreed upon'." The discourses around planetary boundaries only added to this view (Pickering et al. 2020).

Two competing discourses inform criticisms that democracy is not addressing anthropogenic climate change: one positions the fault with the capitalist logic embedded in modern liberal democracies (Fraser 2023), and the other takes a more pessimistic view of democracy and the liberties it fosters (Hulme 2009, 308–309). James Hansen, is an example of the former, telling the *Guardian* (Adam 2009) that corporate lobbying had undermined democratic attempts to curb carbon pollution to the extent that "the democratic process doesn't quite seem to be working." James Lovelock is an example of the latter. Comparing the action needed to address climate change to the austerity endured during the Second World War, Lovelock (2009, 94–95) wrote that "democracy had temporarily to be suspended and we had to accept a disciplined regime that saw our nation as a legitimate but limited safe haven for civilization". Lovelock later told the *Guardian* (Hickman 2010) that "it may be necessary to put democracy on hold for a while."

In these debates, the many versions of possible and existent expressions of democracy are reduced to a singular democracy that is withering, flawed and too cumbersome to help humanity confront its darkest hour. Such handwringing over the state of democracy has inevitably led to some tendering solutions, such as David Shearman and Joseph Wayne Smith (2007, 13) who called for a form of "authoritarian meritocracy" led by "an altruistic, able, authoritarian leader, versed in science and personal skills" to solve the crisis. Such a solution raises a lot of questions (!), such as who will select this authoritarian leader and what will be done to those who resist the proposed solutions? Certainly, examples of recent authoritarian regimes, such as those under Bolsonaro in Brazil, Orbán in Hungary, Duterte in the Philippines, and Modi in India, suggest that the removal of democratic checks and balances, which have included attacks on civil institutions and communication media, tend to favor the transnational extractive industries over environmental protection. As Elizabeth Fisher (2019, 385) observes, the rise of populist governments on both the right and the left has tended toward "the centralized pooling of executive power … [that] sits uncomfortably with the need for an environmental rule of law with the range of institutions it requires." Enforcing even the most benevolent authoritarian regime would also require an unimaginable degree of violence at a global level. Here, Hannah Arendt (1956a, 409) provides a useful caution, writing that attempts to control:

> the unpredictable spontaneity of human beings … demands much more radical measures than the mere transformation of laws into decrees, which is characteristic of all bureaucratic forms of tyranny, where government and due process of law are replaced by administration and anonymous decisions.

In other words, calls for democracy to be suspended to allow scientific expertise to steer us away from catastrophe could just as likely steer us closer to social and environmental calamity.

We might consider the democracies where change is occurring instead. Dryzek and Stevenson (2011) note consensual democracies, rather than their adversarial counterparts, tend to perform better on environmental matters. They suggest it could be the differences in economic systems, with consensual democracies tending to have more cooperative market economies, while adversarial democracies tend to have competitive market economies that are more likely to embrace neoliberal economics. Or, they suggest, it could be that consensual democracies that enable open deliberation also tend to provide better outcomes for environmental issues. What is clearly required, then, is ensuring human cultural systems at a global level align with earth systems in ways that ensure environmental stability. Such a task is not a scientific problem and is distracted by hyperscientific solutions, such as geo-engineering. Instead, realigning human culture to environmental systems requires shifting the dominant human culture, which is the globalized capital systems that increasingly evade the regulating forces of local.

Such work is underway, of course, and captured in initiatives, such as the Green New Deal (e.g. Barbier 2010) that describes pathways to reducing the world's dependency on carbon and the devastating impacts of pollution and biodiversity loss. Communicating these ideas requires keeping an eye on both the past and the present that, neither blinded by cynicism nor ideology, connects what we already know with what could be possible (Zelizer 2019) and deepens, rather than suspends, democratic procedures (Mouffe 2023). This challenge demands deepening the engagement between the natural and social sciences, which requires not only a better understanding of the science informing our understanding of the Anthropocene as a scientific "fact" but also a better understanding of the social, economic and political mechanisms used to stabilize human relations to enable a meaningful response (Vidas et al. 2015). News and other media clearly play an important role in such a project. In short, media can communicate lessons from the past in ways that inform how we understand our present problems and our approach to their solutions (Zelizer 2019). Media can also hold the powerful to account.

While the meddlesome tyranny of an ill-informed public, to borrow from Lippmann, is the phantom that preoccupies many critiques of democracy, other tyrannies warrant our attention. In particular, news and other media focus our attention on the sites of contest between the powerful and the marginalized. In the local clashes between communities and extractive industries, for instance, we see the challenge to the political and economic forces driving globalization, which highlights the desperate need for the international community to rein in the power of transnational corporations, global trade, and financing (Dauvergne 2008). Not only do news and other media raise the alarm, but mediated networks connect local and global communities to share ideas about how we may address the gap between our increasing understanding of the Earth as a complex whole and our currently fragmented regulatory systems (Kim and Kotzé 2022; see also Goodie and Wickham; 2002; Pereira and Viola 2018).

While the discourses of urgency prevail, we not only risk ushering in new tyrannies but also indulging discourses so laden with moral condemnation as to paralyze political action. Jeff Sparrow (2021, 3) warns against talking about climate action in terms that render us "criminally worthless: mindless consumers obsessed only with material satisfaction, too lazy and stupid to even recycle … almost genetically predisposed to selfishness and avarice," which does little to inspire personal or political action (or other expressions of hope). It is time, Sparrow argues, to change how we think about the attribution of liability, guilt, and responsibility. As noted earlier, journalists have long been tasked with describing problems in terms of blame and the responsibility of redress (Altheide 1997), and the courts are increasingly being targeted by activists as the ideal arena in which to define climate change and other environmental problems as problems that governments can, and should, act upon.

The critique of the Anthropocene as a dominant scientific discourse in global climate governance mirrors criticisms of globalization, including imaginaries of a homogenous "global" community, which tend to undervalue diversity, overlook colonial histories and ignore the drivers of industrialization (Chakrabarty 2018; Wodak and Meyer 2016). In their scathing assessment of the Anthropocene, Malm and Hornborg (2014) observe that despite a large proportion of humanity contributing very little to the current climate crisis, the Anthropocene narrative tends to define our current environmental crises as determined by the traits of the entirety of humanity as a species, rather than the practices of a few, which makes the Anthropocene

> an ideology more by default than by design, more the product of the dominance of natural science in the field of climate change and, perhaps, the general blunting of critical edges and narrowing of political horizons in the post-1989 world than of any malicious apologetics. (Malm and Hornborg 2014, 67)

Despite all the possibilities held in democratic imaginaries, and the efforts of many to incorporate an ecological perspective to governance at local, national and international levels, the Anthropocene remains a dominant narrative in scientific circles and beyond that foretells total system collapse, including societal collapse as we head toward the demise of a habitable Earth. Decoupled from its scientific origins once again, the Anthropocene is reimagined as the coming Apocalypse, or end times, which further forecloses opportunities for action.

From the Anthropocene to the Apocalypse

Global pandemics, the invasion of Ukraine and war in Gaza, the ever-widening divide between the miserably poor and the absurdly rich, the shifting baseline of species from abundance to scarcity, the longer, drier "fire seasons," which is what we now call the Australian summer. Such crises are not quite the four horsemen—typically war, famine, wild beasts and pestilence—of the biblical Apocalypse, but such phenomena are frequently described as "apocalyptic" in news and other media, and never more so than during Australia's Black Summer bushfires (Mocatta and Hawley 2020). However, the Apocalypse is more than easy journalistic shorthand to describe the indescribable; it is also favored by environmental activists (Peeples et al. 2014) and those in the de-growth movement, such as Naomi Klein (2020).

With implicit connections to the end of time and reckoning, the Apocalypse carries the same whiff of inevitability implied in some renderings of the Anthropocene. Walter McNeish (2017) usefully problematizes the invocation of the Apocalypse to describe a world where the Earth's tipping points have been passed. Rather than being a new way of looking at environmental crises, McNeish (2017, 1036) writes that the uncritical evocation of the Apocalypse as a "cataclysmic reckoning for humanity … perhaps even annihilation of all life" is not only lodged in the old binary of environment versus human progress but also provides little inspiration for action. Others argue that Apocalyptic conditions started centuries ago for some people with the arrival of colonialism (Kwaymullina 2018, 7; Nixon 2011).

At a time when we urgently need the international community committed to action on climate, the discourses of the Anthropocene and the attendant metaphor of the Apocalypse risk leaving us to "grasp the bars in mediated glee and clap to the sights and sound of the end of the world" (Goodman et al. 2016, 680). Messages of hopelessness proliferate because media logic, including the algorithms designed to capture and keep our attention, privileges sensational claims and the amplification of fear. In turn, our engagement makes a tidy profit for media companies that have close relationships with the networks of industry that prioritize short-term financial gain over climate action (Bladlow and Ladino 2018; McNeish 2017).

In short, global ecological crises may be defined in scientific terms, but their solutions lie in political action. While ecological science gave voice to the early environmental movement and earth systems science has since shown the processes leading to catastrophic climate change, addressing these crises requires engaging with the social, political, and economic drivers of environmental harm. Such engagement involves the institutions of governance and the networks of formal and informal communication, especially networked communication, so we will finish this chapter looking at the challenges and opportunities for news and other media in the challenge of communicating the Earth before turning our attention to law and governance in the next chapter.

Mediated Networks and the Flow of Ideas

Areas of human activity are often described in metaphors including "arenas" (Wolfsfeld 1997), "spheres" (Habermas 1989; Hallin 1984), "fields" (Bourdieu 1986), "networks" (Castells 2009), "capillaries" (Foucault 1980) and, lastly, as "a fragile web" (Arendt 1956b). Webs, networks, and capillaries focus on connections and the diffuse nature of power in modern society, while fields and spheres denote the specific epistemological and institutional communities that are defined by certain practices, structures, actors and expertise through which political, economic and symbolic power is exercised. The theorization of green lawfare offered here draws on Castells' networks and Bourdieu's fields to observe the networked interaction between various spheres during mediated environmental conflict. While Hutchins and Lester (2015) focused on "journalism practices and news reporting" in determining media as a sphere or action, the conceptualization of communication media is extended beyond news and - to capture developments in the mediatization of protest politics since their study.

Not that long ago, "the media" was a useful shorthand for the networks of newspapers, radio and television that brought us "the news." The confidence of the pronoun was unwavering: "the media" was the professional journalists working with familiar news brands whose stories constituted "the news" that would define the political agenda for the days and weeks ahead. This understanding of news media as providing not only information but also scrutiny of the powerful is grounded in the idea of the Fourth Estate which has followed the earliest iterations of journalism (Curran 2002; Schultz 1998). As a major industry and civic institution (Cottle 2006; Couldry and Hepp 2017; Curran 2002; Thompson 1995), news media has long been central to the formation of the public sphere (Habermas 1989) and the "imagined communities" of the nation-state (Anderson 2006) as both "the primary sense-making practice of modernity" (Hartley 1996, 12) and the disrupter of political power (Thompson 1995).

Since the late twentieth century, news and other media have increasingly become embedded in the constitution of our social lives (Castells 2009; Cottle 2006; Couldry and Hepp 2017; Peters and Broesma 2017). The blurring of journalism and entertainment was challenging the democratizing potential of journalism long before the great digital disruption, but the rise of the Internet, especially social media and hand-held devices, has only further blurred the assumed stability of the power-media nexus. More than ever, it is a mistake to regard media, especially in its interactions with politics, as a stable and undifferentiated system (Hannigan 2006, 2). For this reason, understanding media as networks of communication through which information flows and where power is exercised and contested, provides an approach to communication that focuses on the processes that enable or hinder the flow rather than on the specificities of professional roles or platforms.

The complex networks along which information now flows are constituted by a rapidly changing range of communication technologies transforming the practices of production and the content we consume. Castells, especially his conceptualization of *The Network Society* (2004; also, Arsenault and Castells 2008; Castells 2007, 2009), provides a useful framework for observing how social movements engage with power. In the network society, power is not centralized in any one sphere or institution, but "distributed throughout the entire realm of human action" (Castells 2009, 239). Drawing on computer science, Castells describes social networks as defined by the roles, goals and rules of performance—in other words, their operating code—which also enable actors to "switch" the flow of power (Arsenault and Castells 2008). These "switching points" are visible in the contests over leadership, in "landmark" legal cases and in other sites where we see a "switch" in power as a result of changes in power relations and configurations of power.

Definitions of power abound. Manuel Castells (2009, 10) simply defines power as "the relational capacity that enables a social actor to influence asymmetrically the decisions of other social actors(s) in ways that favor the empowered actor's will, interests, and values." For Michel Foucault (1980), whose influential work connected discourse to power, power was envisaged as diffuse and threaded like a network of capillaries in every corner of society. In the network society, news and other media are not so much "the holders of power," but rather constituting the spaces where power is negotiated and decided (Castells 2007, 242) and where power is enacted through the capacity to control mediated visibility (and invisibility) and the struggles to define issues and control agendas (Lester 2010, 5).

For Arjun Appadurai, it is not just the technical apparatus of mediated communication or media as a set of industries that defines the central role of media and communication in the processes of globalization. Adding to these structural forces, he writes (1996, 36) is how they privilege the circulation of the "master narrative of the Enlightenment" and its "chain of ideas, terms, and images, including freedom, welfare, rights, sovereignty, representation, and the master term democracy." In other words, the global network of communication is not the free market of ideas that the techno-utopians might have hoped for but rather a homogenized, globalized mall promoting hegemonic power. As well as the dominant voices in these spaces, we can find those actors calling for differentiation from the tendency for stronger players to define what is possible at a global scale. For instance, when the United Nations General Assembly universally declared that the "right to a clean, healthy and sustainable environment as a human right" (United Nations 2022), Pakistan's representative said that "common but differentiated responsibilities" should have been included in the resolution. In a marketplace spruiking a limited range of possibilities, we find ourselves circling back to democracy's critics to wonder if it is not so much a problem with democracy, but rather how we are communicating what we see as inevitable, rather than possible. News and other media are central to this communication process. As transnational disagreement and conflict about climate and other environmental crises increases, our understanding of the factors influencing the visibility of speakers and their worldviews, actors and their agendas, and the practices and platforms used by journalists and others, remains vital (Post et al. 2019).

Conclusion: Communicating Our Place on Earth

Environmental discourses combine scientific knowledge with the aesthetics, values, and other subjectivities particular to people's daily lives. A gray goshawk (*Accipiter novaehollandiae*) sometimes visits the valley where I live. These snow-white raptors were once shot as vermin but are now largely protected by law and the social opprobrium toward the wanton killing of wild animals. But there is only one goshawk in this valley where once there was a breeding pair. Someone in the valley poisoned its mate because the birds were preying on his chickens. Gray goshawks partner for life, so I imagine this frequent visitor to our valley is lonely, whatever lonely means for a bird. When this lone hunter lands on the tree near my hens, my regard for her shifts a little. She becomes my problem. I have seen her tear into the throat of a terrified hen. Of course, a goshawk flying into my backyard does not compare to the threat to life and livelihood presented by an elephant, tiger or bear wandering close to human habitation. In such moments, though, when I watch that goshawk eyeing off my hens, I am reminded that our understandings and actions in response to our environment are unstable and shifting depending on many contingencies. For nearly a century, the global environment movement has forged a set of recognizable discourses connecting human activity to the natural world on which we all depend. These discourses can be understood as part of a greater effort to reign in the excesses of power. This effort is the focus of the next chapter, which looks at the development of environmental law as a response to the centuries-long resistance to the tyranny of unchecked greed.

References

Abbey, Edward. 1975. *The Monkey Wrench Gang*. Philadelphia: JB Lippencott.

Adam, David. 2009. "Leading Climate Scientist: 'Democratic Process Isn't Working.'" *The Guardian*, March 18. https://www.theguardian.com/science/2009/mar/18/nasa-climate-change-james-hansen (Accessed August 22, 2023).

Agarwal, Anil, and Sunita Narain, eds. 2019. "India in a Warming World: Integrating Climate Change and Development." In *India in a Warming World: Integrating Climate Change and Development*. Oxford: Oxford University Press.

Allan, Stuart, Barbara Adam, and Cynthia Carter, eds. 2000. *Environmental Risks and the Media*. London and New York: Routledge.

Altheide, David. 1997. "The News Media, the Problem Frame, and the Production of Fear." *The Sociological Quarterly* 38 (4): 647–668.

Altheide, David, and Robert Snow. 1979. *Media Logic*. Beverly Hills: Sage Publications.

Anderson, Alison G. 2014. *Environmental Risks, Protest and the Network Society*. London: Palgrave Macmillan UK.

Anderson, Allison, and Libby Lester. 2020. "Foreword." In *The Local and the Digital in Environmental Communication*, edited by Joana Díaz-Pont, Pieter Maeseele, Annika Egan Sjölander, Maitreyee Mishra, and Kerrie Foxwell-Norton, 6–12. Cham: Springer International Publishing.

Anderson, Benedict R. 2006. *Imagined Communities: Reflections on the Origin and Spread of Nationalism*. 2nd ed. London and New York: Verso.

Appadurai, Arjun. 1996. *Modernity at Large: Cultural Dimensions of Globalization*. Minneapolis: University of Minnesota Press.

Arendt, Hannah. 1956b. "Authority in the Twentieth Century." *The Review of Politics* 18 (4): 403–417.

———. 1956a. *The Human Condition*. Edited by Margaret Canovan. 2nd ed. Chicago: University of Chicago Press.

Arsenault, Amelia, and Manuel Castells. 2008. "Switching Power: Rupert Murdoch and the Global Business of Media Politics: A Sociological Analysis." *International Sociology* 23 (4): 488–513.

Banks, Sedina. 2003. "The 'Erin Brockovich Effect': How Media Shapes Toxics Policy." *Environs: Environmental Law and Policy* 26(2): 219–252.

Barbier, Edward B. 2010. *A Global Green New Deal: Rethinking the Economic Recovery*. Cambridge: Cambridge University Press.

Beck, Ulrich. 1987. "The Anthropological Shock: Chernobyl and the Contours of the Risk Society." *Berkeley Journal of Sociology* 32: 153–165.

———. 1995. *Ecological Enlightenment: Essays on the Politics of the Risk Society*. Atlantic Highlands: Humanities Press.

———. 2010. "Climate for Change, or How to Create a Green Modernity?" *Theory, Culture & Society* 27 (2–3): 254–266.

———. 2014. *World at Risk*. Cambridge: Polity Press.

Bladlow, Kyle, and Jennifer Ladino. 2018. "Toward an Affective Ecocriticism." In *Affective Ecocriticism*, edited by Kyle Bladlow and Jennifer Ladino, 1–22. Lincoln: University of Nebraska Press.

Bødker, Henrik, and Hanna E. Morris. 2021. "Climate Change, Journalism, and Time." In *Climate Change and Journalism*, by Henrik Bødker and Hanna E. Morris, 1–9. London: Routledge.

Bourdieu, Pierre. 1986. "The Force of Law: Toward a Sociology of the Juridical Field." *The Hastings Law Journal* 38: 805–813.

Brüggemann, Michael, and Sven Engesser. 2017. "Beyond False Balance: How Interpretive Journalism Shapes Media Coverage of Climate Change." *Global Environmental Change* 42 (January): 58–67. https://doi.org/10.1016/j.gloenvcha.2016.11.004.

Buechler, Steven M. 1995. "New Social Movement Theories." *The Sociological Quarterly* 36 (3): 441–464.

Cappella, Joseph N., and Kathleen Hall Jamieson. 2003. *Spiral of Cynicism: The Press and the Public Good*. Oxford: Oxford University Press.

Carson, Rachel. 1962. *Silent Spring*. Boston: Houghton Mifflin.

Carvalho, Anabela. 2008. "Media(ted) Discourse and Society: Rethinking the Framework of Critical Discourse Analysis." *Journalism Studies* 9 (2): 161–177.

Castells, Manuel, ed. 2004. *The Network Society: A Cross-Cultural Perspective*. Cheltenham, and Northampton: Edward Elgar Publishing.

———. 2007. "Communication, Power and Counter-Power in the Network Society." *International Journal of Communication* 1, 238–266.

———. 2009. *Communication Power*. Oxford: Oxford University Press.

———. 2015. *Networks of Outrage and Hope: Social Movements in the Internet Age*. 2nd ed. Cambridge and Malden: Polity Press.

Chakrabarty, Dipesh. 2018. "Anthropocene Time." *History and Theory* 57 (1): 5–32.

CODEFF. n.d. "Our History." *Committee for the Defense of Fauna and Flora* (blog). www.codeff.cl (Accessed July 21, 2022).

Collingridge, John, Alex Needham, Dan Milmo, Fiona Shields, Jess Cartner-Morley, Mark Oliver, Tim Lusher, Liz Ford, Tanya Aldred, and Dominic Rushe. 2021. "'We're All Climate Journalists Now': How the Weather Took over Everything." *The Guardian*, October 25. https://www.theguardian.com/membership/2021/oct/25/were-all-climate-journalists-now-how-the-weather-took-over-everything (Accessed August 22, 2023).

Cottle, Simon. 2006. *Mediatized Conflicts*. Maidenhead: Open University Press.

Cottle, Simon. 2023. "Reporting Civilizational Collapse Research Notes from a World-in-Crisis." *Global Media and Communication* 19 (2): 269–288.

Couldry, Nick, and Andreas Hepp. 2017. *The Mediated Construction of Reality*. Cambridge and Malden: Polity Press.

Crutzen, Paul J. 2002. "Geology of Mankind." *Nature* 415 (January): 23.

Crutzen, Paul J., and Eugene F. Stoermer. 2000. "The 'Anthropocene.'" *Global Change Newsletter. The International Geosphere–Biosphere Programme*, May 2000. 17–18.

Curran, James. 2002. *Media and Power*. London and New York: Routledge.

Curran, James, and David Hesmondhalgh, eds. 2019. *Media and Society*. 6th ed. New York: Bloomsbury Academic.

Dauvergne, Peter. 2008. *The Shadows of Consumption: Consequences for the Global Environment*. Cambridge: MIT Press.

Dinan, William, and David Miller. 2022. "Managing the Climate Apocalypse." In *The Routledge Handbook of Environment and Communication*, edited by Anders Hansen and Robert Cox, 2nd ed., 132–145. London: Routledge.

Dryzek, John S. 2013. *The Politics of the Earth: Environmental Discourses*. 3rd ed. Oxford: Oxford University Press.

———. 2021. "Discourses." In *The Oxford Handbook of International Environmental Law*, edited by Lavanya Rajamani and Jacqueline Peel, 2nd ed. New York: Oxford University Press.

Dryzek, John S., and Hayley Stevenson. 2011. "Global Democracy and Earth System Governance." *Ecological Economics* 70 (11): 1865–1874.

Entman, Robert M. 1993. "Framing: Toward Clarification of a Fractured Paradigm." *Journal of Communication* 43 (4): 51–58.

Fairclough, Norman. 1995. *Media Discourse*. London: Edward Arnold.

Fernández, Edgar Fernández, and Claire Malwé. 2019. "The Emergence of the 'Planetary Boundaries' Concept in International Environmental Law: A Proposal for a Framework Convention." *Review of European, Comparative & International Environmental Law* 28 (1): 48–56.

Fisher, Elizabeth. 2019. "Unearthing the Relationship Between Environmental Law and Populism." *Journal of Environmental Law* 31 (3): 383–387.

Foucault, Michel. 1980. *Power/Knowledge: Selected Interviews and Other Writings, 1972–1977*. Edited by Colin Gordon. New York: Pantheon Books.

Foxwell-Norton, Kerrie, and Claire Konkes. 2019. "The Great Barrier Reef: News Media, Policy and the Politics of Protection." *International Communication Gazette* 81 (3): 211–234.

Fraser, Nancy. 2023. *Cannibal Capitalism: How Our System Is Devouring Democracy, Care, and the Planet - and What We Can Do about It*. New York: Verso.

Gamson, William A., and Gadi Wolfsfeld. 1993. "Movements and Media as Interacting Systems." *The ANNALS of the American Academy of Political and Social Science* 528 (1): 114–125.

Giddens, Anthony. 2006. "Fate, Risk and Security." In *The Sociology of Risk and Gambling Reader*, edited by James F. Cosgrave. New York: Routledge.

Gitlin, Todd. 1980. "Making Democracy Safe for America." *Columbia Journalism Review* 8 (6): 53–58.

Goodie, Jo. 2011. "The Ecological Narrative of Risk and the Emergence of Toxic Tort Litigation." In *Law and Ecology: New Environmental Foundations*, edited by Andreas Philippopoulos-Mihalopoulos, 65–82. London: Routledge.

Goodie, Jo, and Gary Wickham. 2002. "Calculating "Public Interest": Common Law and the Legal Governance of the Environment." *Social & Legal Studies* 11 (1): 37–60.

Goodman, Michael K., Jo Littler, Dan Brockington, and Maxwell Boykoff. 2016. "Spectacular Environmentalisms: Media, Knowledge and the Framing of Ecological Politics." *Environmental Communication* 10 (6): 677–688.

Grisham, John. 1992. *The Pelican Brief*. New York: DoubleDay.

Habermas, Jürgen. 1989. *The Structural Transformation of the Public Sphere: An Inquiry into a Category of Bourgeois Society*. Cambridge: MIT Press.

Hackett, Robert A., Susan Forde, Shane Gunster, and Kerrie Foxwell-Norton, eds. 2017. *Journalism and Climate Crisis: Public Engagement, Media Alternatives*. Communication and Society. London and New York: Routledge.

Hajer, Maarten A. 1993. "Discourse Coalitions and the Institutionalization of Practice: The Case of Acid Rain in Great Britain." In *The Argumentative Turn in Policy Analysis and Planning*, edited by Frank Fischer and John Forester, 43–75. Durham: Duke University Press.

Hallin, Daniel C. 1984. "The Media, the War in Vietnam, and Political Support: A Critique of the Thesis of an Oppositional Media." *The Journal of Politics* 46 (1): 2–24.

Hannigan, John A. 2006. *Environmental Sociology*. 2nd ed. London and New York: Routledge.
Hansen, Anders, and J. Robert Cox. 2015. *The Routledge Handbook of Environment and Communication*. Oxford: Routledge.
Harcup, Tony, and Deirdre O'Neill. 2017. "What Is News? News Values Revisited (Again)." *Journalism Studies* 18 (12): 1470–1488.
Hardin, Garrett. 1985. "Human Ecology: The Subversive, Conservative Science." *American Zoologist* 25 (2): 469–476.
Hartley, John. 1996. *Popular Reality: Journalism, Modernity, Popular Culture*. London and New York: Arnold.
Hay, Peter. 2002. *Main Currents in Western Environmental Thought*. Sydney: UNSW Press.
Hickman, Leo. 2010. "James Lovelock: Humans are Too Stupid to Prevent Climate Change." *The Guardian*, March. https://www.theguardian.com/science/2010/mar/29/james-lovelock-climate-change#:~:text=Humans%20are%20too%20stupid%20to%20prevent%20climate%20change%20from%20radically,who%20developed%20the%20Gaia%20theory (Accessed August 22, 2023).
Hulme, Mike. 2009. *Why We Disagree About Climate Change: Understanding Controversy, Inaction and Opportunity*. Cambridge and New York: Cambridge University Press.
Humphreys, Sally. 1985. "Law as Discourse." *History and Anthropology* 1 (2): 239–264.
Hutchins, Brett, and Libby Lester. 2006. "Environmental Protest and Tap-Dancing with the Media in the Information Age." *Media, Culture & Society* 28 (3): 433–451.
Hutchins, Brett, and Libby Lester. 2015. "Theorizing the Enactment of Mediatized Environmental Conflict." *International Communication Gazette* 77 (4): 337–358.
IPCC. 2022. *Climate Change 2022: Impacts, Adaptation and Vulnerability. Contribution of Working Group II to the Sixth Assessment Report of the Intergovernmental Panel on Climate Change*. Edited by H.-O. Pörtner, D. C. Roberts, M. Tignor, E. S. Poloczanska, K. Mintenbeck, A. Alegría, M. Craig, S. Langsdorf, S. Löschke, V. Möller, A. Okem, and B. Rama. Cambridge and New York: Cambridge University Press.
Jolley, Connor, and Lauren Rickards. 2020. "Contesting Coal and Climate Change Using Scale: Emergent Topologies in the Adani Mine Controversy." *Geographical Research* 58 (1): 6–23.
Kennedy, David. 2016. *A World of Struggle: How Power, Law, and Expertise Shape Global Political Economy*. Princeton: Princeton University Press.
Kim, Rakhyun E. 2022. "Taming Gaia 2.0: Earth System Law in the Ruptured Anthropocene." *The Anthropocene Review* 9 (3): 411–424.
Kim, R. E. and Kotzé, L. J. 2022. "Planetary Boundaries at the Intersection of Earth System Law, Science and Governance: A State-of-the-Art Review." *Review of European, Comparative & International Environmental Law* 30 (1): 3–15.
Klein, Naomi. 2020. *On Fire: The Burning Case for a Green New Deal*. London: Penguin.
Kwaymullina, Ambellin. 2018. "Aboriginal Nations and the Nation State." In *Indigenous Peoples as Subjects of International Law*, edited by Irene Watson. Oxford: Routledge.
Leopold, Aldo. [1949] 1989. *A Sand County Almanac and Sketches Here and There*. Oxford: Oxford University Press.
Lester, Libby. 2010. *Media and Environment: Conflict, Politics and the News*. Cambridge: Polity Press.

Lester, Libby. 2019. *Global Trade and Mediatized Environmental Protest: The View from Here.* Cham: Springer International Publishing.

Lester, Libby, and Brett Hutchins. 2012. "The Power of the Unseen: Environmental Conflict, the Media and Invisibility." *Media, Culture & Society* 34 (7): 847–863.

Lippmann, Walter. [1927] 1993. *The Phantom Public*. New Brunswick: Transaction.

Lovelock, James. 2009. *The Vanishing Face of Gaia: A Final Warning*. New York: Basic Books.

Lucas, Adam. 2021. "Investigating Networks of Corporate Influence on Government Decision-Making: The Case of Australia's Climate Change and Energy Policies." *Energy Research & Social Science* 81 (November): 1–26.

Maeseele, Pieter. 2022. "Beyond the Post-Political Zeitgeist 2.0." In *The Routledge Handbook of Environment and Communication*, edited by Anders Hansen and Robert Cox, 2nd ed., 441–454. London: Routledge.

Malm, Andreas, and Alf Hornborg. 2014. "The Geology of Mankind? A Critique of the Anthropocene Narrative." *The Anthropocene Review* 1 (1): 62–69.

McCombs, Maxwell. 1997. "New Frontiers in Agenda Setting: Agendas of Attributes and Frames." *Mass Communication Review* 24 (1/2): 32–52.

McNeish, Wallace. 2017. "From Revelation to Revolution: Apocalypticism in Green Politics." *Environmental Politics* 26 (6): 1035–1054.

Mert, Ayşem. 2019. "Democracy in the Anthropocene: A New Scale." In *Anthropocene Encounters: New Directions in Green Political Thinking*, edited by Frank Biermann and Eva Lövbrand, 128–149. Cambridge: Cambridge University Press.

Mocatta, Gabi, and Erin Hawley. 2020. "Uncovering a Climate Catastrophe? Media Coverage of Australia's Black Summer Bushfires and the Revelatory Extent of the Climate Blame Frame." *M/C Journal* 23 (4). https://doi.org/10.5204/mcj.1666

Mouffe, Chantal. 2005. *On the Political*. London and New York: Routledge.

Mouffe, Chantal. 2022. *Towards a Green Democratic Revolution: Left Populism and the Power of Affects*. London and New York: Verso.

Newman, Nic, Richard Fletcher, Kirsten Eddy, Craig T Robertson, and Rasmus Kleis Nielsen. 2023. "Reuters Institute Digital News Report 2023." Oxford: Reuters Institute for the Study of Journalism.

Nixon, Rob. 2011. *Slow Violence and the Environmentalism of the Poor*. Cambridge: Harvard University Press.

Noakes, Jesse. 2022. "The Network behind Direct Action Climate Protests." *Saturday Paper*, November 19, 2022. https://www.thesaturdaypaper.com.au/news/environment/2022/11/19/the-network-behind-direct-action-climate-protests (Accessed August 22, 2023).

Peel, Jacqueline, and Hari M. Osofsky. 2013. "Climate Change Litigation's Regulatory Pathways: A Comparative Analysis of the United States and Australia: Litigation's Regulatory Pathways." *Law & Policy* 35 (3): 150–183.

Osofsky, Hari M., and Jacqueline Peel. 2014. "The Role of Litigation in Multilevel Climate Change Governance: Possibilities for a Lower Carbon Future?" *Environmental and Planning Law Journal* 30: 203–328.

Painter, James. 2021. "The International Coverage of Biodiversity Loss." In *The Handbook of International Trends in Environmental Communication*, edited by Bruno Takahashi, Julia Metag, Jagadish Thaker, and Suzannah Evans Comfort, 173–189. New York: Routledge.

Pathak, Shekhar. 2021. *The Chipko Movement: A People's History*. Ranikhet: Permanent Black.

Peeples, Jennifer, Pete Bsumek, Steve Schwarze, and Jen Schneider. 2014. "Industrial Apocalyptic: Neoliberalism, Coal, and the Burlesque Frame." *Rhetoric and Public Affairs* 17 (2): 227–254.

Pepper, Rachel. 2017. "Ms Onus and Mr Neal: Agitators in an Age of 'Green Lawfare.'" *AIAL FORUM* 90: 52–64.

Peters, Chris, and Marcel Jeroen Broersma, eds. 2017. *Rethinking Journalism Again: Societal Role and Public Relevance in a Digital Age*. London and New York: Routledge.

Pettifor, Ann. 2019. *The Case for the Green New Deal*. London: Verso.

Pezzullo, Phaedra C. 2021. "Environmental Justice and Climate Justice." In *The Routledge Handbook of Environmental Movements*, edited by Maria Grasso and Marco Giugni, 229–244. London: Routledge.

Pickering, Jonathan, Karin Bäckstrand, and David Schlosberg. 2020. "Between Environmental and Ecological Democracy: Theory and Practice at the Democracy-Environment Nexus." *Journal of Environmental Policy & Planning* 22 (1): 1–15.

Pereira, Joana Castro, and Eduardo Viola. 2018. "Catastrophic Climate Change and Forest Tipping Points: Blind Spots in International Politics and Policy." *Global Policy* 9 (4): 513–524.

Post, Senja, Katharina Kleinen-von Königslöw, and Mike S. Schäfer. 2019. "Between Guilt and Obligation: Debating the Responsibility for Climate Change and Climate Politics in the Media." *Environmental Communication* 13 (6): 723–39. https://doi.org/10.1080/17524032.2018.1446037.

Powers, Richard. 2018. *The Overstory*. New York: W. W. Norton & Company.

Ricketson, Matthew. 2004. *Writing Feature Stories: How to Research and Write Newspaper and Magazine Articles*. Crows Nest: Allen & Unwin.

Rockström, Johan, Will Steffen, Kevin Noone, Åsa Persson, F. Stuart Chapin, Eric F. Lambin, Timothy M. Lenton, et al. 2009. "A Safe Operating Space for Humanity." *Nature* 461 (7263): 472–475.

Rockström, Johan, Louis Kotzé, Svetlana Milutinović, Frank Biermann, Victor Brovkin, Jonathan Donges, Jonas Ebbesson, et al. 2024. "The Planetary Commons: A New Paradigm for Safeguarding Earth-Regulating Systems in the Anthropocene." *Proceedings of the National Academy of Sciences* 121 (5): e2301531121. https://doi.org/10.1073/pnas.2301531121.

Sachedina, Hassanali T. 2010. "Disconnected Nature: The Scaling Up of African Wildlife Foundation and Its Impacts on Biodiversity Conservation and Local Livelihoods." *Antipode* 42 (3): 603–623.

Schultz, Julianne. 1998. *Reviving the Fourth Estate: Democracy, Accountability, and the Media*. Reshaping Australian Institutions. Cambridge and New York: Cambridge University Press.

Scoones, Ian. 1999. "New Ecology and the Social Sciences: What Prospects for a Fruitful Engagement?" *Annual Review of Anthropology* 28 (1): 479–507.

Shahar, Dan Coby. 2015. "Rejecting Eco-Authoritarianism, Again." *Environmental Values* 24 (3): 345–366.

Shearman, David J. C., and Joseph Wayne Smith. 2007. *The Climate Change Challenge and the Failure of Democracy*. Westport: Praeger.

Sparrow, Jeff. 2021. *Crimes against Nature: Capitalism and Global Heating*. Brunswick: Scribe.

Steffen, Will, Wendy Broadgate, Lisa Deutsch, Owen Gaffney, and Cornelia Ludwig. 2015. "The Trajectory of the Anthropocene: The Great Acceleration." *The Anthropocene Review* 2 (1): 81–98.

Steffen, Will, Paul J. Crutzen, and John R. McNeill. 2007. "The Anthropocene: Are Humans Now Overwhelming the Great Forces of Nature?" *Ambio* 36 (8): 8.

Stehr, Nico. 2013. "An Inconvenient Democracy: Knowledge and Climate Change." *Society* 50 (1): 55–60.

Stone, D. 1972. "Should Trees Have Standing? Toward Legal Rights for Natural Objects." *Southern California Law Review* 45 (2): 450–501.

Takahashi, Bruno. 2023. "Towards Inclusive International Environmental Communication Scholarship: The Role of Latin America." *International Journal of Cultural Studies* 26 (4): 372–391.

Tănăsescu, Mihnea. 2013. "The Rights of Nature in Ecuador: The Making of an Idea." *International Journal of Environmental Studies* 70 (6): 846–861.

Thaker, Jagadish. 2022. "Environmentalism of the Poor Global South Perspectives on Environmental Communication." In *The Handbook of International Trends in Environmental Communication*, edited by Bruno Takahashi, Julia Metag, Jagadish Thaker, and Suzannah Evans Comfort, 193–205. New York: Routledge.

Thompson, John B. 1995. *The Media and Modernity: A Social Theory of the Media*. Stanford: Stanford University Press.

———. 2005. "The New Visibility." *Theory, Culture & Society* 22 (6): 31–51.

Thoreau, Henry David. [1849] 1983. "Civil Disobedience." In *Walden and Civil Disobedience*. New York: Penguin.

Thorsheim, Peter. 2006. *Inventing Pollution: Coal, Smoke, and Culture in Britain since 1800*. Athens: Ohio University Press.

Vidas, Davor, Jan Zalasiewicz, and Mark Williams. 2014. "What Is the Anthropocene—and Why Is It Relevant for International Law?" *Yearbook of International Environmental Law* 25 (1): 3–23.

Witze, Alexandra. 2024. "It's Final: The Anthropocene Is Not an Epoch, despite Protest over Vote." *Nature* 619 (7970): 441–42. https://doi.org/10.1038/d41586-023-02234-z.

Wodak, Ruth, and Michael Meyer. 2016. "Critical Discourse Studies: History, Agenda, Theory and Methodology." In *Methods of Critical Discourse Studies*. 3rd ed. London and Thousand Oaks: Sage.

Wolfsfeld, Gadi. 1997. *Media and Political Conflict: News from the Middle East*. Cambridge and New York: Cambridge University Press.

Wonneberger, Anke. 2024. "Climate Change Litigation in the News: Litigation as Public Campaigning Tool to Legitimize Climate-Related Responsibilities and Solutions." *Social Movement Studies* 23 (1): 94–112. https://doi.org/10.1080/14742837.2023.2270919.

Worster, Donald. 1994. *Nature's Economy: A History of Ecological Ideas.* 2nd ed. Cambridge: Cambridge University Press.

Vidas, Davor, Jan Zalasiewicz, and Mark Williams. 2014. "What Is the Anthropocene—and Why Is It Relevant for International Law?" *Yearbook of International Environmental Law* 25 (1): 3–23.

Zelizer, Barbie. 2019. "Why Journalism Is About More Than Digital Technology." *Digital Journalism* 7 (3): 343–350.

Case

Greenpeace Australia Ltd v. Redbank Power Co. [1994] 86 LGERA 143.

· 3 ·

FINDING COMMON GROUND

Highlighting the 2008 Global Financial Crisis and the global ecological crisis as marked failures of modern economic theory, George Monbiot (2017, 2019) said we need a new story to lead us out of the mess we are in. He is not the first. For instance, Thomas Berry (1987, 1999) wrote that humanity is caught between two stories: the old biblical cosmology that bestows humans dominance over the Earth and the newer scientific story that explains the origin of the universe and our evolution as a species but does little to offer any satisfying moral direction. What might a new story tell us? With myriad worldviews that do not privilege humanity over other life, and which give meaning and purpose to human action, a new story is likely to be drawn from the deep well of other cosmologies rather than anything imagined entirely anew (Kwaymullina 2018).

Calls to "find new ways of telling a story" carry a whiff of corporate branding about them but the current fashion for story also points to a growing appreciation for the role communication plays in shaping our perception of the world (Couldry and Hepp 2017; van Dijk 1988). A new story for humanity's relationship to the Earth would see a new set of discourses evolve through a radical reappraisal of what we already "know" about culture, politics, economics, religion, and science (Berry 1987). To ask for a new or different story is to ask for new ways to engage with old, seemingly intractable problems. Monbiot's focus on a new political story critiques our systems of governance, whereas Berry's more spiritually oriented explanation for our aporia critiques the scientific stories of modernity, but both challenge the political, economic and social paradigms at the root of our ecological crises. How can we talk about the wicked problems of climate change, declining fish stocks, and unregulated forestry in a way that points to a better, more sustainable future? Such an undertaking would involve close attention to discourse because it is impossible to solve problems without first understanding how we defined and constructed our understanding of the problem (Dryzek 2013, 10).

Conflict is often the result of different discourses about the "same things," which suggests not only the inherent instability of our understanding but also the role of power in defining what is normal and acceptable or what is even possible (Castells 2009). A "clash of worldviews" —which is an important element in Fisher's (2013) idea of "hot law"— describes those moments that reveal different structures of meaning being applied to the subject: the forest is sacred and its values intrinsic; the forest has no value until it is logged; a cleared forest no longer provides valuable ecological services; only cleared land provides agricultural amenity. We are, of course, talking about social, not material, realities. The forest in question does exist in a material sense and to suggest otherwise would be the stuff of madness (Laclau and Mouffe 2001, 112) however, in the case of the forest, the prevailing values and dominant discourse also determines human action in that forest. Power operates in and through contests over definition because what we prioritize and what we ignore, what we celebrate and what we condemn, determines our actions. Defining the forest in terms of having intrinsic value, its ecological services or its potential timber harvest determines if the forest will continue to exist—or not.

In this chapter, we focus on how communication informs our understanding of the environment and its problems in relation to the evolution of environmental law. It approaches environmental law using Elizabeth Fisher's (2017, 1) very broad definition that points out the obvious: that environmental law relates to environmental problems that are the "troubles of politics, society, economics and philosophy." Stepping back, we can define law as a sphere of action with boundaries defined by language, tightly organized processes and expertise that carries its own sets of discourses, principles, and moral and normative values (Bourdieu 1986). From here, we can observe legal ideas—such as harm, causality, responsibility, blame, justice and wrongfulness, legitimate and illegitimate—as both legal concepts, but also ideas informed and shaped by wider society (Tănăsescu 2020). This shaping is usually undertaken through contests over definition with the resulting law carrying the "sedimented authority of prior wins" (Kennedy 2016, 60). Seen this way, law is variously the result of assertions of hegemonic power and the successes of long-fought efforts to challenge power. By treating environmental law as both a distinct field of practice, but also one engaging with the other spheres of civil society that encounter and seek to resolve social, political and economic problems, we can identify the wider forces at play in the constitution and enactment of green lawfare. As Fisher notes, environmental law

> grew and matured because existing legal systems contained little in them to address the complex collective nature of environmental problems. Environmental law is built on existing legal frameworks but often requires the development of new legal obligations and doctrine. This not only means the subject is a mixture of the legally conventional and the legally novel, but this process is unsettling. (Fisher 2017, 3)

It is impossible, and unnecessary, to chart the development of environmental law in one chapter, especially when others (Fisher 2017; Godden et al. 2019; Lazarus 2023) have already done so. Instead, this chapter explores the contests and debates over ideas that can be found at the intersection of environmental discourse and environmental law, which is to say, where some of the old stories about our relationship to our natural world have evolved into the ideas and principles we recognize as environmental law.

Finding A New Story

How far back should we go to find the old stories of law and environmental conflict? Strictly speaking, environmental law emerged alongside the environmental movement in the twentieth century (Fisher 2017) but limiting our gaze to the last century ignores a much longer history of rulemaking and agreement undertaken to maintain an equilibrium between human culture and the natural world. The ancient texts of Asia, including Vedic literature and the Quran, are replete with instructions to not despoil the Earth that gesture to both the sacred and human health and well-being (Ahmad 2021, 359). Around the world, diverse arrangements for the sustainable use of shared resources date back centuries, including shared pastures in Switzerland and India, farmlands in Japan, fisheries in Turkey and Brazil, and irrigation systems in India, Spain, and the Philippines (Ostrom 1990). Similarly, the origin story of Western law contains early discourses about law and environmental conflict are still echoing today.

The story goes something like this. In 1215, on the floodplains of the Thames, England's King John, who had few allies and a weak grip on power, met with some rebellious barons to curtail a brewing civil war. After nine days of talks, the parties assembled in the meadows at Runnymede beside the Ankerwycke Yew—an already mature yew tree (*Taxus baccata*) said to still be standing—to sign an accord that would roll back some of the King's powers. Called magna carta libertatum (Great Charter of Liberties), or Magna Carta, it outlined various legal protections to safeguard the barons and the aristocracy from the tyranny of unfettered royal power. Magna Carta established some of the earliest principles of law still in use today, including the rule of law, the prohibition of torture, and trial by jury. For these reasons, Magna Carta is regarded by some to be the foundational text of liberal democracy, which requires some squint-eyed mythologizing around the intentions of the accord. For instance, describing Magna Carta as an attempt to sort out medieval grievances, David Clark (2015, 50) writes that those at the signing of Magna Carta were thinking of power not democracy. Magna Carta did not treat all people as equal citizens and the protection of rights and interests were limited to the upper classes. However, a second charter, called carta de foresta (or Charter of the Forest) issued by Henry III in 1217 is where we can find some of the earliest efforts to protect shared resources, mediate conflict, and ensure sustainable land use in the foundational texts of English law (Besant 1991; Bollier 2012; Magraw and Thomure 2017).

In medieval England, the Forest described the woodlands, meadows and heath, and the farmlands and town areas that were shared by all people to graze animals, hunt and forage for food, and collect the materials for building and fuel for heating and cooking. Carefully tended for generations, in the years before the troubles that led to the signing of the two charters, the shared forests had gradually been expropriated into "Royal Forests" to be used as the king's hunting grounds. Under the Charter of the Forest, the monarchy was obliged to return enclosed lands to the common people. As a result, the Charter of the Forest is considered one of the first laws to introduce what is today known as the principle of local governance or custodianship (Linebaugh 2010). Unlike Magna Carta, the Charter of the Forest applied to all people and, as such, is considered an early expression of what would now be described as human rights, "such as the rights to water, food, shelter, culture, and an adequate standard of living" (Magraw and Thomure 2017, 3). The Charter of the Forest also addressed privatization and unjust governance and was a "truly radical document" (Standing 2019, 4) that "became a framework through which to reconcile competing environmental claims, then and into the future" (Robinson 2020, 3). Together, the two charters acted as "an emergency brake on accelerating state despotism" (Linebaugh 2008, 22) and for centuries, the Charter of the Forest provided inspiration for those campaigning against the enclosure, privatization, and plunder of the commons. Many were regarded as "dangerous and subversive mob agitators" until the discourses of democracy forged in the American and French Revolutions trickled into Britain in the nineteenth century (Williams 1959, xi).

While Magna Carta is celebrated today, the Charter of the Forest has been gradually erased from common law and popular imagination, especially in the United States because the systems for maintaining the social and ecological equilibrium of shared resources are a problem for those seeking to justify ownership. For instance, the concept of trespass moved from describing the damage of overuse to describing the encroachment onto land and chattels held under private ownership (McDonagh and Griffin 2016, 3). Similarly, waste, which had originally described the over-exploitation of resources, has evolved to describe the lack of economic gain from land and resources (Besant 1991). The gradual erasure of the Charter of the Forest from Western law and the wider popular imagination was not an accident, nor was it any coincidence that the spread of industrialization, colonialization, free-market ideologies and the growth of neoliberalism ran parallel to its disappearance (Babie 2016; Besant 1991). In Britain, the passing of hundreds of separate acts gradually eroded the principle of the commons until the final remnants of the Charter were removed from British statutes in 1971 (Standing 2017). In doing so, a gradual political project oversaw the "deconstruction of an interdependent world and the reconstruction of a world of individual private right where the individual is no longer regarded as embedded within a system" (Besant 1991, 10).

Origin stories and other myths show how ideas travel through culture and time, continually reinvented and reinterpreted to serve new affordances (Babie 2016; Clark 2015; Kennedy 2016). Just as those at Runnymede are unlikely to have had much sense of democracy when they drafted the Magna Carta, they were also unlikely to have cared much for what we now call the environment. But that is not the point. While the environment can be understood as a modern concept, concerns about protecting access to clean water, food, and the other life-sustaining necessities from exploitation and other abuses of power are as old as medieval charters and ancient customs that combine resource management with ideas of the sacred.

What can be learned from treating the dilemmas of environmental law as older than the modern construction of the environment? In short, the dilemma between liberty and responsibility built into the two charters remains a "central antagonism" in the discourses of environmental conflict (Besant 1991, 11). As Paul Babie (2016, 1433) argues:

> in failing to consider the Forest Charter and Magna Carta together, we lose the farmer's commitment to community and obligations that balances the latter's legacy of individual rights. The source of this impoverishment originates in the association of Magna Carta with freedom, or more accurately constitutional freedom, or even more accurately American constitutional freedom. And the adjectives "personal" and "individual" often qualify this understanding of freedom. In other words, those aware of Magna Carta likely view it through American lenses, and those lenses focus on an image of freedom that carries a decidedly individualistic parallax.

A radical reading of the two charters reminds us that the discourses of ecological sustainability and human rights expressed in the idea of the commons have walked together through history into global environmental politics. In this sense, environmental politics predates ecological science or the awareness of risk and, instead, can be seen in the "spontaneous protest against the destruction of everyday culture by the economic and administrative power apparatus" (Gorz 2008 in Mouffe 2023, 1; see also Beck 1995, 48).

The idea of the commons, which includes discourses of interdependence and stewardship, has its intellectual origin in many Indigenous cultures (Tănăsescu 2013, 2020). As Ambelin Kwaymullina, a Palyku woman from Australia's Pilbara, writes (2018, 15–16) "in Indigenous societies, to be a fully realized human being is to be a part of a collective. It is also to be responsible to the collective, including by sustaining the relationships that constitute a lawful way of being." Similarly, Christine Black (2011), and Kombumerri and Munaljahlai woman, provides a radical reimagining of law as a system that comes out of nature to ensure the necessary actions that sustains life. Writing about how "the Land is the Law", Black positions law as independent of human action for its continuity and argues that Western law has diverted from its original duty of ensuring human culture aligns with natural law to instead facilitate technological development and private ownership with ruinous consequences.

From this discussion, we can see that the modern environment movement draws from, or finds connection to, much older ideas and traditions. As such, the coalitions of Indigenous and non-Indigenous activists that form during many environmental protests, such as those who came together at Standing Rock protests in the United States—can be regarded as "conceptual" alliances rather than "marriages of convenience" (Besant 1991, 7). In such instances, the idea of the commons is not just an intellectual construct but, rather, a framework and vocabulary that can be found in the "constellation of self-organized projects around the world that are meeting human needs in more equitable and ecologically responsible ways" (Bollier 2014, 1–2). Centuries of land enclosures in England, repeated across the vast tragedy of colonialism and still echoing today in the neo-colonial projects of globalization, are moments when hegemonic demands for property and capital overwhelm common interests (Linebaugh 2010). This tension between the tyranny of powerful individuals and the ethic of collective responsibility continues today in environmental conflict and the discourses that position economic survival in direct opposition to efforts to maintain ecological integrity or, as is said in many parts of Australia, to care for country. A story that captures that tension is the tragedy of the commons.

The Tragedy of the Commons

The erasure of the logic in the Charter of the Forest included framing the commons as a flawed ideal, rather than a time-tested approach to sustainability. The assertion that human self-interest always trumps collectivity struck a popular chord during the enclosures of the English countryside in the nineteenth century and resurfaced again in the 1960s when the American ecologist, Garret Hardin, described the inevitable tragedy of self-interest in his essay, *The Tragedy of the Commons* (1968).

Written at the height of debates about overpopulation and the limits to growth, Hardin's essay was subtitled: "The population problem has no technical solution; it requires a fundamental extension in morality." Hardin, a biologist, argued that a planet of finite resources required determining an optimum (not maximum) human population that would require "relinquishing the freedom to breed" (1968, 1248). His overall message was that, despite the United States system of private property ownership being unjust, "the alternative of the commons is too horrifying to contemplate [and] injustice is preferable to total ruin" (Hardin 1968, 1247). Several writers have observed with varying degrees of incredulity how Hardin's rambling argument for population control became not only a topic for academics but a truism in scientific writing and common usage. Susan Cox (1985, 4) points out how Hardin's thesis borrowed from the nineteenth-century British economist, William Forster Lloyd, who argued for the enclosure of farmlands. Describing the enduring legacy of Hardin's essay as a "regrettable" example of a "historical event being reported and memorialized inaccurately but consistently until the resulting fiction is believed to be the truth," Cox argues that the root cause of the parlous state of England's commons was not a failure of the commons, but rather the abuse of the rules governing them, including land reforms designed to increase the holdings of a few landowners and changes in agricultural practices. Sharper still, Hardin's explanation for the disappearance of the English countryside was, writes Simon Fairlie (2009, 31), "a travesty of historical interpretation, carried out by a theorist with a pet idea, who knew little about the subject he was writing about." Eventually, Hardin (1994) conceded that the title of his paper should have been The Tragedy of the Unmanaged Commons, but it was too late: the idea of humanity's selfish gene, to evoke another pervasive meme, was established.

The discourse of tragedy illustrates how the distillation of centuries of argument can construct a worldview that appears both authoritative and common sense. What new story might replace Hardin's tragic misrepresentation of the commons? The clue lies in Hardin's pessimistic hypothesis being partly correct: without "regulatory regimes" people tend to exhaust the resources around them (Gardiner 2001, 416). Much has been written in the wake of Hardin's essay to contradict its apparent universalism of self-interest, most notably by the American political scientist and economist, Elinor Ostrom (1990, 2009; Ostrom et al. 1999) who won a Nobel for her work. To demonstrate that Hardin's "tragedy" need not occur, Ostrom sought to identify the rules and mechanisms used by communities that have successfully shared common resources for generations. Ostrom's research found plenty of examples where community-managed fish stocks, pastures, woods, lakes, and groundwater basins were managed as common-pool resources governed by the users. Describing these environmental systems directly affected by human action as socio-economic systems, Ostrom (2009) devised a general framework to identify effective self-organization, or "bottom-up" governance, that maintained social order and ecological sustainability. In this work, she identified the ideal affordances for "bottom-up" governance including scientific knowledge, shared values, and shared economics. By describing the governance structures for long-term sustainability that acknowledged interdependence and the need for specific, context-dependent rules in the politics of sharing, Ostrom's legacy was to discredit the truism that shared resources lead to ecological and social tragedy (Magraw and Thomure 2017, 6) and tell a new story, which was actually an old story, about the commons.

It is difficult to talk about law and the environment without drawing on the discourses of the commons, which are then invariably challenged by Hardin's bleak but enduring metaphor. In matters of environmental law, writes Elizabeth Fisher (2017), the tragedy of the commons as a heurism for the mismatch of supply and demand is too simplistic to be of much use. Indeed, we do need to find a new story for our times. That project can be seen in the occupation of forests and other natural places, in street protests and public rallies, and wherever people gather to challenge assumptions about ownership and property rights around the world (McDonagh and Griffin 2016, 9). The idea of the commons echoes in debates about public housing and food security, access to water and sacred land, biodiversity loss and climate justice. The irreconcilable tension built into discourses about private rights and public duties, not to mention into the mythologies of neoliberalism, is intrinsic to the problems that environmental law is asked to address. If we are to look at the social, political and economic problems informing environmental conflict and thus environmental law and green lawfare, we should pay some attention to the present discourses resisting calls to shift towards an environmental ethic. The most obvious is neoliberalism which, as Nancy Fraser (2023, 12) argues, has inaugurated "a new round of enclosures" such as the commodification of water, that are an assault on the environmental commons. Further, she writes, (2023, 135) neoliberalism is a dominant discourse used to "block popular efforts to plot a new course".

The Present Dilemma

It is almost impossible to write about global ecological crises without some reference to neoliberalism, or at least neoliberal logic. Like fascism, neoliberalism lacks a seminal or defining text and is best described as a set of defining characteristics and principles grounded in a free-market ideology that includes deregulation, privatization, and reduced welfare and taxation (Antonio and Brulle 2011). Its lack of fixed definition, its mutability, gives neoliberalism the necessary agility to enter systems of governance and reshape existing structures to its advantage (Slobodian and Plehwe 2020). First rolled out in the

United States and the United Kingdom in the 1980s, neoliberalism as a dominant discourse has been gradually adopted by developed nations, including Canada and Australia, and forcibly imposed on others in the form of structural adjustment programs (Berry 2019, 58). In other words, neoliberalism has been a particularly contagious, and dangerous, idea that has been "incorporated into the common-sense way many of us interpret, live in, and understand the world" (Harvey 2005, 2–3; see also Birch 2015). Despite neoliberal discourses never explicitly attacking human rights, democracy or the rule of law, policies that undermine wages and the protection of workers, while also neglecting access to education, health care, and other forms of public goods, effectively achieve the same outcomes (Regilme 2019, 158). While sometimes criticized for being a "figment of left imagination" (Peck 2018, xxii), giving a name neoliberalism reflects "a will to name and resist a set of forces that wished to present itself as ineluctable, without alternative, and thus not open to resistance" (Cahill et al 2018, xxv).

We cannot ignore neoliberalism in conceptualizing green lawfare for several reasons. Firstly, the depoliticization of environmental conflicts, which describes the process of removing a problem from the visibility of the mediatized political sphere to the less visible spheres of expertise including the legal sphere, is a classic strategy of neoliberal politics (Harvey 2005, 66–67; Kennedy 2016; Mouffe 2023). Secondly, while neoliberal discourses purport to be against state intervention, neoliberal logic implicitly asks the state to uphold private property rights, monetary governance, and the institutions that support the accumulation of wealth (Regilme 2019, 159). Indeed, David Harvey (2005, 38) argues that neoliberalism is increasingly "authoritarian, forceful, and anti-democratic" in the ways it has "restored power to a narrowly defined capitalist class" through immense concentrations of corporate power, a suspicion of democracy and a preference for governance by experts and elites (Harvey 2005, 66; see also Fraser 2023, 116). An awareness of neoliberalism contributes to any framework seeking to understand the actors and processes informing current environmental debates. Thirdly, in its global reach, neoliberalism can be found in the logics of globalization (Appadurai 2013) and the combination of globalization and neoliberalism forms a "new power" (Castells 2004) that resounds in the global ecological crises we face.

Rather than try to untangle the collective "isms" at play in the global networks of power, green lawfare defines environmental law as the various instruments of arbitration used to check the tendency towards tyranny—or the corruption of power for the benefit of a few—by those seeking to protect the complex structures of relations underpinning communities and place. When protests and other sites of environmental conflict are framed as conflicts between economic and environmental priorities or local interests over corporate rights, we can find remnants of the old sleight of hand that overturned centuries of tradition that ensured the material benefits granted to the few do not come at a terrible cost to the many (Babie 2016, 1443). Tyranny is used here to describe the kind of power that acts in its own interests and makes, or breaks, the rules accordingly (Arendt 1956) and can be found in the violence of colonialization and its reinvention in global debt and transnational corporatism (Fraser 2023).

By not defining tyranny as a particular form of power, but rather as a perpetual force in human affairs, we can observe the paradox of law being a last resort for those affected by tyrannical power and unfettered greed while also being a haven, even hunting ground, for those who wield such power. To further develop the idea of green lawfare, we can look at the broad ideas that inform the way environmental law is invoked by those looking to the courts and other legal mechanisms in their daily struggles against tyranny.

Contagious Ideas in Environmental Law

Natasha Affolder (2019) uses "contagious law-making" to describe how legal ideas are shared. The idea of contagious ideas evokes the virality of social media messages (Finkler and León 2019) and builds on a more orthodox idea of how laws can be transplanted into other jurisdictions to replicate the success of a particular strategy (Lin and Peel 2022, 204). Metaphors abound, including "transplantation," "borrowing" and "judicial cross-fertilization" (Kotzé 2016), and "uploading" and "downloading" (Fisher 2012). An example of a contagious idea was the spread of "climate emergency declarations" in parliaments around the world that began in Australia and found a legally ambiguous footing in public law, politics, and public participation (Stacy 2022).

As noted already, environmental law emerged alongside the fledging environmental movement of the 1960s as governments responded to the growing awareness of environmental problems by reforming existing laws and introducing new laws (Fisher 2017). As Lazarus (2023, 52) notes, making environmental law "places enormous pressure on lawmaking institutions because the essential features of the problem to be addressed are not readily susceptible to legal redress." However, developments in domestic and international law developed in tandem through the sharing of ideas in response to various governments and actors confronting "continuously changing socio-economic, environmental, cultural and political circumstances and regulatory realities" (Kotzé 2016, 71–72). Global environmental problems, summed up in the idea of the Anthropocene, disrupted easier distinctions between international law and the domestic laws of sovereign states, prompting some to adopt "transnational law" as a framework for analyzing the legal response to the global environmental crises (Webster and Mai 2020). Several contagious ideas have informed the evolution of environmental law at local, national and international levels and can be found in the tactics of green lawfare. The following ideas are summarized below to locate the major streams of thought and action, or discourses, informing the development of environmental law and its current trajectories.

Sustainable Development

By developing alongside the environmental movement, the logics of ecology and civil rights are interwoven in environmental law. We have already observed the tension between these two concepts in the two medieval charters that sought to reconcile individual rights with collective responsibility. The tension can be seen in the modern idea of sustainability that emerged in early environmental discourses that argued for a different approach to economic development. The idea of sustainability was mentioned at the 1972 United Nations Conference on the Human Environment held in Stockholm. A decade later, the principle of "sustainable development" was central to the *Our Common Future* report, also known as the Brundtland report, which defined sustainable development as "development that meets the needs of the present without compromising the ability of future generations to meet their own needs" (Brundtland 1987, 54). In 2015, the UN General Assembly adopted the 2030 Agenda for Sustainable Development and Sustainable Development Goals (SDGs). These 17 goals, including 169 underlying global targets, provide a framework by which the international community measures environmental and social governance performance.

That old sleight of hand, that overturns the measures ensuring that the material benefits granted to the few do not come at a terrible cost to many, remains at play. While the idea of sustainability quite simply describes the capacity for humans to live within the limits of ecological systems, the term "sustainable development" evolved as the dominant framework to achieve sustainability (Affolder 2012). As an idea, "sustainable development" reframes the much-criticized practices of industrialization as "development" and thus progress, which associates progress as the ongoing moral advancement of humanity toward an ideal, even spiritual, excellence (Adleman 2018; Du Pisani 2006). As such, the use of the term "sustainable development" perpetually attaches the idea that humanity cannot meet its ecological goals without continuing with a certain kind of industrial development to any effort to align human culture and ecological sustainability. Despite, or perhaps because, Brundtland's definition was vague and open to interpretation, sustainable development was widely and quickly adopted, especially in Europe where the appetite for ecological modernization was strong (Dryzek 2013, 16) or, as Donald Worster (1993, 133) suggests, because it promised an easy path for those "who don't really have a clear notion of what the principal goal of environmentalism ought to be." Others simply describe the concept of sustainable development as oxymoronic (Redclift 2005; see also Kim 2022, 416). What is clear, as Du Pisani (2006, 94) argues, is:

> the term has never been ideologically neutral, because it was intended as an alternative to the zero growth option and was therefore positively inclined towards the growth and modernization viewpoints. The whole debate around sustainable development made it clear that anthropocentric views were stronger than ecocentric views, but that environmental concerns had at least become part of development discourses.

The adoption of the UN's Sustainable Development Goals (SDGs) in 2015 ensured sustainable development remains a dominant discourse in policy, business (Dauvergne 2008) and law (Adelman 2018). Kotzé and French (2018) observe that law has been central to the evolution of sustainable development since its early iteration in Brundtland's report (1987) and continues to be an "instrument of change" at national and international levels and in wider social understanding of the goals. Nevertheless, Kotzé and French also observe that "to say that law can implement the [SDGs] says little about the relative power, and conflicting and diverse interests of the rule- and decision-makers" (Kotzé and French 2018, 4).

What is the power and interests of the rule-makers? Critics of sustainable development argue that the convergence of ecological politics and the rise of neoliberalism, aided by an increasingly global network of media power in the latter part of the twentieth century, ensured the goals of sustainable development served to "conceal a more fundamental class project of accumulation by dispossession through private appropriation of the commons" (Adelman 2018). For instance, in our study of news coverage of campaigns to protect Australia's Great Barrier Reef, Kerrie Foxwell-Norton and I (2019, 230) found sustainable development was used to "question and silence the ecological knowledge and concern that was, ironically, its original ambit" by those privileging the pro-development voices of government and industry. Donald Worster (1993, 137) argues that the idea of sustainability has become "quite simply, another measure of production" that reduces the natural world to a source of materials for human use, based on the assumption that we can determine the carrying capacity of local ecosystems, which "rests on an uncritical, unexamined acceptance of the traditional world view of progressive, secular materialism" (Worster 1993, 142–143; see also Hajer 1993).

Furqar Ahmad (2001) describes the 1972 Stockholm convention as the Magna Carta of environmental law and considers it parallel in significance to the 1948 Universal Declaration of Human Rights. Framed in that way, we can hear the echoes of that much earlier charter on human liberty that was soon followed by a charter drawing attention to our dependence on the natural world, and we can anticipate that the modern discourses on human rights, again, overshadow its ecological counterweight. As such, the tensions inherent in the definition and enactment of sustainable development continue a centuries-old struggle between those who speak for the commons and those arguing for private rights to own and exploit resources on which we all depend, and which are the "common thread linking the remarkable range of issues that we call environmental law" (Plater 1994, 981).

As ever, who gets to define sustainable development and defend that definition by silencing critics determines the legitimacy of actions taken to exploit or protect our natural environment. Sustainable development as a framework for policy and law includes several underlying principles, including the precautionary principle, intergenerational equity, and public participation. As an ambiguous and contestable concept (Affolder 2012), the challenge for translating the goals and principles of sustainable development into law is ensuring that respect for ecological limits guides economic activity (Adelman 2018; Affolder 2019). Without that balance, the framework is only about development. Another approach is to reimagine our understanding of healthy environments through the lens of human rights or, alternatively, to reimagine human rights as an environmental issue.

Environmental Problems as Human Rights Issues

Questions relating to human rights are entwined in how we identify the causes of ecological problems, those most affected by them, and those responsible for addressing the problems (Cole and Foster 2001). As we have already discussed, locating human rights within the context of environmental law risks human concerns overshadowing ecological considerations, however, as Ambellin Kwaymullina (2018, 16) argues, keeping environmental law and human rights law separate ignores how healthy ecosystems and healthy human communities share the same story.

Incorporating human rights into ecological perspectives is central to the environmental and climate justice movements that challenge environment discourses that ignore the suffering of workers, women, Indigenous communities and people of color (Pezzullo 2021, 229; Sandler and Pezzullo 2007). Environmental justice has been a central driver in the modernization of environmental movements and has come to:

> encompass almost everything that is unsustainable about the world, including rampant industrialization, resource depletion, energy use, consumption patterns, food systems, access to environmental amenities, and public policies that adversely affect minority, Indigenous, and low-income communities, other vulnerable groups such as disabled, immigrant, and linguistically isolated populations as well as future generations. (Holifield et al. 2018, 2)

The idea of environmental justice then is invoked whenever we are reminded that, despite affluent societies producing more carbon emissions than the world's least material, it is the latter who often bear the burden of climate mitigation policy. The concept of environmental justice is integral to developments in environmental law to ensure the distributive effects of environmental policy do not privilege top-down governance, often from governments and civil societies from far away, over the participatory decision-making of those most affected (Purdy 2018). In this sense, we can see the inclusion of human rights in the development of environmental law as, once again, being undertaken to ensure the frameworks governing human activity at local, national, and transnational levels support the needs of all people, rather than just the powerful. In July 2022, the United Nations' General Assembly declared that the "right to a clean, healthy and sustainable environment as a human right" (United Nations 2022) which has since been echoed in climate litigation and efforts to describe destruction as a violation of human rights. Another approach is to grant nature its own rights and, in doing so, "enshrine in the law the fundamental symbiosis between human and nonhuman ecological health" (Takacs 2021, 550–551).

The Rights of Nature

The "rights of nature" refers to many approaches that extend rights to non-human entities. For more than a decade, the "rights of nature" as a concept has gained increasing acceptance. The logic is easy enough: if non-human entities, such as corporations and ships, or people who cannot speak for themselves, such as the very infirm or the unborn, can have legal rights, it should be possible for trees, rivers and even whole ecosystems to be recognized having rights that can be defined and defended by those charged with advocating on their behalf (Epstein 2022; Stone 1972, 2010). The rights turn is a good example of law as a constitutive social practice. When Christopher Stone first asked his law class "Should trees have rights?" in 1970, and translated the response into an article titled *Should Trees Have Standing?- Toward Legal Rights for Natural Objects* (1970) he was experimenting with a radical idea that was picked up by legal practitioners and others. Developing the ideas, Stone (2010) explained that giving non-human entities "rights" required seeing the intrinsic values of that entity rather than its relative value as the property of another. In other words, giving a river (or ship or unborn child) the status of personhood provides a legal status not limited to being regarded as the property of another. More recently, Ramiro Ávila, a judge of the Ecuadorian constitutional court, argued that the rights of nature, as a concept, is a specific reaction to the processes of modernity, which are:

> committed to a scientific rationalism, as an exclusive form of knowledge; by capitalism, as a form of human relationship; for coloniality, as a mechanism of cultural imposition; and for the colonization, as a form of exercise of power. Under this logic, nature is seen as a mere resource that can be used by humans and remains passive of cultural imposition; and for colonization, as a form of exercise of power. (Ávila in Gutmann and Naranjo 2021, 335)

From its early, radical origins, the rights for nature movement is now an international movement of activists, researchers, and advocates (Maloney and Burdon 2014) often led by Indigenous peoples (O'Donnell et al. 2020, 403) whose work is providing the discursive momentum for legal and social change.

In 2008, Ecuador was the first to enshrine the rights of nature or Pachamama ("Mother Earth") in its constitution, and Bolivia, Mexico and Colombia have added comparable legal mechanisms in their constitutions since. In other countries, rivers are proving ideal test cases to explore the legal possibilities, with several rivers receiving personhood in the past decade: the first was Aotearoa/New Zealand's Whanganui River in 2017, followed by India's Ganges and Yamuna rivers in 2017, Colombia's Río Atrato in 2018, and, in 2019, every river in Bangladesh. Each of these cases has local histories and legal contexts informing the articulation of their rights, but in each case, the specific nature of the rivers and their defined catchments ensure that governments can formulate the appropriate institutional arrangements, including guardians and funding, to oversee them (O'Donnell et al. 2022). Efforts continue to define the nature of legal personhood of natural systems, such as Australia's Great Barrier Reef (Barcan 2020). For all this progress, there remain difficult questions, such as who enforces the rights granted to nature and who is responsible for harms caused by legal entities, such as a river, that, in the exercise of its rights, have caused harm to others through flooding and other problems (Nellemann et al. 2016).

Transnational Environmental Law

Even the relative containment of a river and its catchments presents problems of law when they cross national boundaries, such as the Mekong River which travels through six countries in southeast Asia, and the Nile, which travels through 11 northeastern African countries. Many environmental problems are also symptomatic of the erosion of state sovereignty and the impact of non-state actors on the domestic sphere (Kotzé 2016; Webster and Mai 2020, 5). In response, some are calling for a "radical alternative to the business-as-usual approaches to environmental law and to the way these juridical interventions are perceived" (Kotzé 2016, 71–73). Transnational environmental law is presented as that radical alternative. It describes a legal framework that supports the migration of legal norms, rules and models across borders, which would include input from local people and non-state actors (Kotzé 2016; Webster and Mai 2020). Transnational environmental law speaks to Nancy Fraser's (2007) conceptualization of the transnational public sphere that challenged the traditional concept of the "public" as being a bounded political community within a territorial state that communicates their concerns in terms of national issues. By questioning the erasure of public opinion as a political force by global capital-driven actors, Fraser invited speculation as to the nature of a transnational public sphere separate from Westphalian notions of citizenship. Fraser (2010, 64) also encountered the dilemma of imagining universal commonality without falling into the pitfall of conformity and cautions against attempts to provide a one-size-fits-all approach to a global humanity. Her call to pay attention to the peculiarities of local contexts echoes Elinor Ostrom's confidence in the capacity for local communities to sustainably regulate resource use.

While a progression toward unified global law sounds appealing, there are, of course, challenges. In the previous chapter, we encountered the problems of the selection of actors and authorities informing "a single global polity" based on Earth system science. Current developments in international law encounter the same concerns. The Paris Agreement provides a good example of the capacity of the international community to differentiate the needs and capacities of developed and developing nations albeit through the frameworks of sovereign states developing national laws. While not satisfying all parties, Lavanya Rajamani (2016) observes the Paris Agreement's current successes lie in combining the "bottom-up" contributions from local communities and governments with the "top-down" pressure applied by the international community made up of both nation states and transnational non-state actors. In short, transnational environmental law responds to the problem of transnational non-state actors, such as large corporations, wielding extraordinary power over the politics of sovereign states and their publics that influence environmental decision-making and other human rights issues, which leads to human rights and environmental problems bleeding across national borders.

Earth Jurisprudence

Another approach to incorporating the planetary boundaries framework into law is the idea of "Earth jurisprudence" or "wild law" that is an emerging legal philosophy that "analyses the contribution of law in constructing, maintaining and perpetuating anthropocentrism and looks at ways in which this orientation can be undermined and ultimately eliminated" (Burdon 2014, 30; see also Pelizzoni 2021). First defined by a Catholic priest, Thomas Berry (1999), but more fully described by Cormac Cullinan (2011), Earth jurisprudence has developed into a critique of the worldviews informing our current ecological crises that offers a radical change in our understanding of governance as a corrective (Burdon 2011; Cullinan 2021; de Lucia 2017; Maloney and Burdon

2014; Murray 2014). As an "ecological theory of law," its central principle is the "Earth community" that locates humanity as existing as part of, and interconnected with, the living and non-living entities of the Earth, which do not exist for human use and exploitation (Burdon 2014). Earth jurisprudence can be seen as a full articulation of the rights of nature (Murray 2014). By addressing criticisms that environmental law has evolved in a piecemeal fashion and lacks a unified coherence, Earth jurisprudence meaningfully addresses the challenge of balancing ecological sustainability with economic sustainability (Lowe 2014, 6). In this approach, we find a return to attempts to "balance human rights and freedoms with responsibilities to contribute to maintaining and enhancing the integrity, functioning, and well-being of Earth" (Cullinan 2021, 235).

Thomas Berry argued that there are two types of law: the Great Law, which would be informed by scientific knowledge, including concepts such as ecosystem health and the Earth's tipping points; and, secondly, Human Law, where the binding prescriptions of law for human activity would be bound to the Great Law (Burdon 2014, 32). In this model, science is given some authority as a translator of the Great Law, but kept separate from governance in Human Law.

Earth systems science has taken this ecological approach to law to describe a new legal framework called "Earth systems law", which first appeared in a paper (Kim and Mackey, 2014) that explored the notion that international environmental law, as a network of treaties and institutions with emergent properties, should be aligned with the complex adaptive systems of the Earth itself. Since then, the idea of Earth systems law has developed (Baber 2021; Cadman 2021; Du Toit and Kotzé 2022) and a more recent articulation can be found in the idea of the "planetary commons" (Rockström et al. 2024) which is described as a fundamental shift from a transnational governance of resources, or "global commons" to a "planetary commons" framework that recognizes the critical biophysical systems that regulate the Earth system. In formulating their fledgling framework, the authors acknowledge the idea of Earth system law, while adding principles including "differentiated degrowth and sufficiency", interconnectivity, and a "new planetary ethic", such as ecological sustainability. In these emerging ideas, we can see the impulse of solidarity that has long informed the idea of the commons being translated through the lens of contemporary Earth systems science and modernity's predilection for global, into imagined directions for international law.

Four key ideas in environmental law—sustainable development, human rights, the rights of nature and Earth jurisprudence—have been briefly described here because these terms, or the tensions they seek to resolve, are woven through the cases and campaigns described in the following chapters. The tensions between ecological sustainability and economic growth, the definition of human rights in the context of ecological damage, and the need to address global problems within local contexts, inform the discourses of green lawfare. Each is a contagious idea about the legal possibilities to address global environmental problems. A quick look at how media, especially books and film, locate environmental law in the popular imagination follows before some discussion on the role of media in the communication of contagious ideas.

Green Lawfare in the Popular Imagination

What are the stories we tell about environmental problems and the law in popular media? In novels, film and television, detectives are the usual heroes of police procedurals and murder mysteries and, similarly, journalists and lawyers, whose professions also use investigation and discovery, are often protagonists in thrillers about conspiracies and cover-ups. Writing on films about journalists, Brian McNair (2010, 28) observed these films "allow film-makers to engage with substantial social issues, and important public debates" and listed a pantheon of directors, including Alfred Hitchcock, Orson Welles and Oliver Stone, who made films "to demonstrate their seriousness and commitment to public affairs." For journalists, think William Alland in Orsen Welle's *Citizen Kane* and the real-life heroes of the Watergate scandal, Carl Bernstein and Bob Woodward in *All the President's Men*. Similarly, popular culture gives lay audiences "a glimpse of law's inner sanctum" (Gies 2008, 7). Lawyers, such as Atticus Finch in Harper Lee's *To Kill a Mocking Bird*, Lieutenant Daniel Kaffee in Rob Reiner's *A Few Good Men*, and John Grisham's Regie Love in *The Client* explore enduring questions relating to law and society through compelling stories using classic narrative structures. While the philosophical debates of environmentalism have attracted plenty of attention in popular culture, stories relating to environmental law and the legal nature of environmental problems are much less prevalent.

Fictional stories engaged explicitly with environmental law, or even lawyers with environmental nous, bring to mind Darby Shaw in John Grisham's *Pelican Brief* (1992) and, more recently, Ray Brinkman in Richard Powers'

The Overstory (2018). More common examples of environmental law in literature and film involve true stories that invariably involve allegations of corporate malfeasance. The award-winning film *Silkwood* (1983) was based on the real-life Erin Silkwood who was collecting evidence about worker safety at a plutonium processing plant when she died in suspicious circumstances. Another real-life female protagonist was chosen for Steven Soderbergh's *Erin Brockovich* (2000), which was based on the true story of Brockovich pursuing a company, Pacific Gas & Electric, that was contaminating drinking water in the southern California town of Hinkley. Like *Silkwood*, the film popularized the idea of individuals pursuing environmental justice and highlighted the role of trust and transparency to counter power and profit in the communication of environmental risk (Ferreira 2004). Similarly, *Civil Action* (1998) was a film about a real-life class action against three companies linked to groundwater contamination and, more recently *Dark Waters* (2019) chronicled true events in a long-running lawsuit against chemical giant DuPont for poisoning its own workers and surrounding communities. DuPont was already in financial difficulties when *Dark Waters* was released and when Chemours, the company that took over the DuPont portfolio, settled the public health lawsuits, it referenced the film and Mark Ruffalo, who starred in and co-produced the film, went on to campaign against such "forever chemicals" (de la Garza 2019). Indeed, *Dark Waters* joins *Silent Spring* and *Erin Brockovich* as examples of popular media playing a role in the United States policy on pollution. Ferreira (2004, 200) notes that films about cover-ups and environmental risk are:

> predicated on beliefs that the "truth" is being held from the public by government agencies and powerful corporations, spelling out issues of unseen radiation or toxic substances contaminating the life needs of unsuspecting neighbors [and] issues of harm to humans and environments are nearly always the result of illegitimate profit and power and knowledge imbalances, accompanied by denial of harm by facility owners and bureaucracies.

The dramatization of these real-life cases are notable for being "true stories" about reluctant heroes who pay a high personal cost for challenging power. Focusing on the personal cost of their activities, serves to reassert the moral weight of actions that, if successful, can provide payouts millions of dollars to victims and their lawyers. These stories position lawyers as "first responders" in a society that offers few avenues for redress (Beck 2020, 80). As Rob Bilott, the lawyer behind the class action portrayed in *Dark Waters*, told *Time* magazine (de la Garza 2019):

> If we can't get where we need to go to protect people through our regulatory channels, through our legislative process, then unfortunately what we have left is our legal process ... If that's what it takes to get people the information they need and to protect people, we're willing to do it.

In this sense, the lawyers who take on the corporate behemoths in environmental cases are portrayed as a kind of whistleblower who challenges the accepted "silences" about institutional and organizational processes (Teo and Caspersz 2011), which is to say, going against the normative assumptions that the law always protects the elite and the social order. Indeed, by presenting lawyers as going against the grain of their professional class and defying expectations to care for the underdog, these films represent the law as being "about who wins, not about who should win" (Ebert 1999). Little wonder there is some unease within the legal sphere about the representation of law in popular culture (Gies 2008). Writing about the "Erin Brockovich effect" (Banks 2003) observes that Hollywood's influence on the public perception of environmental issues was no accident, but the result of groups, such as the Environmental Media Association who make it their mission to mobilize the entertainment "to educate people about environmental problems and inspire them to act on those problems now." These efforts to educate and inspire action are most conspicuously seen in the recent growth of environmental documentary.

Documentaries about environmental problems have grown in popularity in recent years, in part because video streaming has brought larger audiences to the form (Males and van Aelst 2021). While early documentaries, of which David Attenborough is the doyenne, are classic examples of popular science communication, has been a turn to unapologetically campaign-oriented documentaries. However, these documentaries rarely stray into questions of legality or environmental law. The exception here is Tom Berglinger's *Crude* (2009) which, as a long-running legal battle, is discussed in the next chapter.

In the apparent disconnect between public imagination and environmental law, where do people, including future environmental lawyers, find their ideas and inspiration? For now, at least, popular culture represents environmental law as instances of regulation failure and where the activist lawyer, much like the truth-seeking hero journalist, must fight the corporate behemoths while risking their job, family and health along the way. In the popular imagination, then, the ideas and ambitions that we might associate with Earth jurisprudence and other legal approaches have barely penetrated popular imagination. Instead, apocalyptic futures and other dystopian imaginaries dominate the translation of environmental science, philosophy and governance into popular culture. In other words, popular culture is awash with predictions of the ultimate success of tyranny over collective action. These predictions, and the hopelessness they inspire, dominate our engagement with the future. Through the translation of science and economic theory for popular audiences, we have plenty of stories about what will happen if we do not act. Less common are the translations of economic, political and legal thinking about what is possible to sustain life on this planet.

Conclusion: Communicating Contagious Ideas

Having briefly traversed the origins of the environmental movement at the intersections of protest politics, formal politics and civil institutions and the excesses of industrialization in the previous chapter, this chapter looked at the communication of environmental problems as legal issues. By approaching communication as a constitutive practice, we observed the processes and practices that constitute the communication of environmental problems into law and legal thinking. Although quantifying the precise influence of media representations on governmental decision-making is challenging (Preston 2011), the growing use of legal action by environmental groups and other actors suggests environmental law as a set of "contagious ideas" continues to inform, and be informed by, the environmental movement and those working with the legal sphere and those in wider sociolegal frameworks. A substantial body of existing work, especially the theorization of mediatized environmental conflict (Hutchins and Lester 2015), provides a robust theoretical foundation for investigating the people, practices and networked communication processes that enable, and inhibit, the flow of contagious ideas. In such moments and spaces, we can observe how abstract concepts and more concrete examples of environmental law are shared, translated, and repurposed for local contexts across various genres of communication, including news and other media, but also case law and academic journals, books and film, and campaign strategies and communication.

Drawing on a handful of examples to build a unifying idea risks the homogenizing arrogance of universalism and similarly, finding connections between Indigenous and non-Indigenous approaches and worldviews also risks the intellectual colonialism that steals, rather than shares, from the rich diversity of human experience. However, this chapter selected a few of the discourses in environmental philosophy and environmental law to provide a foundation on which to identify legal concepts used by those in, or resisting, the environmental movement. By starting with its earliest roots in Magna Carta and comparing the positions of Hardin and Ostrom as discourses around collective responsibility for resources, this chapter found a universal tension informing the development of environmental law between individual rights and collective responsibilities. As such, the history of global struggle described as environmental conflict, including its most recent incarnation in the politics of climate protest, can be understood as a reaction to the tyrannical forces that ignore the responsibility to the collective or what Romain Francis (2020), in a similar effort to define a universal environmental ethic, calls the "tyranny of the coloniality of nature."

This and the previous chapter have described the elements constituting the enactment of green lawfare, which are: 1) the tension between rights and responsibilities that informs the "clash of worldviews" at the center of mediatized environmental conflict; 2) the various practices and platforms that constitute contemporary media networks; 3) the wide networks of actors engaged in these contests; and, 4) some of the contagious ideas being shared across networks that are informing the conceptualization of environmental problems as matters that can be addressed through legislation and the courts. In the following chapters, we use these tools to observe how the strategic use of law during environmental conflict both challenges and maintains the social, political and economic power at the root of our ecological crises. By drawing on case studies and their representation through news and other media, we will observe the flow of ideas from within and outside the legal sphere along the various networks of power and counter-power and the moments and spaces where these ideas come into material, symbolic and political effect.

This chapter began by reflecting on calls for a new story and presented a range of approaches to environmental law that can be understood as part of that work. We can see the consequences of and reactions to the ecological tyranny unfolding in our daily news feeds, in parliaments, courtrooms and at the physical and virtual sites of protest. The old story about the battles for liberty and responsibility, tyranny and justice, and the newer stories of the Anthropocene and the Apocalypse are played out in the real and mediated spaces of protest and contest. It is not an exaggeration to say that how these stories are told and understood may well determine the future of the world.

References

Adelman, Sam. 2018. "The Sustainable Development Goals, Anthropocentrism and Neoliberalism." In *Sustainable Development Goals*, edited by Duncan French and Louis J. Kotzé, 15–40. Cheltenham: Edward Elgar.

Affolder, Natasha. 2012. "The Legal Concept of Sustainability." Paper presented at the Environment in the Courtroom: Key Environmental Concepts and the Unique Nature of Environmental Damage, University of Calgary, March 23. https://cirl.ca/sites/default/files/teams/1/2012%20Symposium/ENG_The%20Legal%20Concept%20of%20Sustainability_Affolder.pdf

Affolder, Natasha. 2019. "Contagious Environmental Lawmaking." *Journal of Environmental Law* 31 (2): 187–212.

Ahmad, Furqan. 2001. "Origin and Growth of Environmental Law in India." *Journal of the Indian Law Institute* 43 (3): 358–387.

Ahmed, Nabil. 2018. "Proof of Ecocide: Towards a Forensic Practice for the Proposed International Crime Against the Environment." *Archaeological and Environmental Forensic Science* 1 (2): 139–147.

Antonio, Robert J., and Robert J. Brulle. 2011. "The Unbearable Lightness of Politics: Climate Change Denial and Political Polarization." *The Sociological Quarterly* 52 (2): 195–202.

Appadurai, Arjun. 2013. *The Future as Cultural Fact Essays on the Global Condition*. London and New York: Verso.

Arendt, Hannah. 1956. "Authority in the Twentieth Century." *The Review of Politics* 18 (4): 403–417.

Baber, Walter F. 2021. "Earth System Law in the Age of Humanity." In *Earth System Law: Standing on the Precipice of the Anthropocene*, edited by Timothy Cadman, Margot Hurlbert, and Andrea C. Simonelli, 33–54. Abingdon: Routledge.

Babie, Paul. 2016. "Magna Carta and the Forest Charter: Two Stories of Property, What Will You Be Doing in 2017?" *North Carolina Law Review* 94: 1431–1474.

Banks, Sedina. 2003. "The 'Erin Brockovich Effect': How Media Shapes Toxics Policy." *Environs: Environmental Law and Policy* 26 (2): 219–252.

Barcan, Ruth. 2020. "The Campaign for Legal Personhood for the Great Barrier Reef: Finding Political and Pedagogical Value in a Spectacular Failure of Care." *Environment and Planning E: Nature and Space* 3 (3): 810–832.

Beck, Bernard. 2020. "The Last Laugh: *Parasite*, *Joker*, *Dark Waters*, and the Outcasts' Revenge." *Multicultural Perspectives* 22 (2): 79–81.

Beck, Ulrich. 1995. *Ecological Enlightenment: Essays on the Politics of the Risk Society*. Atlantic Highlands: Humanities Press.

Berry, Thomas. 1987. "The New Story: Comments on The Origin, Identification and Transmission of Values." *CrossCurrents* 37 (2/3): 187–199.

———. 1999. *The Great Work: Our Way into the Future*. New York: Bell Tower.

Besant, Chris. 1991. "A Brief History of Environmental Law." *Legal Service Bulletin* 16 (4): 6.

Birch, Kean. 2015. "Neoliberalism: The Whys and Wherefores … and Future Directions: Neoliberalism." *Sociology Compass* 9 (7): 571–584.

Black, C. F. 2011. *The Land Is the Source of the Law: A Dialogic Encounter with Indigenous Jurisprudence*. New York: Routledge.

Bollier, David. 2012. "The Future of International Environmental Law: A Law of the Ecological Commons." In *International Environment Law and World Order*, edited by Jonathan C. Carson and Burns M. Weston. Minnesota: West Publishing.

Bollier, David. 2014. "The Commons: A Template for Transformation." *Great Transition Initiative*, April 2014. https://greattransition.org/publication/the-commons-as-a-template-for-transformation (Accessed July 7, 2023).

Brundtland, Gro Harlem. 1987. "Our Common Future—Call for Action." *Environmental Conservation* 14 (4): 291–294.

Burdon, Peter D., ed. 2011. *Exploring Wild Law: The Philosophy of Earth Jurisprudence*. Adelaide: Wakefield Press.

Burdon, Peter D. 2014. *Earth Jurisprudence: Private Property and the Environment*. Abingdon: Routledge.

Cadman, Timothy. 2021. "Introduction Origins and Evolution of Earth System Law." In *Earth System Law: Standing on the Precipice of the Anthropocene*, by Timothy Cadman, Margot Hurlbert, and Andrea C. Simonelli, 1st ed., 1–11. London: Routledge. https://doi.org/10.4324/9781003198437-1.

Cahill, Damien, Melinda Cooper, Martijn Konings, and David Primrose. 2018. "Approaches to Neoliberalism." In *The SAGE Handbook of Neoliberalism*, edited by Damien Cahill, Melinda Cooper, Martijn Konings, and David Primrose, xxv-xxxiii. London: SAGE.

Carvalho, Anabela, Margit van Wessel, and Pieter Maeseele. 2017. "Communication Practices and Political Engagement with Climate Change: A Research Agenda." *Environmental Communication* 11 (1): 122–135.

Castells, Manuel, ed. 2004. *The Network Society: A Cross-Cultural Perspective*. Cheltenham: Edward Elgar.

———. 2009. *Communication Power*. Oxford: Oxford University Press.

Clark, David. 2015. "Magna Carta in Australia 1803–2015." In *Papers on Parliament: Magna Carta 800 Symposium*, edited by Paula Waring, 43–61. Canberra: Parliament House.

Cole, Luke, and Sheila Foster. 2001. *From the Ground up: Environmental Racism and the Rise of the Environmental Justice Movement*. New York: New York University Press.

Cottle, Simon. 2011. "Taking Global Crises in the News Seriously: Notes from the Dark Side of Globalization." *Global Media and Communication* 7 (2): 77–95.

Couldry, Nick, and Andreas Hepp. 2017. *The Mediated Construction of Reality*. Cambridge: Polity Press.

Cox, Susan Jane Buck. 1985. "No Tragedy on the Commons." *Environmental Ethics* 7 (1): 49–61.

Cullinan, Cormac. 2011. *Wild Law: A Manifesto for Earth Justice*. 2nd ed. White River Junction: Chelsea Green.

———. 2021. "Earth Jurisprudence." In *The Oxford Handbook of International Environmental Law*, 2nd ed. New York: Oxford University Press.

Dauvergne, Peter. 2008. *The Shadows of Consumption: Consequences for the Global Environment.* Cambridge: MIT Press.
De la Garza, Alejandro. 2019. "Dark Waters Tells the True Story of the Lawyer Who Took DuPont to Court and Won. But Rob Bilott's Fight Is Far from Over." *Time*, November 25. https://time.com/5737451/dark-waters-true-story-rob-bilott/ (Accessed July 7, 2023).
De Lucia, Vito. 2017. "Beyond Anthropocentrism and Ecocentrism: A Biopolitical Reading of Environmental Law." *Journal of Human Rights and the Environment* 8 (2): 181–202.
Dijk, Teun van. 1988. *News as Discourse*. Hillsdale: Lawrence Erlbaum.
Dryzek, John S. 2013. *The Politics of the Earth: Environmental Discourses*. 3rd ed. Oxford: Oxford University Press.
Du Pisani, Jacobus A. 2006. "Sustainable Development—Historical Roots of the Concept." *Environmental Sciences* 3 (2): 83–96.
Du Toit, Louise, and Louis J. Kotzé. 2022. "Reimagining International Environmental Law for the Anthropocene: An Earth System Law Perspective." *Earth System Governance* 11 (January): 100132. https://doi.org/10.1016/j.esg.2022.100132.
Ebert, Roger. 1999. "A Civil Action." Roger Egbert, January 8. https://www.rogerebert.com/reviews/a-civil-action-1999#:~:text=%22Civil%20Action%22%20is%20like%20John,t%20necessarily%20arrive%20at%20truth (Accessed October 6, 2022).
Epstein, Seth. 2022. "Rights of Nature, Human Species Identity, and Political Thought in the Anthropocene." *The Anthropocene Review*. https://doi.org/10.1177/20530196221078929
Fairlie, Simon. 2009. "A Short History of Enclosure in Britain." *The Land* 7: 16–31.
Ferreira, Celio. 2004. "Risk, Transparency and Cover up: Media Narratives and Cultural Resonance." *Journal of Risk Research* 7 (2): 199–211.
Finkler, Wiebke, and Bienvenido León. 2019. "The Power of Storytelling and Video: A Visual Rhetoric for Science Communication." *Journal of Science Communication* 18 (5): A02. https://doi.org/10.22323/2.18050202
Fisher, Elizabeth. 2012. "The Rise of Transnational Environmental Law and the Expertise of Environmental Lawyers." *Transnational Environmental Law* 1 (1): 43–52.
———. 2013. "Environmental Law as 'Hot' Law." *Journal of Environmental Law* 25 (3): 347– 358.
———. 2017. *Environmental Law: A Very Short Introduction*. New York: Oxford University Press.
Francis, Romain. 2020. "The Tyranny of the Coloniality of Nature and the Elusive Question of Justice." In *Reimagining Justice, Human Rights and Leadership in Africa*, edited by Everisto Benyera, 39–57. Cham: Springer International.
Fraser, Nancy. 2007. "Transnationalizing the Public Sphere: On the Legitimacy and Efficacy of Public Opinion in a Post-Westphalian World." *Theory, Culture & Society* 24 (4): 7–30.
Fraser, Nancy. 2010. *Scales of Justice: Reimagining Political Space in a Globalizing World*. New York: Columbia University Press.
Fraser, Nancy. 2023. *Cannibal Capitalism: How Our System Is Devouring Democracy, Care, and the Planet - and What We Can Do about It*. New York: Verso.
Gardiner, Stephen M. 2001. "The Real Tragedy of the Commons." *Philosophy & Public Affairs* 30 (4): 387–416.

Garza, Alejandro de la. 2019. "Dark Waters Tells the True Story of the Lawyer Who Took DuPont to Court and Won. But Rob Bilott's Fight is Far from Over." *Time*, November 25. https://time.com/5737451/dark-waters-true-story-rob-bilott/ (Accessed May 5, 2023).

Gellers, Joshua C. 2015. "Greening Critical Discourse Analysis: Applications to the Study of Environmental Law." *Critical Discourse Studies* 12 (4): 482–493.

Gies, Lieve. 2008. *Law and the Media: The Future of an Uneasy Relationship*. Oxford and New York: Routledge-Cavendish.

Godden, Lee, Jacqueline Peel, and Jan McDonald. 2019. *Environmental Law*. 2nd ed. Melbourne: Oxford University Press.

Gunaratne, Shelton A. 2013. "Go East Young 'Man': Seek Wisdom from Laozi and Buddha on How to Metatheorize Mediatization." *Journal of Multicultural Discourses* 8 (3): 165–181.

Gutmann, Andreas, and Viviana Morales Naranjo. 2021. "Should the Absentees Have Standing? The Fundamentals That Justify Nature Accessing Justice in Germany and Ecuador." *VRÜ Verfassung Und Recht in Übersee* 54 (3): 331–351.

Hajer, Maarten A. 1993. "Discourse Coalitions and the Institutionalization of Practice: The Case of Acid Rain in Great Britain." In *The Argumentative Turn in Policy Analysis and Planning*, edited by Frank Fischer and John Forester. Durham: Duke University Press.

Hardin, Garrett. 1968. "The Tragedy of the Commons: The Population Problem Has No Technical Solution; It Requires a Fundamental Extension in Morality." *Science* 162 (3859): 1243–1248.

———. 1994. "The Tragedy of the Unmanaged Commons." *Trends in Ecology & Evolution* 9 (5): 682–683.

Harvey, David. 2005. *A Brief History of Neoliberalism*. Oxford and New York: Oxford University Press.

Higgins, Polly. 2015. *Eradicating Ecocide: Laws and Governance to Prevent the Destruction of Our Planet*. 2nd ed. London: Shepheard-Walwyn.

Higgins, Polly, Damien Short, and Nigel South. 2013. "Protecting the Planet: A Proposal for a Law of Ecocide." *Crime, Law and Social Change* 59 (3): 251–266.

Holifield, Ryan, Jayajit Chakraborty, and Gordon Walker. 2018. "Introduction: The Worlds of Environmental Justice." In *The Routledge Handbook of Environmental Justice*, edited by Gordon Walker, Jayajit Chakraborty, and Ryan Holifield. Abingdon: Routledge.

Kennedy, David. 2016. *A World of Struggle: How Power, Law, and Expertise Shape Global Political Economy*. Princeton: Princeton University Press.

Kim, Rakhyun E. 2022. "Taming Gaia 2.0: Earth System Law in the Ruptured Anthropocene." *The Anthropocene Review* 9 (3): 411–424.

Kim, Rakhyun E., and Brendan Mackey. 2014. "International Environmental Law as a Complex Adaptive System." *International Environmental Agreements: Politics, Law and Economics* 14 (1): 5–24. https://doi.org/10.1007/s10784-013-9225-2.

Kotzé, Louis. 2016. "Transnational Environmental Law: The Birth of a Contemporary Analytical Perspective." In *Research Handbook on Fundamental Concepts of Environmental Law*, by Douglas Fisher, 82–110. Cheltenham: Edward Elgar.

Kotzé, Louis J., and Duncan French. 2018. "The Anthropocentric Ontology of International Environmental Law and the Sustainable Development Goals: Towards an Ecocentric Rule of Law in the Anthropocene." *Global Journal of Comparative Law* 7 (1): 5–36.

Kwaymullina, Ambellin. 2018. "Aboriginal Nations and the Nation State." In *Indigenous Peoples as Subjects of International Law*, edited by Irene Watson. Abingdon: Routledge.

Laclau, Ernesto, and Chantal Mouffe. 2001. *Hegemony and Socialist Strategy: Towards a Radical Democratic Politics*. 2nd ed. London and New York: Verso.

Lazarus, Richard J. 2023. *The Making of Environmental Law*. 2nd ed. Chicago: University of Chicago Press.

Lin, Jolene, and Jacqueline Peel. 2022. "The Farmer or the Hero Litigator? Modes of Climate Litigation in the Global South." In *Litigating the Climate Emergency*, edited by César Rodríguez-Garavito, 187–205. Cambridge: Cambridge University Press.

Linebaugh, Peter. 2008. *The Magna Carta Manifesto: Liberties and Commons for All*. Oakland: University of California Press.

Linebaugh, Peter. 2010. "Enclosures from the Bottom Up." *Radical History Review* 2010 (108): 11–27.

Lowe, Ian. 2014. "Wild Law Embodies Values for a Sustainable Future." In *Wild Law: In Practice*, edited by Michelle M. Maloney and Peter Burdon. Law, Justice and Ecology. Abingdon and New York: Routledge.

Magraw, Daniel, and Natalie Thomure. 2017. "Carta de Foresta: The Charter of the Forest Turns 800." *Environmental Law Reporter* 47: 10934–10940.

Males, Jennifer, and Peter Van Aelst. 2021. "Did the Blue Planet Set the Agenda for Plastic Pollution? An Explorative Study on the Influence of a Documentary on the Public, Media and Political Agendas." *Environmental Communication* 15 (1): 40–54.

Maloney, Michelle, and Peter Burdon, eds. 2014. *Wild Law—In Practice*. Abingdon: Routledge.

McDonagh, Briony, and Carl J. Griffin. 2016. "Occupy! Historical Geographies of Property, Protest and the Commons, 1500–1850." *Journal of Historical Geography* 53 (July): 1–10.

McNair, Brian. 2010. *Journalists in Film: Heroes and Villains*. Edinburgh: Edinburgh University Press.

Monbiot, George. 2017. *Out of the Wreckage: A New Politics for an Age of Crisis*. London and New York: Verso.

———. 2019. "The New Political Story That Could Change Everything." TED Summit 2019. https://www.ted.com/talks/george_monbiot_the_new_political_story_that_could_change_everything?language=en (Accessed August 22, 2023).

Mouffe, Chantal. 2023. *A Green Democratic Revolution*. London and New York: Verso.

Murray, Jamie. 2014. "Earth Jurisprudence, Wild Law, Emergent Law: The Emerging Field of Ecology and Law—Part 1." *Liverpool Law Review* 35 (3): 215–231.

Nellemann, Christian, Rune Henriksen, Arnold Kreilhuber, Davyth Stewart, Maria Kotsovou, Patricia Raxter, Elizabeth Mrema, and Sam Barrat, eds. 2016. *The Rise of Environmental Crime: A Growing Threat to Natural Resources, Peace, Development and Security*. Nairobi: United Nations Environment Programme.

O'Donnell, Erin, Anne Poelina, Alessandro Pelizzon, and Cristy Clark. 2020. "Stop Burying the Lede: The Essential Role of Indigenous Law(s) in Creating Rights of Nature." *Transnational Environmental Law* 9 (3): 403–427.

Ostrom, Elinor. 1990. *Governing the Commons: The Evolution of Institutions for Collective Action*. The Political Economy of Institutions and Decisions. Cambridge and New York: Cambridge University Press.

———. 2009. "A General Framework for Analyzing Sustainability of Social-Ecological Systems." *Science* 325 (5939): 419–422.

Ostrom, Elinor, Joanna Burger, Christopher B. Field, Richard B. Norgaard, and David Policansky. 1999. "Revisiting the Commons: Local Lessons, Global Challenges." *Science* 284: 278–282.

Peck, Jamie. 2018. "Naming Neoliberalism." In *The SAGE Handbook of Neoliberalism*, edited by Damien Cahill, Melinda Cooper, Martijn Konings, and David Primrose, xxi-xxiv. London: SAGE.

Pezzullo, Phaedra C. 2021. "Environmental Justice and Climate Justice." In *The Routledge Handbook of Environmental Movements*, by Maria Grasso and Marco Giugni, 229–244. Abingdon: Routledge.

Plater, Zygmunt J. B. 1994. "From the Beginning, a Fundamental Shift of Paradigms: A Theory and Short History of Environmental Law." *Loyola of Los Angeles Law Review* 27 (3): 981–1008.

Preston, Brian J. 2011. "The Influence of Climate Change Litigation on Governments and the Private Sector." *Climate Law* 2 (4): 485–513.

Purdy, Jedediah. 2018. "The Long Environmental Justice Movement." *Ecology Law Quarterly* 44: 809–864.

Rajamani, Lavanya. 2016. "Ambition and Differentiation in the 2015 Paris Agreement: Interpretative Possibilities and Underlying Politics." *International and Comparative Law Quarterly* 65 (2): 493–514.

Redclift, Michael. 2005. "Sustainable Development (1987–2005): An Oxymoron Comes of Age." *Sustainable Development* 13 (4): 212–227.

Regilme, Salvador Santino F. 2019. "The Decline of American Power and Donald Trump: Reflections on Human Rights, Neoliberalism, and the World Order." *Geoforum* 102 (June): 157–166.

Robertson, Geoffrey. 2023. *Lawfare: How Russians, the Rich and the Government Try to Prevent Free Speech and How to Stop Them*. London: TLS Books.

Robinson, Nicholas A. 2020. "The Charter of the Forest: Evolving Human Rights in Nature." In *The Impact of Environmental Law*, by Rose-Liza Eisma-Osorio, Elizabeth Kirk, and Jessica Steinberg Albin, 54–74. Cheltenham: Edward Elgar.

Sand, Peter H. 2021. "Environmental Dispute Resolution 4,500 Years Ago: The Case of *Lagash v. Umma*." *Yearbook of International Environmental Law* 30 (1): 137–142.

Sandler, Ronald L., and Phaedra C. Pezzullo, eds. 2007. *Environmental Justice and Environmentalism: The Social Justice Challenge to the Environmental Movement*. Urban and Industrial Environments. Cambridge: MIT Press.

Slobodian, Quinn, and Dieter Plehwe. 2020. "Introduction." In *Nine Lives of Neoliberalism*, edited by Dieter Plehwe, Quinn Slobodian, and Philip Mirowski, 1–18. London and New York: Verso.

Stacey, Jocelyn. 2022. "The Public Law Paradoxes of Climate Emergency Declarations." *Transnational Environmental Law* 11 (2): 291–323.

Standing, Guy. 2017. "Why You've Never Heard of a Charter That's as Important as the Magna Carta." *openDemocracy*, November 6. https://www.opendemocracy.net/en/opendemocracyuk/why-youve-never-heard-of-charter-thats-as-important-as-magna-carta/ (Accessed August 22, 2023).

Standing, Guy. 2019. *Plunder of the Commons: A Manifesto for Sharing Public Wealth*. London: Pelican.

Stone, Christopher. 1972. "Should Trees Have Standing? Toward Legal Rights for Natural Objects." *Southern California Law Review* 45: 450–501.

Stone, Christopher. 2010. *Should Trees Have Standing? Law, Morality, and the Environment*. 3rd ed. New York: Oxford University Press.

Takacs, David. 2021. "We Are the River." *University of Illinois Law Review* 2021 (2): 545–606.

Tănăsescu, Mihnea. 2013. "The Rights of Nature in Ecuador: The Making of an Idea." *International Journal of Environmental Studies* 70 (6): 846–861.

———. 2020. "Rights of Nature, Legal Personality, and Indigenous Philosophies." *Transnational Environmental Law* 9 (3): 429–453.

Teo, Hayden, and Donella Caspersz. 2011. "Dissenting Discourse: Exploring Alternatives to the Whistleblowing/Silence Dichotomy." *Journal of Business Ethics* 104 (2): 237–249.

United Nations. 2022. "With 161 Votes in Favour, 8 Abstentions, General Assembly Adopts Landmark Resolution Recognizing Clean, Healthy, Sustainable Environment as Human Right". Media Release. United Nations General Assembly. 28 July https://press.un.org/en/2022/ga12437.doc.htm. Accessed 22 August 2023

Watson, Irene. 2018. *Indigenous Peoples as Subjects of International Law*. Abingdon: Routledge.

Webster, Emily, and Laura Mai. 2020. "Transnational Environmental Law in the Anthropocene." *Transnational Legal Theory* 11 (1–2): 1–15.

Williams, Raymond. 1959. *Culture and Society: 1780–1950*. New York: Anchor Books.

Worster, Donald. 1993. "The Shaky Ground of Sustainable Development." In *Global Ecology: A New Arena of Political Conflict*, by Wolfgang Sachs, 133–145. London and New Jersey: Zed Books.

Zelizer, Barbie. 2004. *Taking Journalism Seriously: News and the Academy*. Thousand Oaks: Sage.

· 4 ·

GREEN LAWFARE AND PROTEST

The history of environmental law runs parallel to the modern environment movement because environmental organizations were quick to use the courts seeking to prevent, mitigate, remediate, or compensate for harm done to the environment (Lazarus 2023; Plater 1994; Preston 2013). That said, faced with ad hoc or negligible environmental rules from which to draw, early environmental campaigners often used whatever administrative or environmental regulations were at hand to achieve a momentary reprieve in development while appealing to media to bring public attention to the issue, often through civil disobedience. These protests sometimes resulted in arrests, which worked to take what was a political speech act into the courts, which then brought more media attention to the cause. This two-pronged approach, of engaging the legal sphere through the front door of whatever administrative or regulative instruments were available and the backdoor of arrest for civil disobedience, continues to bind the environmental movement to the legal sphere.

If mediated visibility is vital for such strategies, then news media treatment of protesters and others—such as framing them as legitimate civil actors or troublemakers, heroes or extremists—is important. However, the complex dynamics at play between journalists and their sources make such strategies difficult to determine or control. The relationship between journalists and their sources is often described as “a structural coupling” (Eskjær and Horsbøl 2023, 3) and a dance in which the source, not the journalist, tends to lead (Carlson 2009; Gans 1979) and environmental activists rarely have the same power relationship with journalists as other political actors might enjoy (Gamson and Wolfsfeld 1993; Lester 2010). Nevertheless, decades of gains in the political and legal spheres have progressed environmental perspectives from being deemed fringe and dangerous ideologies to being taken as mainstream and commonsense practices.

This chapter draws on several key moments in early environmental campaigns to observe the role of news and other media in protest movements that achieved changes to environmental policy and law. Using examples from the United States, Australia, India and Ecuador, it explores the different local contexts informing the interaction of media, activism, government and industry influencing the development of environmental law in these cases. In each, we can find moments and spaces that simultaneously engage with the local and the global without making universalizing assumptions, in order to observe how ideas and strategies are borrowed from other places and jurisdictions to be transformed by local conditions and objectives. In each case we can observe the “bottom-up” pressure on governments from protest and civil society groups, the “top-down” influences of the international community and, into the mix, the horizontal exchange of ideas and strategies across mediated and transnational networks of economics and trade, governance and law, activists and social change agents, and media and communication.

Green Lawfare and the Evolution of Environmental Law

Those engaged in a wide variety of struggles for social change frequently take their problems to the courts and the environmental movement is no different (Gunningham 2009; Plater 1994). When politicians are not listening and the courts offer few remedies, protest action was used to bring attention to environmental problems that articulated the ecological perspective in political and legal terms. Many environmental campaigns use the spectacle of arrest as part of their strategy. Arrests are a compelling visual symbol of the wider conflict—that perennial news value—between powerful interests and defenders of the public interest. Courts, too, provide visibility to the contests between activists, corporate and political actors not normally visible to the public (Nixon et al. 2021). Later, as environmental law developed, litigation provided another way to use the courts to attract media attention to the spectacle of legal contests (Lazarus 2023; Preston 2016; Wickham and Goodie 2013).

News media coverage of such cases can provide a focal point for public debate to further influence political decision-making and highlight issues for law reform (Preston 2006). Media coverage can also test the public mood. A court's decision can be a critical moment in the interpretation of law, but also in public understanding of the changing values being applied to environmental matters. While legal decisions tend to reiterate changes already happening in society—suggesting that success in the courts is an indication of broader cultural change (Rosenberg 2008),—some would also argue that litigation is an ongoing, dynamic process between the development of law and changing social values which present moments where "lines of force intersect" to find "openings within a system of power" (Cox 2010, 128; see also Plater 1994).

As a political response to the problem of civil disobedience and disruption, some argue that early environmental legislation was enacted to channel protesters off the street and into administrative and judicial forums where their grievances could be resolved away from the politically destabilizing antics of protest (see, e.g., Mouffe 2005). Various factors, including international pressure and economic considerations, ensure a myriad of reasons for governments to respond, or not. As the following examples suggest, some governments engage with the bottom-up" demands of grassroots movements to attain political advantage, giving environmentalists "political wins" in policy and legislative reform, while other administrations opt to weather the storms of protest rather than "give in" to demands. In these instances, we can observe how the courts can be used to silence and administrative processes used to hinder and ossify efforts, but we can also see how law reform is vital to social and political change (Kennedy 2016). Four countries—the United States, Australia, India and Ecuador—provide diverse examples of how green lawfare plays a role in the project of advancing domestic and international law to reflect efforts to bring human activity and ecological sustainability into alignment.

United States

It makes sense to start with the United States because of the early successes of its environmental movement in politics and law. In the 1960s, concern for the environment seemed to be everywhere, including images of the Santa Barbara oil spill and Cuyahoga River fire, which provided the right "political ingredients" to support political and legal transformation (Lazarus 2023, 80). In 1969, a newish President Richard Nixon introduced the National Environmental Policy Act (commonly referred to as NEPA) and launched the world's first Environmental Protection Agency (EPA) in part to stop the Democrats from seizing the environmental agenda (Lazarus 2021, 2023). The United States, like other countries, had an ad hoc assemblage of environmental regulation and NEPA was the first national legislation to "raise ecology to star status" (Tarlock 1994, 1126). NEPA also introduced enduring and innovative legal ideas: particularly environmental impact assessment, which is now a common feature in many countries (Lazarus 2023). NEPA also introduced the principle of transparency and disclosure in environmental decision-making, which acknowledges the role of public participation in environmental issues and which went on to be enshrined in international law, namely the United Nations Convention on Access to Information, Public Participation in Decision-making and Access to Justice in Environmental Matters, most commonly referred to as the Aarhus Convention (Nanda and Pring 2013).

Nixon's initial enthusiasm for environmental issues was short-lived because NEPA opened public interest litigation to environmental groups who often found the court amenable to their ambitions (Sabin 2015). Finding environmental matters to be politically difficult, Nixon changed tack in 1972 and aligned himself with industry, but it was too late: NEPA had enabled activists and community groups to file hundreds of suits against federal and state governments (Lazarus 2023), many of which included defendants that read like a "Who's Who" of Nixon's cabinet and administrative agencies (Sabin 2015, 976–977). A classic example of such suits is *Sierra Club v. Morton*. While much has been written on this case, it is a great example of the interplay between media, activism and politics and thus, an early example of green lawfare.

When plans to build a ski resort in California's Mineral King Valley were touted in the mid-1960s, the oldest environmental organization in the United States, the Sierra Club, was initially supportive, but when the Forest Service announced that Walt Disney Enterprises had won the tender, with almost no limits on the extent of the proposed development, the Sierra Club dropped its support for development in national parks. Work on the ski resort came to a halt while a legal battle to stop the proposed ski village ensued. With both sides claiming to be "conservationists," the *New York Times* described the case as a battle between "recreationists and protectionists" (Selmi 2022,) which hints at the transformation occurring within the Sierra Club at the time. Others viewed the case as a protest against the wider problems of "public agency discretion run amuck in the face of effective lobbying by private interests" (Fernandez 2023). When the case made its way slowly to the Supreme Court, the Sierra Club argued that the ski resort would cause significant environmental harm to the area (Selmi 2022). The Court held that the club's concern for the environment was not enough and unless the Sierra Club could demonstrate a personal or particular injury from the proposed development, it had no standing to sue. Importantly, one of the judges, Justice William O. Douglas famously argued:

> The critical question of "standing" would be simplified and also put neatly in focus if we fashioned a federal rule that allowed environmental issues to be litigated before federal agencies or federal courts in the name of the inanimate object about to be despoiled, defaced, or invaded by roads and bulldozers and where injury is the subject of public outrage. Contemporary public concern for protecting nature's ecological equilibrium should lead to the conferral of standing upon environmental objects to sue for their own preservation. This suit would therefore be more properly labelled as *Mineral King v. Morton*. (*Sierra v. Morton*)

In Douglas's words we can hear Christopher Stone's ideas on giving standing to trees—described by one commenter at the time as Stone's "brilliantly serious whimsy" (Baude 1973, 205–206). In his judgment, Douglas also put to rest arguments that if plaintiffs did not have to prove injury as users or property owners, the courts would fill cases with "value-laden controversies" that would "improperly politicize the courts" (Sax 1973). Instead, Douglas argued, a court would be able to distinguish between "those who merely are caught up in environmental news or propaganda and flock to defend these waters or areas" and "those people who have so frequented the place as to know its values and wonders will be able to speak for the entire ecological community." In other words, by distinguishing between those connected to place and the wider political agenda of the environmental movement, Douglas located the court as an arbiter between ecological and economic claims that were not about politics at a time when early environmentalists, such as the members of the Sierra Club, were learning that their concerns were inextricably political.

Sierra Club v. Morton is an early example of how losing a legal battle can still achieve outcomes. Even at the time, the case was treated as a success for conservationists. *Science* magazine (Holden 1972) reported that "the court firmly stated that an individual has as much right to go to court when his aesthetic and environmental well-being is threatened as when he faces economic damage."

The decision was a clear encouragement to the Sierra Club to return to amend its complaint by adding several natural persons as plaintiffs and alleging that club outings in the valley would be harmed by a massive ski resort. With this amendment, the Sierra Club achieved standing, but by then Disney had withdrawn its intention to build the ski resort.

In the development of environmental law, *Sierra Club v. Morton* leaves an uncertain legacy. While largely cited as one of the environment movement's earliest wins, the case was won by determining that people who enjoyed the park, rather than those with any ecological understanding of its intrinsic values, had standing, which left a "dogged anthropocentrism" to its enduring legacy in environmental law (Fernandez 2023, 2).

In his history of the case, Daniel Selmi (2022) observes how media logic informed the *Sierra Club v. Morton* in several ways. Firstly, the Sierra Club did not sue the company behind the resort, Walt Disney Inc., because as one Sierra Club member put it, to sue Disney "would be like suing motherhood, the Flag, and the Boy Scouts all at once" (Selmi 2022, 121). Similarly, as the country's oldest environmental organization, the Sierra Club was associated with two American heroes, John Muir and Walt Disney, who was an honorary lifetime member of the Club because of his ground-breaking nature films. As a result Walt Disney Inc. was also careful not to criticize the actions of the Sierra Club. By suing the Minister of the Interior, Rogers Morton, not the entertainment empire, the Sierra Club kept the focus on government mismanagement, not corporate greed, as it pursued its concerns through the court. As a seminal case in giving standing to public interest groups and exemplifying the role of public participation in the development of environmental law, *Sierra Club v. Morton* is an example of an early environmental win driven by a response to "bottom-up" or grassroots pressure providing the necessary opening in law. As Australian activists were to learn, the strategy was not easily replicated in different political and legal systems (Durbach et al. 2013).

Australia

From the earliest days of the environmental movement to more recent campaigns on climate change, Australian politics stands out for its consistent reluctance to engage with public concern for the environment. One could say a succession of Australian governments at state and federal levels has been dragged into most environmentally focused decisions. Ironically, Australia was one of the first countries, in 1974, to join the World Heritage Convention under the short, but notably progressive, Whitlam Government. However, it would be another decade, marked by protest and international attention, until the *World Heritage Properties Conservation Act* (1983) was enacted. With state governments usually pro-development and "anti-greenie," and with federal governments reluctant to engage in issues over "state rights," being a signatory to UNESCO's World Heritage Convention provided environmental advocates a necessary opening to push for environmental protection. Attaining World Heritage became the central goal of many wilderness campaigns and as a result "the World Heritage Committee often stood amazed as opposing contingents of Australians arrived for World Heritage meetings to support or oppose a listing" (Henry and Boyd 2013, 32). More recent diplomatic showdowns over whether the Great Barrier Reef should be placed on the List of World Heritage in Danger (e.g., Readfern 2023) shows that activists are still forced to take their concerns about Australian environmental and climate policy to the international community. The early battles for the Great Barrier Reef, K'gari (formerly known as Fraser Island,) and the Franklin River all focused on attaining World Heritage status by the strategic use of protest and media. Film and photography, news and subaltern media are woven throughout these campaigns and makes them early examples of green lawfare that drew on both the "bottom-up" pressure of well-organized grassroots campaigns and the "top-down" pressure of international treaties in the context of local and national politics, as the following examples show.

The Great Barrier Reef was the focus of one of Australia's earliest environmental campaigns that started in 1967 when Australian artist, John Büsst, read a notice in his local newspaper that a canesugar farmer wanted to mine limestone on Ellison Reef, a little-known coral atoll just off the North Queensland coast, for cheap fertilizer. The "Save the Reef" campaign resulted in the Great Barrier Reef becoming a national park in 1974 and then being listed by the World Heritage Committee in 1981. Along the way, those involved in these campaigns acknowledged the important role played by individual journalists in bringing the fate of the Reef to national and international audiences (Foxwell-Norton and Lester 2017). Around the same time, but further down the Queensland coast, long-held concerns that sand mining and forestry threatened K'gari—the world's largest sand island—were coming to a head. A Queensland school teacher, John Sinclair, almost single-handedly ran the Fraser Island Defence Organization (FIDO) to save the island from sand mining. As Brian Preston (2007, 18–19) writes, the legal system did not protect Sinclair, who as a teacher was an employee of the same government he was criticizing, nor from the mining company who sued him for publishing a small newsletter against sand mining. Despite the death threats and personal cost, Sinclair and FIDO saved the island which is now, like the Great Barrier Reef, an important part of Australia's tourism industry. While these two early campaigns are notable for the interaction between protest and media and the politics of international pressure, the Franklin River blockade in the southern summer of 1982–83 exemplifies how such protests can engage with the courts to great effect.

The campaign to save the Franklin River in Tasmania from being dammed by a hydroelectricity scheme resulted in a blockade organized by the Wilderness Society that attracted thousands to the remote and beautiful wilderness of the island's southwest. The ongoing physical confrontations between police and protesters, including the arrest and imprisonment of hundreds of protesters, provided spectacular images that attracted international media attention. In particular, the national call to "Save the Franklin" included Peter Dombrovski's famous photograph, *Morning Mist, Rock Island Bend, Franklin River, South-West Tasmania*, being used in a double-page, full-color advertisement with the words "Could you vote for a party that will destroy this?" just days before the 1983 Australian Federal election (Richardson 2018). The incoming Hawke Labor Government fulfilled its election promise to protect the river by enacting the *World Heritage Properties Conservation Act* (1983) which gave the Federal Government power to veto any development that might adversely impact Australia's World Heritage. When the Tasmanian Government challenged the Act on constitutional grounds, the resulting High Court decision, *Commonwealth v. Tasmania* became the leading constitutional case in the development of Australian environmental law and a noteworthy moment in the logic of green lawfare.

When the barrister acting for the Wilderness Society, Michael Black, requested to have Dombrovskis's photographs of the river, which were effectively the Wilderness Society's campaign materials, shown to the court, his request was rejected. Black told the seven judges of the Court that the photographs might explain the beauty of the region at stake better than words could, but the Chief Justice, Sir Harry Gibbs, replied that the beauty of the region was not in doubt and showing the photographs might only "inflame our minds with irrelevances" (Mills 1983, in Lester 2019, 28–29). Black's reply to the judge says something about the challenge of changing established discourses and the way we talk about things. He said:

> But, Your Honours, this is part of Australia. If we were talking about the pyramids, or Leonardo's Last Supper, or Lascaux, all of which are on the list, if the Court did not know them, it could look them. Now, Your Honour, this is a very special part of Australia and, in the crudest way only, a photograph can perhaps tell more than words. And, Your Honours only have words. (LaForgia 2015, 49)

By pointing to the inadequacy of words to describe the river, Black "lifted the veil of legal authority itself" by suggesting that the value of the river was not yet articulated by law (LaForgia 2015, 43) and raised questions about the use of media in the court.[3] The photographs of the region went on to be used by the Commonwealth in its 1982 nomination of the state's southwest wilderness for World Heritage status and its eventual inclusion on the register noted the area's aesthetic values were of global importance (Richardson 2018).

The three places described here are now listed as World Heritage properties and protected under Australian legislation. Despite these wins, and numerous other protests that have unsettled local and national politics, Australia's major environmental parties have struggled to take environmental issues seriously, as equal to economic consideration, or to leverage them for political gain (Walker and Crowley 1999) and have instead used mediated protest as a bellwether for the political and economic viability of projects. As former Australian environment minister Tony Burke (2013, 11) lamented:

> We have tended to judge the value of how well we're looking after the environment by waiting for each project to come along, waiting to see how big the demonstrations were against it, and then seeing whether after all the investments happen at the final hurdle, do we allow it or do we knock it back?

The problem with this approach, Burke said, is that the value of our natural heritage is rarely appreciated "without massive conflict" and Australians only hear about environmental protection if there are "enough conflicts surrounding it." In other words, without mediated protest, Australia would not have many of the environmental protections that it does today.

3 Courts, of course, do permit still images and videos, but there remains a tension as to whether audio and video recordings, for instance of murder victims screaming and sobbing or victims' phone calls during the 9/11 attack on the Pentagon, are legitimate accounts or examples of circumstantial evidence being used strategically to elicit emotion to steer the legal discussion in a certain direction (see Novak 2020).

It was not until 1999, when the rather limited protections set out in the *World Heritage Act* (1983) were replaced by the *Environment Protection and Biodiversity Act* (1999) (EPBC) that some cohesion in Australian environmental policy and law began to emerge (Bowen and Bowen 2002). The EPBC was intended to help Australia fulfill its international obligations relating to world heritage, biodiversity conservation and sustainable development but, with a few exceptions—notably the decision on the Rocky Hill Mine Project (*Gloucester v. Minister for Planning*)—the EPBC has proven to be despairingly inadequate for addressing the environmental degradation or complex and cumulative impacts of climate change and other environmental problems (Samuel 2020, 17). Instead, Australia's environmental policy remains largely reactive to mediated protest and public debate and is thus trapped in a political and politicized process too often directed by powerful lobbyists rather than democratic deliberation.

India

Like Australia, India leaned into international treaties to influence domestic environmental law, but in noticeably different ways. Before the 1972 United Nations Conference on Human Environment held in Stockholm, India's environmental laws were a scattering of provisions inherited from British colonial rule mixed with others introduced after independence. Much like environmental groups elsewhere, Indian campaigners had difficulty getting local governments to engage with their concerns. The Stockholm Conference, however, provided the opening. Not only were Indian Prime Minister Indira Gandhi and Swedish Prime Minister Olaf Palme the only two heads of government to attend (Panjabi 1993), but Swedish diplomats asked domestic participants to provide a report on the state of their nation's environment prior to the conference (Ahmad 2001). Providing a report to the United Nations served as a watershed moment for India because the findings:

> shocked even the most pro-development advocates in India. Stockholm served as the genesis for the series of environmental measures that India passed in the years to come [and] provided the cover Indian officials needed to implement national environment policy without the vitriolic backlash normally expected from industry. (Indian Institution of Ecology and Environment n.d.)

As a result of Stockholm, environmental law became a hot topic in India, not least because "enlightened public opinion" demanded that the country's constitution be amended to include environmental protection (Ahmad 2001, 362). Although never intended to make legally binding law, but rather to provide an arena on which nations would legislate to protect and preserve the environment, the Stockholm Conference is an early example of the openings for change made possible by international forums (Paglia 2021).

Momentum for environmental law in India gathered in the wake of the 1984 Bhopal disaster, in which thousands of residents in the central Indian city of Bhopal were exposed to a deadly cloud of hydrogen cyanide, methyl isocyanate and other chemicals that leaked from a factory owned by Union Carbide India, a subsidiary of the United States chemical company, Union Carbide. The Bhopal tragedy triggered public concern about industry safety, which came to a head a year later when another toxic leak from factory in Delhi killed at least one person. At the time of the leak, a prominent lawyer and social activist, Mahesh Chander Mehta, was seeking the closure of Shriram Industries factories because it was manufacturing hazardous substances in a densely populated area. The resulting landmark case, *Mehta v. Union of India*, established the rule of "absolute liability" to the laws controlling hazardous industrial activities (Abrahams and Abrahams 1991, 364–365) and is an example of how incorporating laws from other places "sensitized judges to the concept of environmental rights" (Gellers 2015, 405). Indian courts can enforce international law without prior legislative reform. While this practice allows international legal norms to slip into domestic law with little parliamentary scrutiny (Chandra 2017), these cases are always grounded in local problems.

Media visibility of environmental problems has a particular role in India because lawyers can initiate litigation. For instance, a landmark case, *Mehta v. Kamal Nath* was triggered by an article published in the *Indian Express* linking a motel development in northern India to the financial interests of then Minister of Environment and Forests, Kamal Nath. The development included the clearing of a large area of forest that altered the flow of the Beas River, which in turn had threatened to flood communities downriver. Mahesh Chander Mehta, widely known in India as a "hero litigator" (Lin and Peel 2022), initiated the case and argued that the land should never have been sold to private interests. The Court ruled that the land be returned to the local government for restoration, and the company was to pay compensation. In a country where "almost every major environmental issue that has made the news ends up before the High Court or the Supreme Court through a petition or is taken up by the Supreme Court of its own volition" (Mir 2020, 286) controlling the mediated visibility of any harmful activity is crucial. Writing about India, but referring also to Bangladesh, Masrur Salekin (2023, 121) observes how successful public interest litigation is dependent on "a collaborative effort between various actors" that includes not only the legal sphere but also "strong networking and consultation among civil society organizations, constant interaction between the organs of the state, collaboration between the government agencies, a trained judiciary, and supportive media." It is not perhaps surprising then that India is considered one of the most dangerous countries in Asia to work as a journalist (Siddiqui 2017, 7).

The role of media coverage in these cases shows the complexity behind assumptions about the mobilizing effect of mediated visibility on achieving justice. Despite the Bhopal disaster killing at least 3,000 people and leaving many more too injured to work, compensation for the victims has been paltry and Union Carbide, now merged with Dow Chemicals, continues to ignore summonses to appear before the Indian courts (Passow and Edwards 2023). Media coverage of the disaster has also been criticized for focusing on the immediate tragedy and blaming a large multinational while overlooking the wider systems that enabled such poor workers' conditions and environmental regulation (Wilkons 1987). While the tendency of news to report on issues as events rather than examples of broader themes is well established (Iyengar 1996), the point here is that the social, media and legal processes that attribute blame and seek remedy in the courts can also shield powerful actors from blame. In the wake of a tragedy, having the power to control media narratives around blame and correctives is a powerful weapon. As Manoj Mate (2014) observes, India's legal system is operated under a form of "elite institutionalism" influenced by a network of legal, political, and intellectual "elites" that include the media. While such networks have the power to bring national attention to environmental matters, environmental and climate news in India is increasingly dominated by international initiatives and perspectives, including "the top-down, scientific discourse from global agencies such as IPCC," that are largely incomprehensible to local residents whose local concerns are marginalized by louder international voices (Ghosh and Boykoff 2019, 10). In summary, India presents unusual challenges for environmentalists, lawyers, politicians and media to keep local issues and voices in the public mind. On the one hand, its active judiciary has plenty of scope to borrow ideas from other places as the country develops its laws, but without an active media engaging with local people about the issues that concern them, progress on environmental progression is grid-locked by a burdened court system and precarious visibility in media.

Ecuador

Ecuador, half-covered by Amazonian rainforests and economically dependent on its petroleum industry, presents a rich case study on the difficulty of adopting environmental law to address local and global concerns. While it is not unusual for Latin American presidents to use constitutional change as a path to major political reform, Ecuador's 2008 constitution was extraordinary and worth examining to see the various ways green lawfare is interwoven in its story.

Under President Rafael Correa, Ecuador became the first country in the world to enshrine the rights of nature in its 2008 constitution that inscribed:

> Nature, or Pachamama, where life is reproduced and occurs, has the right to integral respect for its existence and for the maintenance and regeneration of its life cycles, structure, functions and evolutionary processes.

The 2008 constitution also included a new approach to development based on the worldview of the Quechua peoples of the Andes, called *sumak kawsay*, which focuses more on community, ecological sustainability and culture than "Western" approaches to economic growth (Tănăsescu 2020). It also formally recognized the rights of Indigenous peoples, Afro-descendants and Montubio communities to consultation on matters involving exploration, exploitation and commercialization of non-renewable resources located within their lands and establishing that non-renewable resources belong to the state.

Describing an almost entirely "bottom-up" approach to domestic environmental law, Mihnea Tănăsescu (2013) credits the success of the 2008 constitution to the confluence of several factors, namely: Correa was prepared to imagine a radical alternative for the country; the population was united by a shared distrust of the multinational oil industry; the deliberate inclusion of Indigenous and other minority groups; and, finally, the energy minister and the president of the Constitutional Assembly, Alberto Acosta, was the right person to lead the process. Acosta told Tănăsescu (2013) that he drew on both local Indigenous knowledge and international influences, including Aldo Leopold's Earth Ethic, Christopher Stone and the Chilean environmentalist and lawyer, Godofredo Stutzin. A two-way exchange of "contagious ideas" across transnational digital networks of lawyers and environmentalists can be seen in the formulation of Ecuador's constitution, which included Acosta publishing two papers on the official website for the constitution discussing the idea of giving rights to nature, which caught the attention of other writers, including Uruguay's Eduardo Galeano who, in turn, wrote an article that brought the issue of giving nature rights into Ecuadorian political debate (see Akruin 2015).

As a country with enormous oil deposits and decades of conflict centered on the activities of the petroleum industry, the explicit inclusion of the rights of nature in the constitution can be understood as a response to the influence of globalization on Ecuador's economy, politics and society. A test for Ecuador's ecocentric constitution is how it protects its Amazonian rainforests and the Indigenous people who live in them from these influences. The ongoing conflict between the oil and gas industry and those seeking to protect the Ecuadorian forests is where we can observe how the rights of nature, as a legal construct, is drawn into environmental conflict.

As Tănăsescu (2013, 854) observes, Ecuador's constitution was built not so much from the "bottom-up struggles of resistance and of Indigenous consciousness breaking through into the mainstream" but was orchestrated by the dedicated work "of a handful of people." As well as borrowing ideas from abroad, Ecuador's constitution is also notable for its emphasis on participatory politics that ensured the inclusion of Indigenous beliefs into the constitution (Akchurin 2015). The inclusion of the rights of nature in the constitution was described by one environmental lawyer as

> fundamentally a contribution from Andean civilization to Ecuador's constitution, but a contribution that is, of course, mediated by various other sources. This notion of the rights of nature is something that arose in the US during the 1970s and that in a way coincides with the ancestral vision of the indigenous peoples to view nature not as "something" but rather as "someone" ... Of course, for us it is new; it is novel for Western civilization ... but for them, no. (cited in Akchrin 2015, 954)

Not all agree that the inclusion of Indigenous people in the constitution has been for the benefit of these groups. While Indigenous people were consulted, Patricia Urteaga-Crovetto (2018, 20) argues that transplanting the right to consultation from international law into the context of the national legal system led to public participation becoming "a complex ensemble of legal practices and techniques geared towards procedimentalization" that excluded Indigenous peoples from the participation who needed to master the legal technicalities required to engage consultation. As a result, Indigenous opposition to governmental policies in Ecuador remains a steadfast reminder that the Ecuadorian government failed to maintain its commitment to Indigenous rights and self-determination in its policies for natural resource extraction (Merino 2018).

News and other media have been central to these conflicts. In their study of Ecuador's constitutional court, Castro-Montero and Gijs van Dijck (2017) found the court, unsurprisingly perhaps, tends to favor powerful political actors more than non-political actors—except in matters that receive news media coverage. In other words, mediated visibility plays an important role in bringing issues to public attention, but visibility is determined by a number of issues. Firstly, news media in Ecuador, like most of Latin America, is dominated by the private interests of its "media tycoons" and its state-run media outlets offer no guarantee of a strong watchdog presence (Gutiérrez and Ocampo 2020, 100) and secondly, while the rainforests cover nearly half of Ecuador, most of nation's population live in urbanized areas which keeps protecting the rainforest and the Indigenous populations who live there, consistently low on the political agenda (Lizarazo Rodriguez et al. 2021).

With little government or popular support, Ecuador's Indigenous peoples have turned to national and international litigation to seek redress for the pollution and impact on their lives and livelihood caused by the petroleum industry (Merino 2018). In return, the Correa government responded harshly to their dissent by criminalizing protest and subjecting Indigenous and campesino leaders to politically motivated criminal charges and characterizing activists as violent people rather than citizens campaigning for the right to participate (Amnesty International 2012). Despite enshrining the rights of nature and the crime of ecocide into the constitution, the might of the petroleum industry and the powerful international networks of finance and law, prevail. The decades-long litigation involving Ecuador's battles with the petroleum industry exemplifies how the strategies of green lawfare tie media, environmental law and transnational environmental issues and the struggle for human and ecological rights together, as the following two examples attest.

The first example is the 2007 Yasuní-ITT (Ishpingo-Tambococha-Tiputini) Initiative that was meant to stop drilling in Ecuador's largest oilfield that lies below some of the world's most biodiverse rainforest. The park was designated a World Biosphere Reserve by UNESCO in the late 1980s and in 2007, President Correa's government proposed to the United Nations General Assembly that Ecuador would leave the oil in the ground in exchange for a financial contribution of half the projected profits from drilling the reserves

(Le Quang 2016). The Yasuní-ITT was a test for international cooperation on climate change despite limited local support and presented cooperation with the international community as an alternative to litigation. Three years after the agreement, only US$37 million of the expected US$3.6 billion was committed, and even less deposited into the fund (Sovacool & Scarpaci 2016). In 2010, Correa canceled the initiative, returned the money and authorized oil extraction to start (Lizarazo Rodriguez et al. 2021) telling the nation in a televised address that "the world has failed us … It was not charity that we sought from the international community, but co-responsibility for climate change" (Bawden 2013).

His comments came while his country was embroiled in a massive, and long-running, class action against one of the petroleum companies. In 1993, a group of 30,000 Ecuadorian farmers and Indigenous people represented by the United States attorney, Steven Donziger, filed a class-action suit against Chevron, one of the largest corporations in the United States, alleging that a legacy of poisoned water and pits of toxic sludge remained where Chevron's processor, Texaco, had extracted oil between 1972 and 1992 (Keefe 2012). At the request of Chevron, these legal proceedings were moved to Ecuador, where the legal system does not involve juries, which may have appealed to Chevron perhaps on the assumption it could rely on the political influence of the courts (Lerner 2020). Or, as Donziger suggests, "where they knew the Indigenous peoples had no money or resources to find lawyers" (Hedges 2020). In Ecuador, the court heard testimony about a "rainforest Chernobyl" where the harm could be measured in "cancer deaths, miscarriages, birth defects, dead livestock, sick fish, and the near extinction of several tribes" (Keefe 2012). As part of the lawsuit, Donziger enlisted support from international media celebrities, notably British musician Sting and his partner Trudi Styler, to make sure the world was watching. Filmmaker Joe Berlinger, with financial and logistical support from Trudi Styler, spent three years filming the ongoing fight between the Ecuadorians and Chevron to produce the award-winning film *Crude* (2009).

In 2011, in one of the world's largest pollution judgments, the Ecuadorian Supreme Court ruled against Chevron. It found Texaco guilty of dumping 18 billion gallons of toxic waste, crude oil, toxic wastewater, and other contaminants and ordered Chevron to pay billions of dollars in compensation including environmental remediation, medical treatment, and other relief for those affected. Instead of paying, Chevron declared the ruling "illegitimate and unenforceable," moved its assets out of Ecuador, and then went after

Donziger in the United States claiming Donziger and Ecuadorian lawyers had "corrupted" the lawsuit through fraud, bribery and extortion. Chevron's legal team targeted Berlinger's film on the campaign to a devastating effect.

Firstly, Chevron subpoenaed more than 600 hours of film footage taken by Berlinger over the three years he spent visiting Ecuador. Berlinger's legal team argued that the footage was protected by privilege because Berlinger was an investigative journalist and that turning over the footage would violate confidentiality agreements with his subjects and his First Amendment rights, but the court found that Berlinger could not invoke the journalists' privilege because he did not have sufficient "independence" from Donziger (Itzkoff 2010). The emails exchanged between Chevron and their legal team regarding Berlinger's footage provide an insight into the strategies that set out to "demonize Donziger" (see Lerner 2020). The selection of Berlinger's outtakes shown in court exposed an unflattering side of Donziger as a public relations-savvy lawyer and the judge, Lewis Kaplan, described Donziger as "the field general of a political and media offensive" (Keefe 2012). Chevron also asked to see Donziger's documents on the grounds that "much of what Donziger did was fund-raising and publicity, rather than lawyering" (Keefe 2012). Again, Judge Kaplan agreed and Donziger was forced to hand over his entire case file relating to his work in Ecuador. Just as forcing Beringer to hand over his outtakes had sent a chilling message to other filmmakers—and those who might trust them with their story—the professional and personal humiliation of handing over his private file sent a chilling message to other attorneys and their clients (Isler 2012). The result of having access to these documents contributed to Judge Kaplan's finding that Donziger and his legal team had obtained the judgment in the Ecuadorian court through corrupt means, including fraud, bribery, extortion and coercive behavior (Isler 2014). After two decades of work to get compensation and redress for some of Ecuador's most disadvantaged people, Donziger was placed under house arrest in 2019 or, in his words, was made a "corporate political prisoner" (Lerner 2020).

As a classic example of green lawfare, where the strategic use of law and media collide, a few have observed how news media in the United States has largely ignored the legal attacks on Donziger (North 2021). Writing in the *Guardian*, Erin Brockovich (2022) asked readers to

> imagine if instead of a movie telling my story, I'd gone to jail. That's essentially what has happened to Steve Donziger. And, since this litigation started in 1993, Chevron has not paid a cent or performed any clean up. So far, the only people who have paid for Chevron's alleged behaviour are Donziger and those affected by the

contamination—the poor and Indigenous Ecuadorians who continue to live every day with the pollution's effects.

These stories from the United States, Australia, India and Ecuador provide a glimpse of how mediatized environmental conflict has long been implicated in the formation of environmental law. In each of these examples, Hutchins and Lester's (2015) four spheres of action—activist strategies and campaigns; journalism practices and news reporting; formal politics and decision-making processes, and industry activities and trade—are variously engaged. The interactions between actors and the moments and events that follow can be seen as switching points where power is enforced or challenged: a theoretical paper on the rights of nature shifts the thinking of a judge during a landmark case; a political campaign, high court case and international treaty hinge on the beauty seen in a single photograph; bureaucrats from afar call for a report that reveals the unimaginable; and, networks of corporate power avoid the rule of law. A question was asked, a photograph was taken, a report was written, a journalist's outtakes subpoenaed. In each of these examples, the interactions between actors involves mediated communication and the exchange of ideas about the environment informed by and expressed through media where events and practices and various networks interacted with the legal sphere in order to assert or challenge power.

Green Lawfare and Transnational Environmental Conflict

So far, we have considered how environmental law has developed over decades from diverse tributaries of action inspired by a range of philosophies, worldviews, and political aims but, the discussion has not fully captured the transnational nature of many environmental problems, and the difficulty of addressing these in the absence of any enforceable global mechanisms. Efforts to protect the world's oceans illustrate green lawfare at a transnational scale because the high seas are, along with the deep seabed, the atmosphere, and outer space, regarded as "global commons" (Garcia 2021). International law relating to the sea is unique because it is not developed to satisfy the needs of any particular nation. As Elinor Ostrom and colleagues (1999) observed, stark warnings of the tragedy of the commons looms when common-pool resources are shared by multiple and diverse actors across a wide area. In her later work, Ostram (2009) suggested that a combination of multi-level organizations, ranging from the global to the local can provide the focus on these truly global concerns, as well as technological advances, such as fish-tracking technology to monitor populations. For this reason, two examples of green lawfare involving transnational spaces present another view of the legal sphere in mediatized environmental conflict.

Sea Shepherd and the High Seas

To the dismay of many, efforts to protect our planet do not end when laws are in place, which leaves NGOs to officially and unofficially engage in law enforcement. Eilstrup-Sangiovanni and Sharman (2022) argue that environmental NGOs play a crucial role in environmental governance because they are adept at mobilizing public concern, producing scientific knowledge, and providing independent expertise. The international NGO, the Sea Shepherd Conservation Society, stands out here as possibly the most media-savvy and legally-adept group involved in the conflict surrounding commercial whaling and fishing, and other maritime activities. Gray Wolf and Hummingbird (1993) observe that the world's oceans are

> a frontier beyond the reach of the laws of most nation-states. Within the realm of this non-territorial zone there is no legal jurisdiction other than a confusing and conflicting quagmire of international treaties and regulations. Into this lawless territory it is possible for the intrepid defender of marine ecosystems to move and operate in a guarded but overt manner.

Founded by former Greenpeace activist Paul Watson in 1971, the Sea Shepherd Conservation Society is renowned for harassing whale operations and other exploitative activities in international waters. For Watson, the problem is not the lack of environmental laws but the lack of enforcement of laws. Under Watson, Sea Shepherd challenged, at times confronted, whaling fleets and other fishing vessels to material and symbolic effect. Not only did Sea Shepherd stop whales and other creatures from dying, but the compelling images of industrial-scale whaling, colliding ships and smoke bombs appealed to media to ensure images of their derring-do were shared with the world. Under Watson's leadership, Sea Shepherd combined legal logic and media logic to achieve its goals. In an interview with Libby Lester (2011, 128–129,) Watson said, "I set up Sea Shepherd to intervene, not to protest. And we intervene against illegal activities involving marine wildlife or habitat. So we're … an enforcement group than anything else," which left Lester to reflect that his insistence on being more than a protest group was "fundamental to his continuing mediated visibility." Watson also told Lester (2011, 129):

> We have to walk a very fine line on strategies: one to make sure that we don't break the law but we walk very close to breaking the law; certainly that we don't injure anybody. It's good to maintain an image of aggressiveness; it's good even to maintain an image of violence, in a way as long as you don't actually hurt anybody.

Sea Shepherd also argues that its members are legally empowered to intervene in protecting marine environments under provisions in the *World Charter for Nature* (1982) which is the United Nations' code of conduct for the protection and preservation of global natural habitats and resources. This claim to uphold the spirit of international law tends to shield Sea Shepherd activists from political and legal prosecution because potential plaintiffs want to avoid disputing the facts of their operations, especially in the glare of mediated publicity that Sea Shepherd generate (Eilstrup-Sangiovanni and Bondaroff 2014).

Sea Shepherd maintained a reputation of being a self-appointed law enforcement organization until 2022 when Watson was stood down from Sea Shepherd because its board of directors decided to be less confrontational and instead work more closely with authorities on issues including overfishing or, as Watson described, to provide an "Uber service for government bureaucrats" (Seecombe 2022). It remains to be seen if Sea Shepherd can maintain its high media profile while working with authorities and whether its diminished appeal to media will translate to diminished effectiveness.

While Sea Shepherd focuses on enforcing laws they deem broken or ignored, the final case study in this chapter looks at the network of lawyers and activists calling for new transnational laws using sophisticated ways of communicating legal ideas to international audiences within and outside the sphere of law.

Ecocide: The Fifth Crime

If ever a new(ish) concept could be carried in a single word to broad audiences, it would be ecocide. With genocide a familiar concept and the ubiquity of "eco" as a prefix for ecology, imagining the concept of ecocide is not difficult. Nor is the frequent association of ecocide with war. However, the journey to make ecocide the fifth law against peace has not been easy and recent efforts, namely by the late barrister and activist, Polly Higgins, and colleagues, shines another light on the role of media in strategies aimed at influencing the development of environmental law. But first, the origin story of this law also hints at networks of less–than–visible actors involved in burying the idea.

The first recorded use of the term ecocide can be found at the Conference on War and National Responsibility held in Washington in 1970 when Professor Arthur W. Galston proposed a new international ban on "ecocide" as a direct response to the use of Agent Orange on forests and crops by the United States in Vietnam (Weisberg 1970, 4). At the 1972 United Nations Conference on the Environment in Stockholm, Sweden's Prime Minister, Olof Palme, used the term "ecocide" in calling for an international law against the mass-scale destruction of ecosystems, which was regarded as a pointed comment on the use of defoliants in Vietnam. Russell E. Train, the chairman of the United States delegation, rebuked Palme's suggestion, describing it as "a gratuitous politicizing of our environmental discussions," which, writing for the *New York Times*, Gladwin Hill (1972) described as the "first harsh exchange" at the conference. In that moment, we cannot know where Palme got his idea to mention ecocide. Determining how a conversation, something read, or a protester's sign on the way to a meeting might inform a person's actions on any given day remains in the "black box" of much communication work, but we do know attached to the Stockholm Conference was The Folket's Forum (People's Forum) for citizen groups that was meant to be a "sideshow" to the event but had turned into a quasi-forum in its own right. At the time, the *New York Times* (1972) reported that one of the "sideshows" was a particular effort "to get specific mention of 'ecocide' in Vietnam into the declaration." While the concept was understood as the intentional and extensive destruction of ecosystems, ecocide was yet to be criminalized.

While no reference was made to ecocide in the official outcome document of the Stockholm Conference, the idea caught on and became a familiar topic among NGOs and in academic debate, especially whether the intention to cause harm was a necessary element of the crime (Gauger et al. 2012, 5-6). Polly Higgins (2015) provides a fascinating account of how ecocide was listed as the fifth crime against peace, alongside genocide, crimes against humanity, war crimes, and the crime of aggression in the drafting of the *Rome Statute of the International Criminal Court* (Rome Statute) in 1998 but was "removed completely, and somewhat mysteriously" from the final draft. Despite this setback, ecocide and the idea of "structural violence against ecosystems" gradually gained acceptance in international and domestic law (Kreike 2021).

A glance at *Google Trends* using the search term "ecocide" shows that 2005 was a big year for mainstream interest in ecocide.[4] The spike in Google searches can be linked to the promotion of Jared Diamond's book *Collapse* (2005), which explored historical examples of how human populations that have a catastrophic impact on their local environment are eventually wiped out.[5] Diamond wrote these "mysterious abandonments" were the result of:

> people inadvertently destroying the environmental resources on which their societies depended. This suspicion of unintended ecological suicide—ecocide—has been confirmed by discoveries made in recent decades by archaeologists, climatologists, historians, palaeontologists, and palynologists.

In 2010, Polly Higgins, submitted a proposal to the United Nations Law Commission that defined ecocide as "extensive loss, damage to or destruction of ecosystems of a given territory, such that peaceful enjoyment by the inhabitants has been or will be severely diminished," which attracted a lot of media attention followed by funding. Higgins went on to found the Netherlands-based Stop Ecocide Foundation, along with a coalition of environmentalists, lawyers and human rights advocates, and organized a mock trial in 2011 that demonstrated the legal viability of such a crime and brought Higgins to international attention. Here, she argued the case for the need to name actions in ways that define them as a crime. Prior to the idea of genocide being used to explain the Holocaust, Higgins (2012, xii) wrote, the mass killing of people

> wasn't recognized as an international crime, which made it almost impossible for people like Sophie Scholl to stand up and object. She and others in Nazi Germany were fighting against something that had been endorsed by their government and the media as the norm, no matter how unpleasant it was. In so doing, the people were

4 Google Trends provides data collected from Google searches that shows fluctuations in public interest in topics and, for this reason, has been used in a wide range of studies, including voter intentions, public interest in climate change and correlations between public interest, policy formation and news coverage (Foxwell-Norton and Konkes 2021).

5 Diamond, of course, was not the first to connect the demise of civilizations with ecological collapse. Tim Flannery's (1995) *Future Eaters* described how humans arriving in new environments typically consume the resources they find available to their limits was closely followed by Diamond's (1998) *Guns, Germs, and Steel: The Fates of Human Societies*, which observed how technological advance increased health and population growth, but consumption, inexorably leading to conflict over resources. Such popular books provide a "deep time" perspective to human history that suggests ways human culture might adapt to what we know about ecological constraints (Richardson 2017, 40).

> effectively silenced. Without the word for genocide in their vocabulary, it was almost impossible to identify what was a crime.

The Stop Ecocide Foundation is adept at using the affordances of video streaming to share ideas and activities and to build a network of relationships with international media, which includes using the power of celebrity in media campaigns. In 2019, Stop Ecocide brought Greta Thunberg and French President Emmanuel Macron together with Pope John Francis in a well-orchestrated media event where Pope Francis said conduct that could be considered ecocide included "the massive contamination of air, land and water resources, the large-scale destruction of flora and fauna, and any action capable of producing an ecological disaster or destroying an ecosystem" (Funnell 2021). This combination of celebrity and religious authority works on many levels, not least by ensuring that a message targeting millions of Catholics across the globe gave the term a moral as well as legal force. Higgins also attended the annual meetings of the International Criminal Court's management oversight and legislative body (the Assembly of State Parties to the Rome Statute) for four consecutive years and used her visibility at these meetings to campaign on behalf of Pacific Island states.

Vietnam was the first to codify ecocide in its domestic law in 1990, ecocide is mentioned in Ecuador's 2008 constitution and, in 2021, France was the first country in the European Union to put ecocide into law. At the time of writing, 10 countries around the world have criminalized ecocide in domestic law and Ukraine was investigating whether Russia was prosecutable for breaching the Nova Kakhovka dam. It has been suggested (Bianchi et al. 2024, 4) that adoption of "the right to a clean, healthy and sustainable environment as a human right" by the UN General Assembly in 2022 "provides a relevant lens through which to address the challenges related to the investigation and prosecution of crimes that are committed by means of, or that result in, environmental damage under the Rome Statute". In other words, defining the wilful destruction of the environment as a war crime is being reimagined as a human rights issues.

But for now, the dualism of the natural world and human culture remain in expressions of international solidarity leaving humanitarian efforts "based almost entirely on the wellbeing of individual humans rather than with concern for the natural world that sustains them" (Eichler 2020, 104).

Conclusion: Green Lawfare as a Grassroots Force

By starting with the early environmental campaigns in the United States that spun from Rachel Carson's ground-breaking work in the 1960s to recent efforts to prosecute illegal fishers and make ecocide a crime against peace this chapter described how environmental law has evolved alongside, and in response to, the actors and events that constitute the environmental movement. Protest that conforms to media logic are instrumental in these developments at local, national and international levels by facilitating the sharing, responding and translation, and the evolution of ideas into action.

The challenge for those resisting a ski resort in California or toxic dumps in Ecuador's forests, from threatening whalers with violence to calling ecocide a crime against peace, is to engage with legal systems that privilege private rights over collective responsibility. Bringing an ecological perspective to law across many jurisdictions has been the result of decades of work identifying environmental harm, giving it a name, describing the harm endured and attributing blame to its causes that has been undertaken by scientists, journalists, lawyers, activists and others.

The evolution of environmental law can be seen in the myriad efforts to answer the question of who gets to speak for nature (Lazarus 2023, 97; Sabine 2015). While the environmental movement can be regarded as global and many environmental problems extend across national boundaries and through networks of global trade, environmental issues are encountered in local contexts through the daily experiences of people and the avenues for action and redress they have at hand. As such, this chapter has observed the development of environmental law to be often driven by grassroots campaigns more often than not inspired and informed by the exchange of ideas from other places that travel through communication media and enable the activities of protest and civil disobedience, parliamentary debate, international diplomacy, and courts and tribunals. While litigation has accompanied the earliest environmental law, climate change litigation, or climate litigation hereon, stands out as a rapidly growing area of legal activity and is the focus of the next chapter, which looks at the development of climate litigation since the early campaigns of the 1990s.

References

Abraham, C. M., and Sushila Abraham. 1991. "The Bhopal Case and the Development of Environmental Law in India." *International and Comparative Law Quarterly* 40 (2): 334–365.

Ahmad, Furqan. 2001. "Origin and Growth of Environmental Law in India." *Journal of the Indian Law Institute* 43 (III): 358.

Akchurin, Maria. 2015. "Constructing the Rights of Nature: Constitutional Reform, Mobilization, and Environmental Protection in Ecuador." *Law & Social Inquiry* 40 (04): 937–968.

Amnesty International. 2012. "'So That No One Can Demand Anything' Criminalizing the Right to Protest in Ecuador?" London: Amnesty International. https://www.amnesty.org.uk/files/ecuador_report_-_report_eng.pdf (Accessed August 23, 2023).

Baude, Patrick L. 1973. "Sierra Club v. Morton: Standing Trees in a Thicket of Justiciability." *Indiana Law Journal* 18 (2): 197–215.

Bawden, Tom. 2013. "Blow to Climate Change Battle as President Correa Tears up $3.6bn UN Agreement." *The Independent*, August 16, 2013. https://www.independent.co.uk/news/world/americas/the-world-has-failed-us-ecuador-ditches-plan-to-save-amazon-from-oil-drilling-8771506.html (Accessed May 5, 2023).

Bianchini, Flaviano, Pablo Gavira Díaz, Joe Holt, Pauline Martini, Maud Sarliève, and Rupert Stuart-Smith. 2024. "Comment on OTP Environmental Crimes Policy." https://www.smithschool.ox.ac.uk/sites/default/files/2024-03/20240316_Comment_on_OTP%20Environmental_Crimes_Policy_Sarlieve_et_al.pdf.

Bowen, James, and Margarita Bowen. 2002. *The Great Barrier Reef: History, Science, Heritage.* Cambridge and New York: Cambridge University Press.

Brockovich, Erin. 2022. "This Lawyer Should Be World-Famous for His Battle with Chevron but He's in Jail." *The Guardian*, February 9, 2022. https://www.theguardian.com/commentisfree/2022/feb/08/chevron-amazon-ecuador-steven-donziger-erin-brockovich (Accessed August 22, 2023).

Burke, Tony. 2013. "Australia's World Heritage—Keeping the Outstanding Exceptional." In *Keeping the Outstanding Exceptional: The Future of World Heritage in Australia*, edited by Penny Figgis, Andrea Leverington, Richard Mackay, Andrew Maclean, and Peter Valentine, 8–13. Sydney: Australian Committee for IUCN Inc.

Carlson, Matt. 2009. "Dueling, Dancing, or Dominating? Journalists and Their Sources: Journalists and Their Sources." *Sociology Compass* 3 (4): 526–542.

Castro-Montero, José Luis, and Gijs Van Dijck. 2017. "Judicial Politics in Unconsolidated Democracies: An Empirical Analysis of the Ecuadorian Constitutional Court (2008–2016)." *Justice System Journal* 38 (4): 380–398.

Chandra, Aparna. 2017. "India and International Law: Formal Dualism, Functional Monism." *Indian Journal of International Law* 57 (1–2): 25–45.

Cox, J. Robert. 2010. "Beyond Frames: Recovering the Strategic in Climate Communication." *Environmental Communication* 4 (1): 122–133.

Diamond, Jared. 1998. *Guns, Germs and Steel.* London: Vintage.

Diamond, Jared. 2005. *Collapse: How Societies Choose to Fail or Succeed*. New York: Viking.

Durbach, Andrea, Luke McNamara, Simon Rice, and Mark Rix. 2013. "Public Interest Litigation: Making the Case in Australia." *Alternative Law Journal* 38 (4): 219–223.

Eichler, Lauren J. 2020. "Ecocide Is Genocide: Decolonizing the Definition of Genocide." *Genocide Studies and Prevention* 14 (2): 104–121.

Eilstrup-Sangiovanni, Mette, and Teale N. Phelps Bondaroff. 2014. "From Advocacy to Confrontation: Direct Enforcement by Environmental NGOs." *International Studies Quarterly* 58 (2): 348–361.

Eilstrup-Sangiovanni, Mette, and J. C. Sharman. 2022. *Vigilantes beyond Borders: NGOs as Enforcers of International Law*. Princeton: Princeton University Press.

Eskjær, Mikkel Fugl, and Anders Horsbøl. 2023. "New Environmental Controversies: Towards a Typology of Green Conflicts." *Sustainability* 15 (3): 1914. https://doi.org/10.3390/su15031914

Fernandez, Angela. 2023. "Environmental Law, Standing, and the History of Sierra Club v. Morton." *Jotwell: The Journal of Things We Like (Lots)* 3 (March 2023): 1–2.

Flannery, Tim. 2002. *The Future Eaters: An Ecological History of The Australasian Lands and People*. New York: Grove Press.

Foxwell-Norton, Kerrie, and Claire Konkes. 2021. "Is the Great Barrier Reef Dead? Satire, Death and Environmental Communication." *Media International Australia* 184 (1): 106–121.

Foxwell-Norton, Kerrie, and Libby Lester. 2017. "Saving the Great Barrier Reef from Disaster, Media Then and Now." *Media, Culture & Society* 39 (4): 568–581.

Funnell, Antony. 2021. "'Ecocide' Proposal Aiming to Make Environmental Destruction an International Crime." *ABC RN*, February 13, 2021. https://www.abc.net.au/news/2021-02-13/will-ecocide-become-an-international-crime/13136912 (Accessed May 5, 2023).

Gamson, William A., and Gadi Wolfsfeld. 1993. "Movements and Media as Interacting Systems." *The ANNALS of the American Academy of Political and Social Science* 528 (1): 114–125.

Gans, Herbert. 1979. *Deciding What's News*. New York: Pantheon.

Garcia, Denise. 2021. "Global Commons Law: Norms to Safeguard the Planet and Humanity's Heritage." *International Relations* 35 (3): 422–445.

Gauger, Anja, Mai Pouye Rabatel-Fernel, Louise Kulbicki, Damien Short, and Polly Higgins. 2012. "The Ecocide Project: Ecocide is the missing 5th crime against peace: " London: Human Rights Consortium.

Gellers, Joshua C. 2015. "Environmental Constitutionalism in South Asia: Analyzing the Experiences of Nepal and Sri Lanka." *Transnational Environmental Law* 4 (2): 395–423.

Ghosh, Aditya, and Maxwell Boykoff. 2019. "Framing Sustainability and Climate Change: Interrogating Discourses in Vernacular and English-Language Media in Sundarbans, India." *Geoforum* 99 (February): 142–153.

Gray Wolf and Hummingbird. 1993. "Marine Monkeywrenching." In *Ecodefense: A Field Guide to Monkeywrenching*, edited by Dave Foreman and Bill Haywood, 3rd ed. Chico: Abbzug Press.

Gunningham, N. 2009. "Environment Law, Regulation and Governance: Shifting Architectures." *Journal of Environmental Law* 21 (2): 179–212.

Gutiérrez, Fernando, and Alejandro Ocampo. 2020. "Latin America: From Media Censorship to Media Ownership." In *Transnational Media: Concepts and Cases*, edited by Suman Mishra and Rebecca Kern-Stone, 97–106. Hoboken: Wiley-Blackwell.

Henry, Don, and Denise Boyd. 2013. "Celebrating the Role of World Heritage in Australia's Environmental and Cultural History." In *Keeping the Outstanding Exceptional: The Future of World Heritage in Australia*, edited by Penny Figgis, Andrea Leverington, Richard Mackay, Andrew Maclean, and Peter Valentine, 30–35. Sydney: Australian Committee for IUCN Inc.

Higgins, Polly. 2012. *Earth Is Our Business: Changing the Rules of the Game*. London: Shepheard-Walwyn.

———. 2015. *Eradicating Ecocide: Laws and Governance to Prevent the Destruction of Our Planet*. 2nd ed. London: Shepheard-Walwyn.

Hill, Gladwin. 1972. "U.S. at U.N. Parley on Environment, Rebukes Sweden for 'Politicizing' Talks." *New York Times*, June 8, 1972. https://www.nytimes.com/1972/06/08/archives/us-at-un-parley-on-environment-rebukes-sweden-for-politicizing.html (Accessed August 23, 2023).

Holden, Constance. 1972. "Sierra Club Foiled in High Court." *Science* 176 (4034): 494–494.

Holden, William. 2022. "Climate Change, Neoauthoritarianism, Necropolitics, and State Failure: The Duterte Regime in the Philippines." *Asian Geographer*, February 1–23.

Indian Institution of Ecology and Environment. n.d. "Environmental Legislation in India." Indian Institution of Ecology and Environment (website) https://www.ecology.edu/environmental-legislation.html (Accessed October 6, 2022).

Isler, Tom. 2012. "Chevron Corp. v. Berlinger and the Future of the Journalists' Privilege for Documentary Filmmakers." *University of Pennsylvania Law Review* 160 (3): 865–920.

———. 2014. "What Chevron Corp v. Donziger Continues to Get Wrong about Documentary Filmmaking" (blog) https://www.law.upenn.edu/live/news/4608-what-chevron-corp-v-donziger-continues-to-get/news/documentaries-news.php#sthash.msr1zfqJ.dpbs (Accessed May 5, 2023).

Itzkoff, Dave. 2010. "Judge Rules That Filmmaker Must Give Footage to Chevron." *New York Times*, May 6. https://archive.nytimes.com/artsbeat.blogs.nytimes.com/2010/05/06/judge-rules-that-filmmaker-must-give-footage-to-chevron/ (Accessed May 5, 2023).

Iyengar, Shanto. 1996. "Framing Responsibility for Political Issues." *The ANNALS of the American Academy of Political and Social Science* 546 (1): 59–70.

Keefe, Patrick Radden. 2012. "Reversal of Fortune." *The New Yorker*, January 2. https://www.newyorker.com/magazine/2012/01/09/reversal-of-fortune-patrick-radden-keefe (Accessed May 5, 2023).

Kennedy, David. 2016. *A World of Struggle: How Power, Law, and Expertise Shape Global Political Economy*. Princeton: Princeton University Press.

Kreike, Emmanuel. 2021. *Scorched Earth: Environmental Warfare as a Crime against Humanity and Nature*. Human Rights and Crimes against Humanity. Princeton: Princeton University Press.

LaForgia, Rebecca. 2015. "Limitlessness in Australian Constitutional Legal Narrative: The Memory of Black's Address in the *Tasmanian Dam Case*." *Griffith Law Review* 24 (1): 41–57.

Lazarus, Richard J. 2001. "The Greening of America and the Graying of United States Environmental Law: Reflections on Environmental Law's First Three Decades in the United States." *Virginia Environmental Law Journal* 20 (1): 75–106.

Lazarus, Richard J. 2023. *The Making of Environmental Law*. 2nd ed. Chicago and London: University of Chicago Press.

Le Quang, Matthieu. 2016. "The Yasuní-ITT Initiative: Toward New Imaginaries." *Latin American Perspectives* 43 (1): 187–199.

Lerner, Sharon. 2020. "How the Environmental Lawyer Who Won a Massive Judgment Against Chevron Lost Everything." *The Intercept*, January 29. https://theintercept.com/2020/01/29/chevron-ecuador-lawsuit-steven-donziger/ (Accessed May 5, 2003).

Lester, Libby. 2011. "Species of the Month: Anti-Whaling, Mediated Visibility, and the News." *Environmental Communication* 5 (1): 124–139.

———. 2019. *Global Trade and Mediatised Environmental Protest: The View from Here*. Cham: Springer International.

Lin, Jolene, and Jacqueline Peel. 2022. "The Farmer or the Hero Litigator? Modes of Climate Litigation in the Global South." In *Litigating the Climate Emergency*, edited by César Rodríguez-Garavito, 187–205. Cambridge: Cambridge University Press.

Lizarazo Rodriguez, L., D. Montag, E. Verhaeghe, M. A. Tigre, and J. De Freitas. 2021. "Governance Challenges for Preserving the Amazon Region." Curiae Virides (blog). June 23. https://www.curiaevirides.eu/post/governance-challenges-for-preserving-the-amazon-region (Accessed May 5, 2023).

Mate, Manoj. 2014. "The Rise of Judicial Governance in the Supreme Court of India." *SSRN Electronic Journal*. https://doi.org/10.2139/ssrn.2544307 (Accessed August 23, 2023).

Merino, Roger. 2018. "Reimagining the Nation-State: Indigenous Peoples and the Making of Plurinationalism in Latin America." *Leiden Journal of International Law* 31 (4): 773–972.

Mir, Waqqas Ahmad. 2020. "From Shehla Zia to Asghar Leghari: Pronouncing Unwritten Rights Is More Complex than a Celebratory Tale." In *Climate Change Litigation in the Asia Pacific*, edited by Jolene Lin and Douglas A. Kysar, 261–293. Cambridge: Cambridge University Press.

Mouffe, Chantal. 2005. *On the Political*. London and New York: Routledge.

Nanda, Ved, and George (Rock) Pring. 2013. *International Environmental Law and Policy for the 21st Century*. 2nd rev. ed. Leiden: Martinus Nijhoff.

New York Times. 1970. "… And a Plea to Ban 'Ecocide.'" *New York Times*, February 26. https://www.nytimes.com/1970/02/26/archives/and-a-plea-to-ban-ecocide.html (Accessed August 23, 2023).

New York Times. 1972. "Environment Conference Will Offer Some Sideshows" *New York Times*, June 5. https://timesmachine.nytimes.com/timesmachine/1972/06/05/80791702.html?pageNumber=24 (Accessed August 23, 2023).

Nixon, Cynthia, Claire Konkes, Libby Lester, and Kathleen Williams. 2021. "Mediated Visibility and Public Environmental Litigation: The Interplay between Inside and Outside Court during Environmental Conflict in Australia." *Laws* 10 (2): 35. https://doi.org/10.3390/laws10020035

North, James. 2021. "Is Chevron's Vendetta Against Steven Donziger Finally Backfiring?" *The Nation*, October 4. https://www.thenation.com/article/environment/steven-donziger-chevron-sentencing/ (Accessed January 23, 2023).

Novak, Marko. 2020. "Multi-Modal Argumentation and Rhetoric in Judicial Proceedings." *Argumentation and Advocacy* 56 (1): 41–60.

Ostrom, Elinor. 2009. "A General Framework for Analyzing Sustainability of Social-Ecological Systems." *Science* 325 (5939): 419–422.

Ostrom, Elinor, Joanna Burger, Christopher B. Field, Richard B. Norgaard, and David Policansky. 1999. "Revisiting the Commons: Local Lessons, Global Challenges." *Science* 284: 278–282.

Paglia, Eric. 2021. "The Swedish Initiative and the 1972 Stockholm Conference: The Decisive Role of Science Diplomacy in the Emergence of Global Environmental Governance." *Humanities and Social Sciences Communications* 8 (1) https://doi.org/10.1057/s41599-020-00681-x

Panjabi, Ranee Khooshie Lal. 1993. "From Stockholm to Rio: A Comparison of the Declaratory Principles of International Environmental Law," Denver Journal of International Law and Policy 21 (2): 215-288.

Passow, Judah, and Tim Edwards. 2023. "The Long, Dark Shadow of Bhopal: Still Waiting for Justice, Four Decades On." *The Guardian*, June 14. https://www.theguardian.com/global-development/2023/jun/14/bhopal-toxic-gas-leak-chemical-environmental-disaster-waiting-for-justice-union-carbide-dow (Accessed August 22, 2023).

Plater, Zygmunt J. 1994. "From the Beginning, a Fundamental Shift of Paradigms: A Theory and Short History of Environmental Law." *Loyola of Los Angeles Law Review* 27 (3): 981–1008.

Preston, Brian J. 2013. "Environmental Public Interest Litigation: Conditions for Success." Paper presented at the *Towards an Effective Guarantee of the Green Access: Japan's Achievements and Critical Points from a Global Perspective*, International Symposium. Awaji Island, Japan, March 30. https://lec.nsw.gov.au/documents/speeches-and-papers/preston_environmental%20public%20interest%20litigation.pdf (Accessed July 23, 2023).

Preston, Brian J. 2016. "The Contribution of the Courts in Tackling Climate Change." *Journal of Environmental Law* 28 (1): 11–17.

Richardson, Benjamin J. 2017. *Time and Environmental Law: Telling Nature's Time.* Cambridge: Cambridge University Press.

Richardson, Benjamin J. 2018. "Aesthetics and Environmental Law: Valuing Tasmania's 'Ordinary' Nature." *Griffith Law Review* 27 (1): 1–30. https://doi.org/10.1080/10383441.2018.1477364.

Rosenberg, Gerald N. 2008. *The Hollow Hope: Can Courts Bring About Social Change?* Chicago: University of Chicago Press.

Sabin, Paul. 2015. "Environmental Law and the End of the New Deal Order." *Law and History Review* 33 (4): 965–1003.

Salekin, Masrur. 2023. "Role of the Courts of India and Ireland in Ensuring Access to Environmental Justice." *South Asian Journal of Environmental Law and Policy* 1 (2): 501–517.

Samuel, Graeme. 2020. *Independent Review of the EPBC Act—Final Report*. Department of Agriculture, Water and the Environment, Canberra, Australia.

Sax, Joseph L. 1973. "Standing To Sue: A Critical Review of The Mineral King Decision." *Natural Resources Journal* 13 (1): 76–88.

Seccombe, Mike. 2022. "The Last Pirate: Paul Watson Splits with Sea Shepherd." *The Saturday Paper*, October 15. https://www.thesaturdaypaper.com.au/news/environment/2022/10/15/the-last-pirate-paul-watson-splits-with-sea-shepherd (Accessed August 17, 2023).

Selmi, Daniel P. 2022. *Dawn at Mineral King Valley: The Sierra Club, the Disney Company, and the Rise of Environmental Law*. Chicago: University of Chicago Press.

Siddiqui, Furquan Ameen. 2017. *Threats to Journalists in India: Journalism in the Age of Intolerance and Rising Nationalism*. Oxford: Reuters Institute.

Sohn, Louis B. 1973. "The Stockholm Declaration on the Human Environment." *The Harvard International Law Journal* 14 (3): 423–515.

Sovacool, Benjamin K., and Joseph Scarpaci. 2016. "Energy Justice and the Contested Petroleum Politics of Stranded Assets: Policy Insights from the Yasuní-ITT Initiative in Ecuador." *Energy Policy* 95 (August): 158–171.

Tănăsescu, Mihnea. 2013. "The Rights of Nature in Ecuador: The Making of an Idea." *International Journal of Environmental Studies* 70 (6): 846–861.

———. 2020. "Rights of Nature, Legal Personality, and Indigenous Philosophies." *Transnational Environmental Law* 9 (3): 429–453.

Tarlock, A. Dan. 1994. "The Nonequilibrium Paradigm in Ecology and the Partial Unraveling Of Environmental." *Loyola of Los Angeles Law Review* 27: 1121–1144.

Urteaga-Crovetto, Patricia. 2018. "Implementation of the Right to Prior Consultation in the Andean Countries: A Comparative Perspective." *The Journal of Legal Pluralism and Unofficial Law* 50 (1): 7–30.

Walker, Kenneth, and Kate Crowley, eds. 1999. *Australian Environmental Policy 2: Studies in Decline + Devolution*. Sydney: UNSW Press.

Weisberg, Barry. 1970. *Ecocide in Indochina: The Ecology of War*. San Francisco: Canfield Press.

Wickham, Gary, and Jo-Ann Goodie. 2013. *Legal and Political Challenges of Governing the Environment and Climate Change*. London and New York: Routledge.

Wilkons, L. 1987. *Shared Vulnerability: Media Coverage and Shared Public Memory of the Bhopal Disaster*. Westport: Greenwood Press.

Cases

Commonwealth v. Tasmania (1983) 158 CLR 1 (July 1, 1983).

Gloucester Resources Limited v. Minister for Planning (2019) NSWLEC 7.

M. C. *Mehta v. Kamal Nath and Others* (1997) 1 SCC 388.

M.C. *Mehta v. Union of India* (AIR 1987 SC 1086).

Sierra Club v. Morton, 405 U.S. 727 (1972).

· 5 ·

GREEN LAWFARE AND CLIMATE LITIGATION

In 2013, Typhoon Haiyan (locally known as Yolanda) struck the central Philippines. Thousands of people died, millions were displaced and the Philippine government declared a state of national calamity. In 2015, Greenpeace and other groups asked the Philippines' Commission on Human Rights (CHR), a constitutional body with the power to investigate human rights violations, to investigate the extent to which fossil fuel and cement producers were responsible for violations caused by their contribution to climate change. Hearings held in Manila, New York City and London considered scientific and legal evidence and witness testimonies. In 2016, the CHR released its report, in which it named 47 Carbon Majors —which describes the fossil fuel and cement producers responsible for most industrial carbon emissions (Heede 2014)—and accused them of knowing their products would contribute to climate change and engaging in "willful obfuscation" of climate science to spread doubt and misinformation to prevent the transition to clean energy. "All acts to obfuscate climate science and delay, derail or obstruct this transition may be bases for liability," the commissioners wrote. "At the very least, they are immoral" (Schonhardt and Clark 2022).

The CHR report made world headlines, with various sources noting the report augured a change in global climate litigation and approaches to corporate responsibility for climate change and action on climate. While none of the 47 companies assessed in the inquiry were headquartered in the Philippines, the report invited judges and other legal actors to look beyond carbon emissions as a matter of pollution and instead, as the result of companies willfully contributing to environmental harm and human rights abuses. As Joana Setzer said in response to the report (Schonhardt and Clark 2022):

> What litigation is doing is raising awareness. And, very importantly, the risk of litigation makes decision makers at the corporate and government level think twice before they commit or don't commit to something ... It's almost like the risk of litigation is more beneficial than the litigation itself because it is changing behavior before, hopefully, litigation is needed.

As Setzer points out, climate litigation is a key strategy in green lawfare undertaken to change government and corporate attitudes and behavior and climate litigation is growing, but our understanding of how climate litigation is represented in media or understood by those engaged is only just beginning to emerge. Certainly, the relationship between news media and entrenched climate denialism is well understood (eg. Tschötschel et al. 2020), but less is known about how climate litigation is being used to reframe climate change as a problem that can be addressed by holding certain parties responsible for action. Early studies suggest, however, that climate litigation is indeed raising awareness. For instance, Anke Wonneberger (2024) found news coverage of key climate litigation in the Netherlands, including *Urgenda*, tended to be favorable to the claims of plaintiffs, which were all NGOs. As such, a better understanding of how climate litigation is represented in news media and the factors influencing mediated visibility is useful for anyone interested in social and political engagement with climate change (Brüggemann and Engesser 2017).

This chapter begins by looking at the rise of climate litigation and the role of mediated visibility in strategies involving litigation before tracing early efforts to get climate action into the courts. It discusses three waves of climate action: the early "eclectic" cases, the "next wave" based on human rights law and government obligations to address climate change, and the most recent wave targeting corporations for misleading customers and investors about their green credentials, or "greenwashing".

The Rise of Climate Litigation

By the end of 2022, more than 2,180 climate-related cases had been filed worldwide, representing a steady increase from just 884 cases in 2017 (Burger and Tigre 2023). Most of these cases were filed in the United States, followed by Australia despite it being a much smaller nation. Australia's enthusiasm for climate litigation illustrates what happens when "a very active and engaged civil society" tackles the problem of having a carbon-intensive economy and significant fossil fuel exports yet a dearth of national climate policy (Peel 2023). When we look at other resource-rich economies in Africa, South America and Asia-Pacific, each with varying degrees of environmental law and government inaction, we can anticipate more climate litigation to come especially if governments fail to adapt to extreme weather events and large numbers of people become displaced (Carvalho et al. 2017; Lin 2012). Already more than 80 cases have been filed in less materially affluent countries, such as Pakistan and the Philippines, since 2017 (Barritt and Sediti 2019; Selzer and Higham 2022).

These figures do not, however, present the full picture of the use of litigation to address the causes and impacts of climate change. The figures above are limited to those involving issues specific to climate science, climate policy and climate law, but do not include cases involving "peripheral" claims that impact climate governance, such as those involving biodiversity protection in the Amazon forests (Peel and Lin 2019; Tigre et al. 2023). Here we can return to the early and eclectic efforts discussed in the previous chapter to observe that in the absence of specific environmental or climate laws, climate litigation continues the practice of using whatever approaches and legal instruments are at hand to stop specific projects or activities, as well as to encourage political action and legal reform. Such litigation can appear in local news as a small story about planning laws, but on closer inspection, be part of a larger strategy to address climate change (Langford 2023). Effective and equitable access to action on climate requires an understanding of the social dynamics that inform and support these cases (Setzer and Vanhala 2019) and news and other media are central players in this process. To understand litigation as a strategy in green lawfare, we will step back to consider the role of mediated visibility in public issues, which includes the treatment of courts by media as arenas of conflict, before looking at examples of such actions.

Visibility and the Courts

Malcolm Langford (2023, 8) suggests that climate litigation confronts judges with three complex adaptive systems: the legal system, the climate system, and the climate governance system. If we treat law as a sealed sphere where reason and rhetoric are untroubled by public opinion, political contest, or interpersonal communication, we might focus solely on the three adaptive systems of law, climate science and climate governance. However, law is not a closed system (Preston 2023) and news and other media play a vital role in the processes that make climate law "hot" (Fisher 2013). Indeed, we might consider news and other media as a fourth system contributing to the process of climate litigation. If we want to understand how climate litigation raises awareness, and influences political decision-making or consumer behavior, or if we are curious about how changing social practices and attitudes inform law reform, then the question of the mediatization of climate litigation is where we should look.

Activists have a long history of employing spectacle to transform environmental protest sites into arenas of confrontation to appeal to media logic of what makes an event "newsworthy" or otherwise interesting to audiences (Lester 2010). Like other protest strategies that adopt media logic to raise awareness, litigation can also be used strategically to appeal to media appetite for conflict and its preference for clearly defined arenas of contest (Nixon et al. 2021). So too, climate litigation can be seen as an example of social change campaigns that find openings within systems to enact change (Cox 2010, 128). Richard Lazarus (2009, 1156) warns that changes to law should be seen as only "moments" because changing political moods, limited budgets and lack of enforcement can work to ensure the most uncompromising mandate can slip away "into nothing more than a symbolic aspirational statement", but such statements are not entirely meaningless. Another way of looking at such "moments" is through the idea of "critical discourse moments," which describes those moments of intense media coverage where assumed knowledge and conventional assumptions are challenged. In such moments, news and other media do not play a passive role (Gamson and Modigliani 1992, 68; also Carvalho 2008; Cottle 2006) as "the nature of what everyone knows becomes widely established and remains part of the common store of understanding even after media attention moves on" (Brown and Ferree 2005, 7–8). Climate litigation can provide the conditions for a "critical discourse moment" because court action provides an ideal arena to challenge or support the legitimacy of claims. Even in cases where litigation fails, climate litigation can gauge public support for further legal reforms and signal to stakeholders the extent of public concern (Schuijers 2017). When seen beyond what happens in court, we can see litigation as a communicative action. Observing where climate change is communicated, the language used and the struggles to define these terms can reveal the dynamics of power in politics and society that is shaping knowledge and public attitudes about climate change (Ghosh and Boykoff 2019). While not as visually spectacular as other sites of protest, litigation can be undertaken with a clear view to stimulating debates that inform political decisions on adopting, amending, or repealing laws in response to public pressure (Preston 2016). Litigation can also exert political pressure by exposing stakeholders' complicity in violating laws and otherwise causing environmental harm.

Courts seldom engage directly with news media: they rarely issue press releases, hold media conferences, or participate in case-related interviews and their primary mode of communication is written documents that employ language tailored for legal audiences, which leaves journalists and other newsmakers responsible for translating the issue and events for the wider public. Like other forms of news production, court reporting relies on sources for commentary and interpretation of the day's events and the interplay between lawyers, journalists, and activists, and the practices and strategies of journalists and their sources, informs how these legal challenges are described and interpreted (Konkes and Lester 2016). Drawing on landmark cases, we can observe the involvement of media during the various stages of climate litigation that range from drawing on an eclectic range of local legal instruments in the absence of specific climate law; litigation framing action on climate as a human rights issue; and, finally, litigation focusing on corporate responsibility and malfeasance.

Early, Eclectic Efforts

Early climate litigation is made up of "eclectic" efforts because, with little to no laws in place, groups use what is available to initiate proceedings (Langford 2023). For instance, some of the earliest climate litigation in the United States, United Kingdom and Australia involved zoning and planning laws, as well as pollution and heritage statutes, tort law and trust law to bring matters to court, and focused on individual, emissions-intensive projects with the aim of improving the regulations and decision-making related to that project as well as similar projects (Lin and Peel 2022). For instance, in 1994, Australia's first climate case, *Greenpeace v. Redbank* challenged the approval of a coal-fired power station for its potential to contribute to climate change. While that case was unsuccessful in its aims to stop a coalmine, it catalyzed further climate litigation in Australia based on the notion that adaptation, mitigation and environmentally sustainable development principles should all be considered as part of the "public interest" during the approval process (Melrose 2022). Two decades later, in 2007, *Massachusetts v. EPA* attracted media attention as the first case in the United States, and the world, to identify greenhouse gases as a source of pollution.

Such early cases received national, sometimes global, media attention but, as Setzer and Vanhala (2019) observe, most early efforts in climate litigation occur as small, local cases involving planning and administrative law, which rarely have news value beyond the local. Even then, coverage does not necessarily associate the matter before the courts with climate action. However, local news not only tell the stories of local people but also hold local authorities to account and, as such, play a role in communicating climate science and the local initiatives taken to address mitigation and adaptation (Myers et al. 2020; Nettlefold and Pecl 2022). Such stories are easy to overlook in the global narrative of climate action, especially when they come from countries and communities at the "peripheries" (Connell 2020).

The limited scholarly attention given to climate litigation in India and South Asia generally is a missed opportunity to better understand global efforts in climate action (Lin and Peel 2022, 190). If, as Chris Hilson (2023, 25) observes, climate litigation is resulting in case law that is "strategically designed to be contagious," then the transmission of these ideas, to continue the metaphor, through various networks would include paying closer attention to the early, eclectic cases that target individual projects.

Using International Law

From early efforts focused on specific projects, climate litigation has developed through repurposing old legal precedents and well-established mechanisms in other areas of law to a "next wave" holding governments and corporations directly to account for the impact of climate change on individuals and their communities (Lin and Peel 2022; Peel et al. 2020, 182). The signing of the Paris Agreement in 2015 marked a particular turn (Peel and

Osofsky 2017). While the connection between environmental protection and human rights has been recognized in international law since the 1972 United Nations Conference on the Human Environment, the Paris Agreement is the first global environmental agreement to recognize human rights as an integral element of the regime it establishes (Knox 2020, 323). As well as its stated objectives of holding action to increases in global temperature, the preamble to the Paris Agreement calls on states, when taking action to address climate change, to "respect, promote and consider their respective obligations on human rights." The inclusion of human rights in the Paris Agreement provides a bridge across the separation of nature and human culture by making climate change about people, not polar bears (Peel and Osofsky 2017) and while the Paris Agreement does not stipulate how human rights are to be protected, the inclusion serves to normalize the inclusion of human rights in climate action (Knox 2020, 324). As a legally binding treaty, the Paris Agreement provides the "top-down" pressure from international agreements to get national governments to act but also raises important questions about what power constitutes these agreements and who holds these processes to account. In particular, the Paris Agreement has provided people worldwide an important opening in which to argue for climate action on the grounds of government obligations to meet human rights as the following two high-profile cases, one from Europe and the other from South Asia, illustrate.

The *Urgenda* Case

Perhaps the most famous, for now at least, case drawing on the Paris Agreement was initiated by the Dutch environmental group, the Urgenda Foundation, and 900 Dutch citizens in 2015. In *Urgenda v. Netherlands*, a Dutch District Court ordered the Dutch Government to lower its greenhouse gas emissions by the end of 2020. Unsurprisingly, the Dutch Government appealed the decision (*Netherlands v. Urgenda*), but the Hague Court of Appeals upheld the District Court's decision and found the State was "failing to pursue a more ambitious reduction" to greenhouse gas emissions and agreed with the earlier decision that the State should reduce its emissions by at least 25 percent by 2020. Further, the Hague Court acknowledged Urgenda's claim that under the European Charter of Human Rights, the Dutch Government has an obligation to protect the right to life, privacy and family life and home from the genuine threat posed by climate change.

As the first case in the world to establish that a government has a legal duty to protect its citizens from the dangers of climate change, Urgenda was a win for climate change inside and outside the court (Peel and Osofsky 2017, 38). The Urgenda Foundation ran the case with a "media strategy as sophisticated as their case strategy" ensuring their claim in the Supreme Court was anticipated around the world in the run-up to the 2015 Paris COP (Barritt 2020, 296). In their study of news coverage of the case, Anke Wonneberger and Rens Vliegenthart (2021) found the *Urgenda* case provided Dutch news media with a focal point for attention on climate policy and climate issues more generally, which was reflected in parliamentary attention to climate policies during the case and afterward. They also describe the dynamic processes that enable media coverage of a specific case to carry the ideas and a debate from the courtroom into both the public sphere and the spheres of political decision-making. While the *Urgenda* case prompted predictions of a "global civil movement" (eg. Howard 2019), one was already well underway, especially in the so-called Global South (Peel and Lin 2019).

Asghar Leghari v. Federation of Pakistan

In 2015, Asghar Leghari, a law student and drought-affected farmer, sued the Pakistan government for failing to tackle the impacts of climate change. Drawing from Pakistan's National Climate Change Policy, Leghari claimed his human rights were being violated because of the government's failure "to ensure water, food and energy security in the face of the challenges posed by climate change" (Gill 2015). Curiously, Leghari is almost always described as a farmer, and only occasionally as a law student and a member of the Lahore High Court Bar Association, which not only says something about media's preference for a "David" to take on the Goliaths of industry and government, but also prompts the question of whether Leghari got his idea to sue his government from the *Urgenda* case that was unfolding in the Netherlands. Instead of suing for compensation, Leghari argued that his government should act on its promises to address climate change. The High Court of Lahore found in his favor and the decision read "like the scolding of naughty children" including criticisms about "the delay and lethargy of the State" in addressing the fundamental rights of its citizens (Barritt and Sediti 2019, 204).

The *Leghari* case was a classic example of green lawfare. While not the first climate case in a developing country, Leghari received a lot of media in Pakistan and throughout South Asia, which put a global spotlight on the region as a leading jurisdiction for climate litigation. Like its neighbor India, Pakistan has an active civil society and progressive legal culture, which includes an active judiciary, which is supporting this move (Barritt and Sediti 2019; Ohdedar 2021). As Waqqas Ahmad Mir (2020, 265) observes, anyone familiar with Pakistani case law, including journalists, would have found nothing remarkable about Leghari's petition to the court, but the "magnitude" of Leghari's claim and the questions it raised for Pakistan made the claim remarkable. In *Leghari*, "the court acted as a forum of solutions-oriented dialogue between the state and its citizens" and drove the national agenda on the importance and gravity of climate change (Mir 2020, 326). In his assessment of the case, Mir (2020) suggests the courts serve as a forum "for many stakeholders to come together to familiarize themselves with each other's positions, concerns, and limitations", which echoes the idea of "critical discourse moments", and raises important questions about how a citizenry can engage in this deliberation, or at least have faith in the transparency of the legal process, if they cannot see these forums in their local news. In Pakistan, however, the picture is all too familiar: shrinking newsrooms, climate remaining low in editorial priority, and a lack of access to reliable data means Pakistani journalists are limited to reporting climate change as extreme weather events or using "indirect angles" such as stories linking NGO activities to policy (Sharif and Medvecky 2018). Reporting on the *Legari* case then, not only provided journalists with news angles outside of the "usual," but it also presented reporters with new, or at least different, ways to frame climate change.

News reporting on climate litigation, whether coming from the Hague or Lahore, provided new stories about action on climate. As a form of green lawfare, such cases not only inform law and the discourses of climate governance, but also use the discourses of law to talk about climate change in ways that point to action, not hopelessness. In conclusion, we can see the shift in climate litigation from early efforts that focused on single projects to larger claims targeting governments' human rights obligations as a powerful shift from communicating climate change as a scientific problem, often carrying the symbolism of collapsing ice sheets and starving polar bears, to framing climate change as a political problem, carried by the faces of people already impacted by a changing world. In other words, the human rights turn in climate litigation is delivering a powerful way to tell human stories of climate change in ways that subvert hopelessness into radical calls for governments to change the trajectory. That said, some of those most affected by climate change are looking beyond their governments to the global community for action.

Sinking Islands in the Pacific

Climate change presents extraordinary and unprecedented challenges everywhere, but the loss of entire nations to rising sea levels raises particular questions about sovereignty and human rights (Stewart 2023). For the nations in the Pacific, distance from the political and economic centers of the world presents another set of challenges. In 2021, Tuvalu's foreign minister, Simon Kofe, grabbed international attention by recording his address to the widely publicized Conference of the Parties to the United Nations Framework Convention on Climate Change (COP26) while standing thigh-deep in the sea. The incongruous image of Kofe—standing at his watery lectern in a suit and tie with his message "we are sinking"—went global, not only carried by news organizations covering the event but also shared widely on social media (Guardian 2021). It was a stunt with spectacular symbolism and Kofe's words echoed those of Kiribati's President Anote Tong, who told the 2014 United Nations Climate Summit in New York that "Our plight is the plight of the global community further down the line" (Tong 2014, 3). While images abound of the literal devastation already impacting Pacific Island states, media strategies that ask politicians and others to "perform" being inundated by rising seas appeal to media's appetite for the unusual by providing striking images that include a human face. Despite the performativity, they send a compelling message that climate change has already arrived.

Communicating climate change for international audiences involves, writes Katerina Teaiwa (2019), a combination of diplomatic discussions and negotiations, images to attract media attention, film and documentary, and cultural performances, and an interplay between the literal and symbolic. In such communication, writes Teaiwa (2019, 55), global audiences "rarely see the Indigenous knowledge and cultures themselves as in need of safeguarding" but

> [a] Pacific song or dance is rarely only an empty form of entertainment—a dance and its accompanying chant may contain centuries of corporeal, social and environmental knowledge reflecting the need for balance between human societies and their natural environments.

In other words, the impact of climate change on cultural diversity is, like its impact on biodiversity, taking away the very things we need for balance in this world. The importance of media to record, share, and archive these stories described by Teaiwa is being acknowledged at a time when resources to support media are diminishing. For instance, Kofe's video statement was recorded by Tuvalu's public broadcaster TVBC, but journalists in Tuvalu are reporting the difficulty of protecting equipment and archives from the encroaching sea. In such circumstances, it might be tempting for news organizations to accept financial support from foreign governments and corporations to buy cameras, cars and other equipment, which raises questions about the quality of climate reporting when media are funded by actors who may not welcome such reporting (Ross 2020).

Stories from the Pacific Islands must travel beyond the local to find friends in the international forums that are deciding on climate action. How those stories are told is important. Teaiwa (2019) observes how the tendency of Australian news media to frame Pacific Islands politics as hopelessly corrupt stands in contrast to showing these cultures on the cusp of annihilation and needing help. In other words, the soft diplomacy of communicating climate action must include attention to news and other media to ensure that public opinion in faraway places is sympathetic to the issues their governments are being asked to adopt. For instance, in 2023, the United Nations adopted a landmark resolution put forward by Vanuatu and co-supported by 132 countries including Australia, seeking an opinion on the obligations that countries have to act on the climate crisis, with particular attention to the harm experienced by small island developing countries (United Nations 2023). Vanuatu's draft resolution asked the International Court of Justice to lay out the legal consequences for countries that "by their acts and omissions" have caused significant harm to the climate system and other parts of the environment. Such a request builds on previous work in framing climate change, in law and in the public imagination, as an issue of human rights and cites a range of sources for these obligations, including the Paris Agreement (Hurst 2023). While not legally binding, a decision issued by the United Nations will be another moment providing both the "top-down" pressure of international opprobrium as well as a discursive framework for those putting "bottom-up" pressure on their governments. The mediated images and messages coming from the region and circulating among international audiences ensure that the apparently distant nature of international diplomacy maintains a human face and conveys urgency rather than abstraction. While Kofe's watery lectern speech used the symbolic to convey the complex, the symbolism in any communicative act, no matter how performative, can capture people's attention and challenge them to think differently. In other words, if law (in the broadest sense of the word) is made in moments when various actors find an opening for change, then news and other media are vital to ensure that moment remains in people's minds not only as an idea, but as a possibility.

Youth v. The State

Symbolism is obviously at play in the smiling faces of school students who are not only striking for action on climate but also initiating climate litigation. To date, at least 32 cases involving young plaintiffs have been lodged in 14 countries (Parker et al. 2022). Each of these provides a glimpse into the mediated networks that are sharing ideas about intergenerational duty and global connection, as well as strategies for getting attention and action. The symbolic power of news and other media lies in its capacity to produce and transmit such symbols (Thompson 2005), which includes attaching a universal value or ideal to a single event or person. The juxtaposition of hopeful young faces and the sober gravity of the legal system, then, symbolizes not only how climate litigation is reshaping traditional legal assumptions and norms (Preston 2016) but also the dominant framing of environmental problems as an issue for "future generations" by showing that those who will be profoundly disadvantaged by climate change are already born and demanding action (Morris 2021). Indeed, the faces of youth litigation are the faces of the Anthropocene, which is marked by shifting temporalities in political decision-making to include the future (Kotzé and Knappe 2023). Of course, the image of young people talking about climate evokes the familiar, often scowling, face of Greta Thunberg, who was only 15 years old in 2018 when she started sitting alone with a sign on the steps of the Swedish parliament each Friday. In 2019, Thunberg attended the United Nations Climate Action Summit in New York City where she made her short, but now famous, "how dare you" speech in which she berated the adults gathered before her, declaring:

> This is all wrong. I shouldn't be up here. I should be back in school on the other side of the ocean … You have stolen my dreams and my childhood with your empty words … and all you can talk about is money and fairy tales of eternal economic growth. How dare you! (Gladstone and Yuhas 2019)

From this moment, Thunberg became the face of future generations furious with the missed opportunities to act on climate. While Thunberg has little to say on solutions and nothing "akin to a revolution" (Morris 2021), the power of Thunberg's rhetoric lies in her use of temporal themes to speak of the future, such as this excerpt from *Time* magazine where she tells journalists (Alter, Haynes and Worland 2019):

> "We can't just continue living as if there was no tomorrow, because there is a tomorrow," she says, tugging on the sleeve of her blue sweatshirt. "That is all we are saying."

Thunberg's simple message resonates with young people worldwide because her words and sentiments and the apparent simplicity of her actions—school strikes and speaking truth to power—are transmutable. As such, "The Greta effect" has come to describe the influence of her message on other young people, which includes inspiring the global Strike 4 Climate movement (Calibeo 2023). She has inspired a wave of young people, especially young women, to speak out about climate. For instance, echoing Thunberg's "I shouldn't be up here," prominent Australian climate activist Daisy Jeffrey (2020) wrote in *Vogue* magazine:

> How do I balance activism and school? It's all a bit of a shemozzle, really. My mind is always in a million different places at once—trig over here, Adani over there, and a desperate need for coffee at the front. I should not have to be doing this. This is the government's responsibility, not mine.

The digital networks carrying the contagious idea of youth activism have led some young people into dangerous territory, such as Indian climate activist Disha Ravi who was arrested and charged with sedition in 2021 for re-posting a tweet by Thunberg that included a "toolkit," including instructions on how to use hashtags and petitions, that Thunberg had created to support Indian farmers who were striking. Sharing the toolkit had made Ravi a "key conspirator" in the farmers' protest and a widespread denunciation of the "toolkit" followed in news and other media, including claims the toolkit was evidence of foreign interference and proof of a coordinated international conspiracy "to wage economic, social, cultural, and regional war against India" (Ellis-Petersen 2021). The convergence of activism, media, and legal frameworks that constitute global efforts for improved climate governance, and which are seen in instances such as Ravi's arrest, are areas of conflict that can be regarded as examples of green lawfare whether they make it to court or not.

Anjali Sharma, often photographed in a school blazer that seemed too big for her slim shoulders, looked like a typical Australian school student when she became the public face of Australian climate litigation in 2022.

Sharma and her fellow litigants had all been involved in organizing the School Strike for Climate in September 2019, when about 100,000 students and their supporters marched in Melbourne. The case of *Sharma v. Minister for the Environment* involved eight young people, aged between 13 and 17, led by Sharma and assisted by an 86-year-old nun, Sister Brigid Arthur, who sought to block the approval of an extension to a coal mine project. Instead of waiting to challenge an administrative decision, which is a more usual course of action in Australia, the young people took an unusually pre-emptive approach by asking the Federal Court to stop the Australian Government from approving the extension to the Whitehaven Vickery coal mine on the grounds that the federal environment minister had a common law duty of care for young people. In an interesting twist on the temporal rhetoric of the past and future, Sharma brought a spatial logic to her motivation as an activist, writing that as a migrant from India, she had "listened as family members describe the reality of living in a country being transformed by climate change" (Sharma 2021). The Court recognized the Environment Minister's duty of care to protect young people which, as one lawyer (Pender 2022) said owed to the "uncontested scientific evidence in *Sharma*" that no amount of legal sophistry could deny. *Sharma* was also a classic example of the symbolic power of climate litigation to gain advantage even when a case is lost. When then Environment Minister, Susan Ley, successfully appealed against the court's decision, cartoonists and satirists had a field day showing a jubilant minister celebrating her relief that she did not have any duty of care to protect young people!

In the United States, Rikki Held was the public face of a similar case where the first-ever constitutional climate trial in the United States. *Held v. Montana*, was brought by young activists on the grounds that Montana's state constitution promises "the right to a clean and healthful environment." At the same time, another case, sometimes called the "children's case," was in progress. In 2015, 21 young plaintiffs in *Juliana v. United States* claimed that the government had violated their constitutional rights, including a claimed right under the Fifth Amendment to a "climate system capable of sustaining human life." They also sought to hold individuals in government accountable for allegedly misleading the public and obstructing climate action, such as by deliberately hiding or distorting climate science, misrepresenting the costs and benefits of climate regulations, or undermining public understanding of the issue. At the time of writing, *Juliana* has yet to make it to trial because the Obama, Trump and Biden administrations have continually fought to delay the trial (Danesha 2024).

In these cases, we can see how an idea, carried by Greta Thunberg, but with a history older than her short years, travels across the world, connecting mediated images of street protests and youthful hope to more complex and arcane legal concepts. In each instance, the young litigants can look to their global hero for inspiration but must work with what they have at a national, or more local, level. Some have access to more generous legal mechanisms, such as those in Colombia where there is constitutional recognition, or tutela, which enables Colombians to bring claims of violations against their human rights before a judge. For instance, in 2018, 25 young Colombians filed a lawsuit, *Future Generations v. Ministry of the Environment and Others*, against various government bodies, municipalities, and corporations claiming that climate change, combined with the government's failure to curb deforestation to meet zero-net deforestation targets, as agreed under the Paris Agreement and in national policy, was endangering their fundamental rights. More recently, six Portuguese youths lodged a claim against 27 European Union member states and six other countries, *Duarte Agostinho and Others v. Portugal and 32 Other States*, arguing that each of these governments has violated their human rights obligations by not implementing emission-reduction policies in line with the Paris Agreement. Drawing on the *European Convention of Human Rights* (ECHR), these young plaintiffs argue that environmental hazards threaten life, disrupt family life, and may result in discrimination.

The list of youth-led climate litigation will no doubt continue to grow as the symbolism of youth and protest is carried by news and other media to students who begin their activism with a street march or climate strike and learn not only about the connection between public participation and governance but also the role of law in these matters. Along the way, their strategies will invariably target news and other media to spread their message and garner political legitimacy.

Targeting the Greenwashers

A third area of litigation is using domestic commercial law to target misleading representations in advertising, marketing, and shareholder communications. Such cases focus on what has long been called "greenwashing," which describes the disjunction between the promotion of a company or brand's green credentials to consumers, stakeholders and regulatory authorities and the actual practices of the company (Burger and Tigre 2023). This section begins with litigation in relation to the more familiar practice of greenwashing in advertising and marketing campaigns before looking at litigation targeting the disingenuous communication practices targeting shareholders and regulators. Green lawfare that targets greenwashing puts media in a conspicuously central role because these actions specifically target the contemporary communication logics and practices.

It is hard to avoid those pernicious, and increasingly ubiquitous, marketing campaigns promoting a company's dubious environmental credentials, such as those that promote the net-zero credentials of companies still committed to mining fossil fuels. Corporations in various sectors employ basic strategies to meet social and environmental regulations, as well as to gain stakeholder legitimacy, but sometimes the promotion of these activities involves such ambiguity and euphemism that they can be interpreted as deceitful (Sarfraz 2023). Greenwashing is about vague claims, such as Nespresso's reassurances that its coffee pods were recyclable without mentioning that recycling the pods required consumers to deliver them to a limited number of special facilities that landed coffee pod manufacturer Keurig in court for false advertising (Fraser 2023). Greenwashing is also about using false data in promotional material, such as when car manufacturer Volkswagen, which claimed to have the cleanest options available in the combustion-engine market, was shown to emit up to 40 times more pollutants than they advertised (Mujkic and Klingner 2019).

Greenwashing cases are gaining pace as more companies commit to net-zero targets but fail to meaningfully change their activities (Benjamin et al. 2022). In 2021, three environmental groups, Global Witness, Greenpeace and Earthworks, filed a false advertising complaint against the oil giant Chevron with the United States Federal Trade Commission alleging Chevron had overstated its investment in renewable energy and actions to curb greenhouse gas emissions in its marketing campaigns (Benjamin et al. 2022, 12). The first greenwashing case targeting Europe's energy sector was instigated in 2022 by several NGOs who raised concerns about French multinational TotalEnergies's net-zero advertising campaign. In *Greenpeace v. TotalEnergies*, the claimants argue the company's "reinvention" marketing campaign broke European consumer law by suggesting TotalEnergies could reach net-zero carbon emissions by 2050 was misleading. In a similar case in Australia, *ACCR v. Santos*, the Australasian Centre for Corporate Responsibility (ACCR), a climate-focused shareholder advocacy group, argued that oil and gas company, Santos, was breaching Australian consumer protection and corporation laws by claiming to provide clean energy natural gas and plans for net-zero emissions by 2040 while, at the same time, increasing its natural gas operations. The group also claimed the company was misleading investors about its net-zero plans. ACCR's strategy was a clear example of green lawfare that used the court system as part of a wider communication campaign. As its executive director, Brynn O'Brien told the *Australian* newspaper (Loussikian and Williams 2023), companies need a credible plan to deliver their net-zero commitments and Santos's "targets, and the feasibility of meeting them in real-world terms, deserve close scrutiny. We have asked the courts to do that."

Strategies targeting greenwashing are a particular example of green lawfare because the public-oriented claims of companies in advertising and other communication are at the heart of these cases. Such actions, and the consumer laws designed to protect consumers from false claims, highlight the considerable power of media, especially branding and advertising, to influence consumer behavior and public opinion more generally. In turn, litigation targeting false and misleading activity is a form of green lawfare that not only uses the courts to reveal dishonest claims but also to highlight poor practices and corporate behavior.

While the idea of greenwashing has its roots in calling out false claims in advertising, litigation is increasingly targeting claims made to shareholders and government regulators on the grounds that certain statements are deceptive and misleading about business activities that put others at risk (Elkateb et al. 2023). Governments and investor groups have initiated cases to enforce securities disclosures and consumer protection laws and are challenging public disclosures made by companies when they are deemed to be misleading or fraudulent. These suits cover claims made by companies relating to transitioning away from fossil fuels, potential impacts on business or investment assets, and the risks posed by climate change to infrastructure, operations, and supply chains. As the regulatory landscape for climate disclosures is in constant flux, we can see this area of litigation as a good example of what Elizabeth Fisher (2013) described as "hot law." For instance, chair of the United Kingdom's Environment Agency, Emma Howard Boyd told an investment forum:

> If we fail to identify and address greenwashing, we allow ourselves false confidence that we are already addressing the causes and treating the symptoms of the climate crisis. Greenwash makes it more likely that we won't realize this deception until it is too late … Companies that believe their own greenwash are embedding liability, storing up risk for their investors. (Groves 2022)

The fossil fuel industry is a particular target for allegations of greenwashing (Wentz et al. 2023). In the United States, at the time of writing, the state of Massachusetts is prosecuting ExxonMobil for greenwashing (*Commonwealth v. ExxonMobil*) arguing the corporation promoted its investment in lower-emission energy solutions, while it continued to invest large sums in fossil fuel operations (McGreal 2021).

Cases against the greenwashers are likely to grow as a form of green lawfare notable for targeting communication as the egregious practice. As Setzer and Vanhala (2019) observe, some industries remain noticeably absent from climate-related litigation to date, including aviation, international shipping, and the meat industry. Similarly, they note, little scholarship has explored the role of the finance sector, which includes banks, institutional investors, insurance companies, corporate borrowers, financial supervisory authorities, and regulators, in the dynamics of action and inaction on climate. Banks and pension fund schemes are also facing mounting pressure to integrate climate risk into their strategies. In short, the flow of commodities, manufactured consumables, and finance remains the source of much global power (Appadurai 1996; Lester 2019) and therefore provides plenty of potential targets for pursuing action on climate and other environment problems through the courts.

Conclusion: Conspicuous Ideas at Work

A typhoon in the Philippines triggers an inquiry into what the fossil fuel industry knew about the effects of carbon emissions on climate change. The inquiry becomes an investigation of the misinformation campaigns used by the fossil fuel industry to shift attention away from the world's worst polluters that points to future directions in global climate litigation. Approaching climate litigation as a form of green lawfare means observing lawsuits as single moments in law and law-making that draw on ideas and strategies from a wide network of actors. In an increasingly globalized world, the reach of transnational investment and influence means that even the most local story about climate litigation is likely to involve a network of actors beyond the local. In cases that draw on international law, we see human rights and environmental rights being brought together to bring a human face to the impacts of corporate tyranny because when the soil of an Ecuadorian forest is soaked with the toxic waste left by oil drilling, the human cost and the ecological cost are one and the same. Such cases also intersect with the global forces that drive international trade and finance that deflect the ecological costs of consumption away from the affluent. While climate litigation is an established area of law, new strategies and approaches, such as lawsuits targeting financial entities that support and profit from major polluters, are still emerging and will require analysis that includes the often-hidden networks of international trade that until recently have evaded liability.

Green lawfare is most conspicuous when litigants incorporate media into their campaign strategies, including cultivating close relationships with interested journalists and deploying media strategies that spread their message to key actors and the broader public. As a campaign strategy, litigation provides a new arena of contest to attract the "mediated visibility" essential for enacting social change that includes raising public awareness and putting an issue on the political agenda. Some cases before the courts trigger wider public debates, while in others, public concern about an issue crystalizes around a particular case. Either way, climate litigation is increasingly being used to test government commitments on climate action in ways that not only progress the development of environmental and climate law but also stimulate ongoing discussion in public and political spheres.

While extensive research exists on the role of framing and news sources in media representations of environmental issues, limited knowledge exists about how the mediatization of climate litigation informs public opinion (Konkes 2018) and how legal actors are informed by and, in turn, influence media coverage (Nixon et al. 2021). Research in this area may find that a lack of engagement between the legal sphere and those working in news and other media continues to foster a culture of antagonism between lawyers and journalists which serves to hinder the communicative potential of such actions. Research into climate litigation could also involve looking at the material, symbolic, and political implications of these strategies (Konkes 2018). For instance, courts have the material power to halt or delay projects that contribute to climate change and other harms, but observing climate litigation also requires watching the symbolism at play, especially outside of the court: youthful faces, leaders thigh-deep in rising waters, and the symbolic power of international bodies that sends powerful messages to those watching proceedings unfold, which can influence public sentiment about the case and the issues around it. As well as material and symbolic power is the political consequence of climate litigation undertaken by grassroots actors seeking to apply "bottom-up" pressure on governments through protest and other mediated spectacles or using international law to apply "top-down" pressure. By considering the material, symbolic, and political dimensions of climate litigation as communicative action, we can find deeper insights into the implications and effectiveness of green lawfare strategies.

Climate litigation is an example of "hot law" (Fisher 2013) because climate change and action on climate continue to develop on an unstable knowledge base, where the identities of actors, including plaintiffs and defendants but also other interested parties, continue to fluctuate, as do the sources of complaint and the targets of attribution and blame. Increasingly, and as covered in more detail in the next chapter, cases are being filed directly against companies and, in turn, governments and the corporate sector are turning to litigation and other tactics to fight back.

Climate litigation continues to evolve alongside domestic and international efforts to enact meaningful action on climate. While some champion the human rights turn, which places the focus on human suffering and social justice, others are calling for a more radical shift from anthropocentric legal frameworks to more ecocentric structures that prioritize the integrity of ecological systems or, indeed draw inspiration from Earth systems. Each of these approaches argue for our knowledge of the planet to inform human culture, including our legal systems. Climate litigation, then, is just one part of green lawfare. Importantly, successful litigation relies on a diverse network of actors bringing expertise and funding to campaigns and communication strategies that mobilize not only interest but also public support for systemic social, political, economic and legal change. While climate litigation is an established area of green lawfare, scientific advances in the detection and attribution of drivers of global warming, the ongoing impacts of extreme weather events, and the increasing evidence of corporate malfeasance ensure that climate litigation will remain an area of "hot" law for years to come.

References

Alter, Charlotte, Suyin Haynes, and Justin Worland. 2019. "Greta Thunberg: TIME's Person of the Year 2019." *Time*, 2019. https://time.com/person-of-the-year-2019-greta-thunberg/?utm_source=twitter&utm_medium=social&utm_campaign=person-of-the-year&utm_term=_&linkId=78763203 (Accessed August 22, 2023).

Appadurai, Arjun. 1996. *Modernity at Large: Cultural Dimensions of Globalization*. Minneapolis: University of Minnesota Press.

Barritt, Emily. 2020. "Consciously Transnational: Urgenda and the Shape of Climate Change Litigation: The State of the Netherlands (Ministry of Economic Affairs and Climate Policy) v. Urgenda Foundation." *Environmental Law Review* 22 (4): 296–305.

Barritt, Emily, and Boitumelo Sediti. 2019. "The Symbolic Value of *Leghari v. Federation of Pakistan*: Climate Change Adjudication in the Global South." *King's Law Journal* 30 (2): 203–210.

Benjamin, Lisa, Akriti Bhargava, Benjamin Franta, Karla Martínez Toral, Joana Setzer, and Aradhna Tandon. 2022. "Climate-Washing Litigation: Legal Liability for Misleading Climate Communications." Policy Briefing, The Climate Social Science Network. January 2022.

Brown, Jessica Autumn, and Myra Marx Ferree. 2005. "Close your eyes and think of England: Pronatalism in the British print media." *Gender & Society* 19 (1): 5-24.

Brüggemann, Michael, and Sven Engesser. 2017. "Beyond False Balance: How Interpretive Journalism Shapes Media Coverage of Climate Change." *Global Environmental Change* 42 (January): 58–67. https://doi.org/10.1016/j.gloenvcha.2016.11.004.

Burger, Michael, and Maria Antonia Tigre. 2023. "Global Climate Litigation Report: 2023 Status Review." Sabin Center for Climate Change Law, Columbia Law School & United Nations Environment Programme.

Calibeo, Diletta Luna. 2024. "'We Became Our Own Media!': Australian Perspectives on the Beneficial Potentialities of New Media for Environmental Activism." *Journal of Environmental Studies and Sciences*, January. https://doi.org/10.1007/s13412-023-00885-y.

Carmichael, Jason T., and Robert J. Brulle. 2017. "Elite Cues, Media Coverage, and Public Concern: An Integrated Path Analysis of Public Opinion on Climate Change, 2001–2013." *Environmental Politics* 26 (2): 232–252.

Carvalho, Anabela. 2008. "Media (Ted) Discourse and Society: Rethinking the Framework of Critical Discourse Analysis." *Journalism Studies* 9 (2): 161–177.

Carvalho, Anabela, Margit van Wessel, and Pieter Maeseele. 2017. "Communication Practices and Political Engagement with Climate Change: A Research Agenda." *Environmental Communication* 11 (1): 122–135.

Connell, Raewyn. 2020. *Southern Theory: The Global Dynamics of Knowledge in Social Science.* London: Routledge.

Cottle, Simon. 2006. *Mediatized Conflicts*. Maidenhead: Open University Press.

Cox, J. Robert. 2010. "Beyond Frames: Recovering the Strategic in Climate Communication." *Environmental Communication* 4 (1): 122–133.

Daneesha, Neel. 2024. "The Climate Lawsuit Three Presidents Tried to Kill is Finally Going to Court". *Heatmap News*. January 5, 2024.
https://heatmap.news/politics/juliana-climate-lawsuit-biden-trump-obama

Dauvergne, Peter. 2008. *The Shadows of Consumption: Consequences for the Global Environment.* Cambridge: MIT Press.

Elkateb, Maha, Ouidad Yousfi, and Abdelwahed Omri. 2023. "Perspective Chapter: Rethinking CSR Strategies in the Era of COVID-19." In *Business, Management and Economics*, edited by Muddassar Sarfraz. Vol. 4. IntechOpen. https://doi.org/10.5772/intechopen.106248

Ellis-Petersen, Hannah. 2021. "India: Activist Arrested over Protest 'Toolkit' Shared by Greta Thunberg." *The Guardian*, February 15, 2021. https://www.theguardian.com/world/2021/feb/15/india-activist-arrested-over-protest-toolkit-shared-by-greta-thunberg (Accessed August 22, 2023).

Fermeglia, Matteo. 2020. "Climate Science Before the Courts: Turning the Tide in Climate Change Litigation." In *Ecological Integrity in Science and Law*, edited by Laura Westra, Klaus Bosselmann, and Matteo Fermeglia, 23–36. Cham: Springer International.

Fisher, Elizabeth. 2013. "Climate Change Litigation, Obsession and Expertise: Reflecting on the Scholarly Response to Massachusetts v. EPA." *Law & Policy* 35 (3): 236–260.

Fraser, Connor J. 2023. "Recycled Misrepresentation: Plastic Products, Consumer Protection Law & Attorneys General." *NYU Environmental Law Journal* 31. http://dx.doi.org/10.2139/ssrn.4346171

Fraser, Nancy, and Kate Nash. 2014. *Transnationalizing the Public Sphere*. Hoboken: Wiley.

Ghosh, Aditya, and Maxwell Boykoff. 2019. "Framing Sustainability and Climate Change: Interrogating Discourses in Vernacular and English-Language Media in Sundarbans, India." *Geoforum* 99 (February): 142–153.

Gill, Anam. 2014. "Farmer Sues Pakistan's Government to Demand Action on Climate Change." *Reuters*, November 14. https://www.reuters.com/article/pakistan-climatechange-lawsuit-idUSL8N1383YJ20151113 (Accessed July 7, 2023).

Gladstone, Rick, and Alan Yuhas. 2019. "What Happened at the U.N. General Assembly." *New York Times*, September 24. https://www.nytimes.com/2019/09/24/world/united-nations-general-assembly-recap.html (Accessed July 7, 2023).

Greenpeace. 2022. "COP27 Sponsor the Coca-Cola Company Named Worst Plastic Polluter for Five Years in a Row According to 2022 Brand Audit." Greenpeace USA News (blog). November 15, 2022. https://www.greenpeace.org/usa/news/cop27-sponsor-the-coca-cola-company-named-worst-plastic-polluter-for-five-years-in-a-row-according-to-2022-brand-audit/ (Accessed December 17, 2022).

Groves, Matthew. 2017. "Lawfare and the Enemy within Our Public Law." *AIAL Forum* 90: 32–51.

Guardian, The. 2021. "Tuvalu Minister to Address COP26 Knee Deep in Water to Highlight Climate Crisis and Sea Level Rise." *The Guardian*, November 8. https://www.theguardian.com/environment/2021/nov/08/tuvalu-minister-to-address-cop26-knee-deep-in-seawater-to-highlight-climate-crisis (Accessed July 21, 2023).

Heede, Richard. 2014. "Tracing Anthropogenic Carbon Dioxide and Methane Emissions to Fossil Fuel and Cement Producers, 1854–2010." *Climatic Change* 122 (1–2): 229–241.

Hilson, Chris. 2023. "Trends in Environmental Law Scholarship: Marketisation, Globalisation, Polarisation, and Digitalisation." *Journal of Environmental Law* 35 (1): 21–31.

Hurst, Daniel. 2023. "Australia Joins Vanuatu Bid for International Court to Rule on Obligation to Prevent Climate Harm." *The Guardian*, March 1. https://www.theguardian.com/world/2023/mar/01/australia-joins-vanuatu-bid-for-international-court-to-rule-on-obligation-to-prevent-climate-harm#:~:text=7%20months%20old-,Australia%20joins%20Vanuatu%20bid%20for%20international%20court%20to,obligation%20to%20prevent%20climate%20harm&text=Australia%20will%20co%2Dsponsor%20Vanuatu's%20histo

ric%20bid%20for%20the%20international,for%20causing%20significant%20environmental%20harm (Accessed August 22, 2023).

Jeffrey, Daisy. 2020. "Teenage climate-change campaigner Daisy Jeffrey on what it's really like to be a young activist." *Vogue*, June 2. https://www.vogue.com.au/culture/features/teenage-climatechange-campaigner-daisy-jeffrey-on-what-its-really-like-to-be-a-young-activist/news-story/4b7442757e6e066df7d3ce31f07410cd (Accessed August 22, 2023).

Knox, John H. 2020. "The Paris Agreement as a Human Rights Treaty." In *Human Rights and 21st Century Challenges*, edited by Dapo Akande, 323–347. Oxford: Oxford University Press.

Konkes, Claire. 2018. "Green Lawfare: Environmental Public Interest Litigation and Mediatized Environmental Conflict." *Environmental Communication* 12 (2): 191–203.

Konkes, Claire, and Libby Lester. 2016. "Justice, Politics and the Social Usefulness of News." *Crime, Media, Culture: An International Journal* 12 (1): 17–35.

Kotzé, Louis J, and Henrike Knappe. 2023. "Youth Movements, Intergenerational Justice, and Climate Litigation in the Deep Time Context of the Anthropocene." *Environmental Research Communications* 5 (2): 025001. https://doi.org/10.1088/2515-7620/acaa21.

Langford, Malcolm. 2023. "Climate Change in Courts: A Responsive Approach." Annual Lecture, Centre for Environmental Law, Macquarie University, April 6. https://www.jus.uio.no/ior/english/people/aca/malcolml/lecture-climate-change-courts.pdf (Accessed August 12, 2023).

Lazarus, Richard. 2009. "Super Wicked Problems and Climate Change: Restraining the Present to Liberate the Future." *Cornell Law Review* 94 (5): 1153–1234.

Lazarus, Richard J. 2023. *The Making of Environmental Law*. 2nd ed. Chicago and London: University of Chicago Press.

Lester, Libby. 2010. *Media and Environment: Conflict, Politics and the News*. Cambridge: Polity.

———. 2019. *Global Trade and Mediatised Environmental Protest: The View from Here*. Cham: Springer International.

Lin, Jolene. 2012. "Climate Change and the Courts." *Legal Studies* 32 (1): 35–57.

Lin, Jolene, and Jacqueline Peel. 2022. "The Farmer or the Hero Litigator? Modes of Climate Litigation in the Global South." In *Litigating the Climate Emergency*, edited by César Rodríguez-Garavito, 187–205. Cambridge: Cambridge University Press.

Loussikian, Kylar, and Perry Williams. 2023. "ASIC Monitoring Santos Court Action over Greenwashing Claims." *The Australian*, January 23. https://www.theaustralian.com.au/business/mining-energy/asic-monitoring-santos-court-action-over-greenwashing-claims/news-story/cae64b6e05a6a73b6efb1e9d24577251 (Accessed July 21, 2023).

McGreal, Chris. 2021. "Exxon and BP Called to Testify on Climate after 'Troubling' New Documents." *The Guardian*, September 16. https://www.theguardian.com/business/2021/sep/16/exxon-bp-congress-climate-crisis (Accessed January 19, 2023).

Melrose, Laura. 2022. "Emerging Trends in Australian Climate Change Litigation: Bringing the Heat." *Alternative Law Journal* 47 (3): 187–193.

Mir, Waqqas Ahmad. 2020. "From Shehla Zia to Asghar Leghari: Pronouncing Unwritten Rights Is More Complex than a Celebratory Tale." In *Climate Change Litigation in the Asia Pacific*, edited by Jolene Lin and Douglas A. Kysar, 261–293. Cambridge: Cambridge University Press.

Morris, Hanna E. 2021. "Generational Anxieties in United States Climate Journalism." In *Climate Change and Journalism*, edited by Henrik Bødker and Hanna E. Morris, 68–84. London: Routledge.

Mujkic, Edin, and Donald Klingner. 2019. "Dieselgate: How Hubris and Bad Leadership Caused the Biggest Scandal in Automotive History." *Public Integrity* 21 (4): 365–377.

Myers, Teresa A., Edward W. Maibach, Bernadette Woods Placky, Kimberly L. Henry, Michael D. Slater, and Keith L. Seitter. 2020. "Impact of the Climate Matters Program on Public Understanding of Climate Change." *Weather, Climate, and Society* 12 (4): 863–876.

Nettlefold, Jocelyn, and Gretta T. Pecl. 2022. "Engaged Journalism and Climate Change: Lessons from an Audience-Led, Locally Focused Australian Collaboration." *Journalism Practice* 16 (1): 19–34.

Nixon, Cynthia, Claire Konkes, Libby Lester, and Kathleen Williams. 2021. "Mediated Visibility and Public Environmental Litigation: The Interplay between Inside and Outside Court during Environmental Conflict in Australia." *Laws* 10 (2): https://doi.org/10.3390/laws10020035

Ohdedar, Birsha. 2021. "Litigating Climate Change in India and Pakistan: Analysing Opportunities and Challenges." In *Climate Change Litigation: Global Perspectives*, edited by Ivano Alogna, Christine Bakker, and Jean-Pierre Gauci. Leiden: Koninklijke Brill NV.

Parker, Larissa, Juliette Mestre, Sébastien Jodoin, and Margarentha Wewerinke-Singh. 2022. "When the Kids Put Climate Change on Trial: Youth-Focused Rights-Based Climate Litigation around the World." *Journal of Qualitative Research in Tourism* 13 (1): 65–89.

Peel, Jacqueline. 2023. "Climate Litigation Is on the Rise around the World and Australia Is at the Head of the Pack." *The Conversation*, July 27, 2023. https://theconversation.com/climate-litigation-is-on-the-rise-around-the-world-and-australia-is-at-the-head-of-the-pack-210375 (Accessed August 21, 2023).

Peel, Jacqueline, Hari Osofsky, and Anita Foerster. "'Next Generation' Climate Change Litigation in Australia." In *Climate Change Litigation in the Asia Pacific*, edited by Jolene Lin and Douglas A. Kysar, 1st ed., 175–206. Cambridge University Press. https://doi.org/10.1017/9781108777810.009.

Peel, Jacqueline, and Jolene Lin. 2020. "Climate Change Adaptation Litigation: A View from Southeast Asia." In *Climate Change Litigation in the Asia Pacific*, edited by Jolene Lin and Douglas A. Kysar. Cambridge: Cambridge University Press. 294–328.

Pender, Kieran. 2022. "In the Sharma Decision the federal court says: we see the climate risk but cannot act." *The Guardian*, March 16, 2022. https://www.theguardian.com/commentisfree/2022/mar/16/in-the-sharma-decision-the-federal-court-says-we-see-the-climate-risk-but-cannot-act#:~:text=1%20year%20old-,In%20the%20Sharma%20decision%20the%20federal%20court%20says%3A%20we%20see,climate%20risk%20but%20cannot%20act&text=It%20has%20become%20a,posed%20by%20the%20climate%20crisis (Accessed July 21, 2022).

Preston, Brian. 2023. "Mainstreaming Climate Change in Legal Education" Paper presented at the Te Piringa Faculty of Law, University of Waikato and IUCN Academy of Environmental Law Webinar, July 6, 2023. https://lec.nsw.gov.au/documents/speec

hes-and-papers/Preston_CJ_-_Mainstreaming_Climate_Change_in_Legal_Education.pdf (Accessed July 21, 2023).

Preston, Brian. 2016. "The Contribution of the Courts in Tackling Climate Change." *Journal of Environmental Law* 28 (1): 11–17.

Puvimanasinghe, Shyami. 2021. "The Role of Public Interest Litigation in Realizing Environmental Justice in South Asia: Selected Cases as Guidance in Implementing Agenda 2030." In *The Cambridge Handbook of Environmental Justice and Sustainable Development*, edited by Sumudu A. Atapattu, Carmen G. Gonzalez, and Sara L. Seck, 137–151. Cambridge: Cambridge University Press.

Rogers, Nicole. 2015. "'If You Obey All the Rules You Miss All the Fun': Climate Change Litigation, Climate Change Activism and Lawfulness." *New Zealand Journal of Public and International Law* 13(1): 179–199.

Ross, Tara. 2020. "Pacific Media." In *Oxford Research Encyclopedia of Communication*, by Tara Ross. Oxford University Press. https://doi.org/10.1093/acrefore/9780190228613.013.987.

Sarfraz, Muddassar. 2023. *Corporate Social Responsibility in the 21st Century*. London: IntechOpen.

Schonhardt, Sara, and Lesley Clark. 2022. "How a Philippine Inquiry Could Shape Global Climatelitigation." *ClimateWire*, May 16. https://www.eenews.net/articles/how-a-philippine-inquiry-could-shape-global-climate-litigation/ (Accessed August 22, 2023).

Schuijers, Laura. 2017. "Environmental Decision-Making in the Anthropocene: Challenges for Ecologically Sustainable Development and the Case for Systems Thinking," *Environmental and Planning Law Journal* 19 (3). 179–197.

Setzer, Joana, and Catherine Higham. 2022. *Global Trends in Climate Change Litigation: 2022 Snapshot*. London: Grantham Research Institute on Climate Change and the Environment and Centre for Climate Change Economics and Policy, London School of Economics and Political Science.

Setzer, Joana, and Lisa C. Vanhala. 2019. "Climate Change Litigation: A Review of Research on Courts and Litigants in Climate Governance." *WIREs Climate Change* 10 (3). https://doi.org/10.1002/wcc.580

Sharif, Asim, and Fabien Medvecky. 2018. "Climate Change News Reporting in Pakistan: A Qualitative Analysis of Environmental Journalists and the Barriers They Face." *Journal of Science Communication* 17 (1). https://doi.org/10.22323/2.17010203

Sharma, Anjali. 2021. "Sharma v. Environment Minister." *The Saturday Paper*, June 5. https://www.thesaturdaypaper.com.au/news/politics/2021/06/05/sharma-v-environment-minister/162281520011815 (Accessed August 22, 2023).

Stewart, Melissa. 2023. "Cascading Consequences of Sinking States." *SSRN Electronic Journal*. https://doi.org/10.2139/ssrn.4321214

Teaiwa, Katerina. 2019. "No Distant Future: Climate Change as an Existential Threat." *Australian Foreign Affairs* January (6): 51–70.

Thompson, John B. 2005. "The New Visibility." *Theory, Culture & Society* 22 (6): 31–51.

Tigre, Maria Antonia, Natalia Urzola, and Alexandra Goodman. 2023. "Climate Litigation in Latin America: Is the Region Quietly Leading a Revolution?" *Journal of Human Rights and the Environment* 14 (1): 67–93.

Tong, Anote 2014. "Statement by H. E President Anote Tong." 69th United Nations General Assembly, New York, September 26. https://www.un.org/en/ga/69/meetings/gadebate/pdf/KI_en.pdf (Accessed August 23, 2023).

Tschötschel, Robin, Andreas Schuck, and Anke Wonneberger. 2020. "Patterns of Controversy and Consensus in German, Canadian, and US Online News on Climate Change." *Global Environmental Change* 60 (January): 101957. https://doi.org/10.1016/j.gloenvcha.2019.101957.

United Nations. 2023. "General Assembly Adopts Resolution Requesting International Court of Justice Provide Advisory Opinion on States' Obligations Concerning Climate Change." Meetings Coverage and Press Releases. 29 March 2023

https://press.un.org/en/2023/ga12497.doc.htm

Wentz, Jessica, Delta Merner, Benjamin Franta, Alessandra Lehmen, and Peter C. Frumhoff. 2023. "Research Priorities for Climate Litigation." *Earth's Future* 11 (1). https://doi.org/10.1029/2022EF002928

Wonneberger, Anke. 2024. "Climate Change Litigation in the News: Litigation as Public Campaigning Tool to Legitimize Climate-Related Responsibilities and Solutions." *Social Movement Studies* 23 (1): 94–112. https://doi.org/10.1080/14742837.2023.2270919.

Wonneberger, Anke, and Rens Vliegenthart. 2021. "Agenda-Setting Effects of Climate Change Litigation: Interrelations Across Issue Levels, Media, and Politics in the Case of Urgenda Against the Dutch Government." *Environmental Communication* 15 (5): 699–714.

Cases

Ashgar Leghari v. Federation of Pakistan. Case No: W.P. No. 25501/2015.

Australasian Centre for Corporate Responsibility v. Santos Limited NSD858/2021 (Federal Court of Australia).

Duarte Agostinho and Others v. Portugal and 32 Other States (2020) 39371/20.

Commonwealth v. Exxon Mobil Corp., 489 Mass. 724.

Future Generations v. Colombia (STC 4360-2018).

Greenpeace Australia Ltd v. Redbank Power Co. [1994] 86 LGERA 143.

Greenpeace France, Amis de la Terre France, Notre Affaire à Tous v. TotalEnergies SE, TotalEnergies Electricité, Gaz France, Court of Paris (France).

Held v. Montana, No. CDV-2020–307 (1st Dist. Ct. Mont., August 14, 2023).

Juliana v. United States, 947 F.3d 1159.

Massachusetts v. EPA, 549 U.S. 497 (2007).

Sharma and others v. Minister for the Environment (2022). Federal Court of Australia, VID 389, April 22 (Australia).

The State of the Netherlands v. Urgenda Foundation Supreme Court of the Netherlands (December 20, 2019).

Urgenda Foundation v. The Netherlands [2015] HAZA C/09/00456689 (June 24, 2015).

· 6 ·

GREEN LAWFARE AND SCIENCE

Watching their homes in northern Australia threatened by rising sea levels, two Torres Strait Islander elders, Uncle Pabai Pabai and Uncle Paul Kabai, asked the Australian Federal Court to require the Australian Government to reduce Australia's greenhouse gas emissions "consistent with the Best Available Science" and asked whether its greenhouse gas emissions reduction targets are "consistent with the Best Available Science" (capitalizations in original) (*Pabai Pabai v. Commonwealth of Australia*). At the heart of their case was whether the Australian Government had failed to implement measures to reduce Australia's greenhouse gas emissions and, in so doing, failed in their duty of care to protect the islanders, their traditional way of life, and their environment from harm caused by climate change. The plaintiffs provided scientific evidence to support their claims and hearings were held on Boigu, Badu, and Saibai islands (three of 38 inhabited islands between mainland Australia and Papua New Guinea), so the court could see the damage already inflicted on "Australia's first climate change refugees" (Ruben 2023).

The discussion so far has largely observed the influence of science, especially ecology and Earth systems science, on the environmental movement and institutional action on environmental problems. This chapter focuses on the science of detection and attribution being used in climate litigation.

Science has, of course, a long history with the legal system (Feldman 2009). Scientific expertise is called on to provide evidence and to translate scientific information in ways that conform to the logic of the court. Forensic science, in which evidence collected from crime scenes is interpreted for the court, is the obvious example. Science is also used to show causal connections between dangerous substances, such as tobacco and asbestos, and human health and disease. These cases have proven to be powerful outside of court, too. Public opinion, in the United States and elsewhere, turned against major tobacco companies following lawsuits that led to the discovery that the tobacco industry had misled the public about their knowledge of the harm to health caused by smoking and courts directed tobacco companies to cease fraudulent communications. This capacity for scientific findings to be used to attribute harm to industries has provided a pathway for cases to not only uncover information about corporate responsibility for climate change but to do so in a way that affects corporate reputations and their social license to operate (Wentz et al. 2023, 3).

Climate litigation is using the emerging science of detection and attribution to link extreme weather events and other climate-related problems to anthropogenic climate change (Marjanac and Patton 2018, 280). In these instances, the courts are "sites of repeated re-representations of scientific knowledge" uniting law and science in "communicative, persuasive, even argumentative activity" (Jasanoff 2008, 123). News and other media are also involved throughout this communicative or discursive activity that brings science into the courtroom. Before an issue makes it to court, news and other media have been involved in translating science and other knowledges and claims to define the problem, which usually includes the mediatization of protest activity as well, and involves news and other media rendering an issue "visible" and requiring action. Having been identified in policy and legislation, another process of translation articulates the problem in terms that apply to existing laws or, in the absence of law, in ways that call attention to new laws or new interpretations of law (Otto et al. 2022; Vanhala 2018). Once a matter is before the court, a further process of interpretation and re-representation occurs when news and other media report on the issue before the courts. As such, this continual cycle of interpretation and reinterpretation of scientific information binds science, as a body of knowledge and field of practice, to the social forces at play in the mediatization of environmental law.

The prominence of science in environmental and climate matters raises questions about the authority given to science in democratic decision-making, which includes concerns about the "politicization of science" (Gauchat 2012) and the "scientization of politics" (Doremus and Tarlock 2005; Kinchy 2010; Stehr 2022). When social problems are brought before the courts, the legal sphere becomes an arbitrating actor between the spheres associated with mediatized environmental conflict, namely activism, industry, government and media (Hutchins and Lester 2015), and the prominence of science in these matters suggests that science has a particular role in green lawfare. Or, to put it another way, observing the prominence of science in green lawfare can provide insight into the role of science in political decision-making. This chapter treats science as a sphere of action, or field, which describes an area of structured, socially patterned activity, or "practice," that is disciplinarily and professionally defined (Bourdieu 1986). It also recognizes that suggestions that science is a separate and identifiable field are contested, with some arguing science is not a singular monolithic field but better understood as practiced in the "spaces between fields" occupied by "knowledge brokers or expert interventions in formal politics" (Baker 2017, 863). Whether a field or a space between fields, or a discourse practiced by both scientists and non-scientists, scientific actors and discourse can be seen in mediatized environmental conflict, and thus, green lawfare.

This chapter begins by problematizing the apparent simplicity in the phrase "best available science" in the context of the science-policy nexus before focusing on the "best available science" in terms of the emerging field of detection and attribution science in climate litigation that is shaping climate law and the discourses and direction of green lawfare.

The Best Available Science?

When Greta Thunberg turned down the Nordic Council's annual environmental prize in 2019, she posted on Instagram:

> The climate movement does not need any more awards. What we need is for our politicians and the people in power to start listening to the current, best available science. (ABC 2019)

The phrase "best available science" has long appeared in legislation in the United States and elsewhere but gained particular salience with the signing of the Paris Agreement in 2015 (Cook 2018). In its preamble, the signatories to the Paris Agreement recognized "the need for an effective and progressive response to the urgent threat of climate change on the basis of the best available scientific knowledge" and "the best available science" is mentioned twice within the Paris Agreement: firstly, in Article 2, which sets out a long-term temperature goal and, secondly, in Article 4, which establishes the binding commitments by all Parties to pursue domestic measures to achieve their contribution toward reducing greenhouse gas emissions.

In these two articles lies the nexus between science, policy, government, and law. As Michael Gerrard (2015) points out, Article 4 is

> [a] heavily negotiated sentence that, when closely read, seems to call for the virtual end of fossil fuel use in this century unless there are major advances in carbon sequestration or air capture technology. That, in turn, has important legal implications.

A wide range of interlocking scientific uncertainties fuels the political, and therefore legal, implications of the Paris Agreement (Hanekamp and Bergkamp 2016). For instance, Glen Peters (2016, 648) observes the Paris Agreement requires the "best available science" to inform climate policy despite gaps in scientific knowledge and political uncertainty over what are the technically and politically feasible options for reducing emissions. In other words, the best available science can be used to monitor and assess mitigation efforts but offers little direction as to how governments can achieve these goals. As Kate Cook (2018, 389) writes, the Paris Agreement "combines requirements for 'bottom-up' national action on mitigation … with 'top-down' international support and review" including giving climate scientists a central role in calculating the global carbon budget and assessing the collective progress of each signatory to meet their promise. In other words, the "best available science" is being used to not only guide government policy but to hold governments to account. In doing so, the Paris Agreement provides courts around the world with the scientific evidence used to judge the adequacy of a government's emissions reduction policies or the environmental significance of a particular emissions-intensive project (Peel et al. 2020, 185–186). But who determines the "best available science" and how it should be translated into policy action (Ryder et al. 2010)?

Just as "the public interest" and "open justice" are ideals that most experts and lay people intuitively understand but which defy definition, the phrase "best available science" also promises more certainty than it can deliver. The qualifier "best" alludes to the mutability of scientific knowledge and the complex human interactions involved in its production. Even the best available science involves incomplete data or scientific information, which can then be selected or ignored to support a pre-determined decision and reinterpreted by others; not to mention the logic of funding priorities and political sensitivities that inform the pathways of research (Kim et al. 2022). As Donald Worster (1994, 420) writes, science

> is not a single-minded monolithic force marching through time. It is not the pure, disinterested search for knowledge many of its supporters make it out to be … Science has had as many schisms, conflicts, dissensions, and personality contrasts as any human activity. A less protean enterprise could never have accommodated so many minds or described so many of nature's patterns.

Or, as Bernd Hamm (2005, 64–65) more bluntly asserts:

> Those concerned with science as an institution will perceive a complicated network of universities, institutes, and research departments in government and private corporations, and cannot ignore the permanent struggle for competitive advantages, reputation, money, power, and influence among them … [that results in science being] dominated by the perceptions, interests, and worldviews of those who can afford to pay for it.

Determining what is "best" then is not an entirely objective process. The authority and legitimacy of science may be relatively unquestioned by many within the boundaries of the scientific enterprise, but such assumptions are not so steadfast when science engages with the other arenas of social and political life where objective truths encounter various processes of interpretation and other subjectivities. As Doremus and Tarlock (2005) found in conflict over conservation issues, some actors associate the idea of "best available science" with better environmental goals and outcomes, whereas others anticipate the "best available science" will deliver the evidence needed to cut through red tape holding back projects.

Outside its epistemological endeavors and internal battles, "the science" and its advocates can find a world indifferent, and even downright hostile, to scientific perspectives. During environmental conflict, scientific claims must compete with social, political, and economic interests that "contribute to differing outcomes depending on who is speaking, how they are framed, and what the claims are directed towards" (Hutchins and Lester 2015, 344). When observing the enactment of mediatized environmental conflict, we can see how quickly scientific knowledge— "the science"—is separated from those involved in its production, who are "the scientists." Various non-scientific actors draw on scientific discourses with varying levels of accuracy and good faith, to describe the causes and impacts of environmental problems and the responsibilities for redress. In such moments, the apparent certainty of scientific claims is unsettled as various actors "cherry pick" and "bend" the science to suit their argument and legitimize their claims (McGarity and Wagner 2008). Science then remains a source of symbolic power for administrations, while also holding the potential to destabilize bureaucratic capital (Baker 2017). The symbolic power of scientific claims have led some to suggest that our systems and processes of governance, including environmental governance, have become "scientized" (Doremus and Tarlock 2005; Stehr 2022), which has resulted from a process of scientization "granting experts a high level of political authority, and narrowing the regulatory domain to matters that can be adjudicated on the basis of scientific information or 'managed' by environmental experts" (Kinchy 2010, 506).

While scientific decision-making is privileged as more rational than the subjectivities that influence political decision-making (Doremus and Tarlock 2005, 3), the authority granted to the "best available science" carries with it the legacies of those with the "capacity to exploit discretion, facility to organize protection, authority to speak, ability to mobilize defiance and capacity of avoidance" (Stehr 2022, 64–65). In other words, the authority of science is constituted in the capacity to control not only the production of knowledge, but the visibility of that production and its communication. Such legacies are formed by silencing the contribution of other knowledge systems, such as local, traditional, or First Nation knowledges that reflect the complex interweaving of social, economic, and political elements that support human society (Black 2011). Such legacies can be found in environmental conflict when local actors use scientific claims as a proxy for powerful political-economic interests, which are overwhelmingly pro-technology and pro-development (Hamm 2005; Lester 2019). While we might consider that it is not science, per se, that does the damage but rather the misuse of science by those with the power to finance it, it can also be argued that the development of Western science since the early Enlightenment has been so deeply aligned with powerful economic interests that it is difficult to separate the products of scientific research from its powerful masters (Foxwell-Norton 2018).

To summarize, scientific knowledge is a form of knowledge produced through a network of institutions, including universities, that—like all fields of human endeavor—are structured by hierarchies and fiefdoms and the struggle for power, position and relevance. Remaining cognizant of how such struggles contribute to the mutability of scientific knowledge is not to undermine trust in science or to deny the benefits of certain advancements and technologies. Rather, such awareness serves to challenge the illusion of absolute certainty in phrases like the "best available science" so that we can better understand the sources, values, worldviews, and discourses at play in conflicting accounts about science, the use of science in decision-making, and the evaluation of decisions, especially in the courtroom.

Science in the Courtroom

As noted earlier, science is not uncommon in legal settings. However, legal actors are often ill-equipped to evaluate the relevant scientific literature or to engage with scientists as witnesses and scientists, in turn, are similarly unfamiliar with the legal realm (Wentz et al. 2023, 2). In this space, between the use of science as an instrument and the actors using the instrument, falls the role of science communication, which has been called a science in itself (Jamieson et al. 2017). Indeed, the "science of science communication" (Kahan 2015) has evolved from treating science communication as a one-way delivery of scientific fact from experts to the scientifically illiterate to involving multiway dialogues that encompass risk, ethics, values, and the consideration of the societal consequences, including legal implications, of the scientific enterprise (Akin 2017). Calling on decision-makers to draw on the "best available science" in the courtroom, then, requires a dialogic encounter between those from formal institutions of science as well as those engaging at the peripheries of science, such as actors from NGOs using scientific methods to monitor the causes and effects of environmental issues, and the testimonies of Indigenous peoples. As Lieve Gies (2008, 139) suggests, the challenge for the courtroom is establishing "how law can still operate as law, that is as something we recognize as distinctly legal, while also taking its place in a rich cultural tapestry where its symbols readily spill over into many different spheres." Similarly, how do the dialogic engagement with science in the court reconcile competing scientific claims? Examining the politicization inherent to scientific processes, Doremus and Tarlock (2005) suggest that courts should require those called to present scientific information to also explain the processes that informed their research and choices—in other words, the subjectivities that shape their judgments and decisions. Indeed, calling "the best available science" into the courtroom or other arenas of arbitration gives a particular set of actors a degree of symbolic power and legitimacy but, in such an antagonistic arena, their authority and legitimacy can be challenged. In other words, Thunberg can echo the Paris Agreement by calling for the best available science to inform policy, and the Paris Agreement can be evoked in legal claims, but the legal process itself diminishes the symbolic power of such claims by exposing the uncertainty inherent in science including conflicts over the interpretation of data (Angelo 2008; see also Jasanoff 1992). Unsurprisingly, some scientists are skeptical about translating science for a process that seems "purposefully designed to avoid getting at the truth" (Diamond and Lempert 2018, 54). As one scientist described the experience of being an expert witness:

> Science is about truth. The legal system is about spinning, distorting or suppressing the truth in order to win. The ethos of the two fields is fundamentally different. Even judges are biased and not objective. For these reasons, participation in the legal system is very frustrating for a scientist. (Diamond and Lempert 2018, 42)

Such frustrations were summed up by James Hansen, a climate scientist who has advised or served as an expert witness in dozens of climate lawsuits since 2005. As an expert witness in the case of *Juliana v. United States*, Hansen said after months spent preparing a report on climate change, his work was "buried in court proceedings and hardly considered by the judges" (Schiermeier 2021). As Sheila Jasanoff points out, critics of the legal system frequently assume that

> representation within the sciences is neutral, impartial, and objective; by contrast, legal representation is seen as deviant ("junk science"), because it incorporates such distorting factors as the interests of parties, their experts, and their legal counsel. (Jasanoff 2008, 127)

In these statements we can see the authority of scientific claims and speakers jostling for relevance and authority in a process that seeks not so much "a dispassionate truth" but a fair and just outcome within a wider societal context (Breyer 1998, 4; also, Otto et al. 2022).

Having been translated for the courts, "the science" is translated again in the reporting and commentary by news and other media where it often comes under renewed attack (Jasanoff 2008). In moments when scientific claims are used and disputed by all sides in the conflict, or otherwise challenged, we can observe how the uncertainty inherent to the scientific method can become part of the rhetorical weaponry of all actors (Maeseele 2009) and such contests are framed in media as battles that position activists as heroically pitted against industry that use science to defend their activities (Latour 1987, 44;

Selmi 2022) or, alternatively, between those with "sound scientific expertise" and the otherwise "anti-scientific public" (Stirling 2008, 95).

In summary, the challenge for those observing the communication of science during mediatized environmental conflict is to balance the acknowledgment of scientific knowledge as a credible source of authoritative information while remaining cognizant of the individual subjectivities and institutional structures that inform, define and assert these claims. From this deliberately generalized discussion of the role of science in the legal context, which focused on the inherent instability of scientific claims, we can now turn our attention to the rise of detection and attribution science in climate litigation.

Detection and Attribution Science

We have been detecting greenhouse gases for a long time, certainly as far back as the 1950s with Charles Keeling's continuous measurements at Hawaii's Mauna Loa volcano (for a concise timeline, see Heede 2022). Climate science, which draws on long-term weather records, climate models, numerical simulations, and powerful computer modeling, continues to find the causal links between human activity and climate change and these findings inform the targets in the Paris Agreement (Stuart-Smith et al. 2022). Increasingly, climate science is detecting sources of emissions and finding causal links between greenhouse gas emissions and climate events including heatwaves, storms, droughts, and long-term climate shifts that can be attributed to certain industries and other human activities (Osaka et al. 2020; Provant and Carey 2022; Stuart-Smith et al. 2021). Consequently, climate science is playing an increasingly central role in the politics of action on climate change, which includes legal action to hold governments and corporations to account for failing to mitigate greenhouse gas emissions (Osaka et al. 2020). Climate change litigation translates the information behind the scientific consensus on climate change into legal principles and political action (Peel and Orofsky 2017). In terms of green lawfare, we are seeing the rise in attribution science being used both inside and outside the courts to connect extreme weather events to human-induced climate change (Otto et al. 2022).

Climate litigation draws on three subsets of climate science that *detect* greenhouse gas emissions and their sources, *calculate* carbon budgets as part of mitigation efforts, and *attribute* greenhouse gas emissions to specific extreme weather events, such as floods and drought (Fermeglia 2020). As discussed in the previous chapter, the first subset has proven useful for identifying individual projects as sources of greenhouse gas emissions, such as in the early *Massachusetts* and *Redbank* cases, and the calculation of carbon budgets informs arguments that governments are not reducing national emissions, such as in the case of *Urgenda*. While attributing climate change to specific events, which is the third subset, has proven more difficult, recent developments in this area of climate science have resulted in attribution becoming one of the "hotter" areas of environmental law (Burger et al. 2020) and the "major missing link" in climate litigation (Suzuki and Khan 2021).

A Short History of Detection and Attribution Science

The earliest attempt by climate scientists to quantify how human-caused climate change increased the risk of extreme weather events dates to a study (Stott et al. 2004) of the 2003 European heatwave which, even then, was seen as a potential pathway for lawsuits against major emissions producers (Khamsi 2004). Around the same time, Myles Allen (2003) was writing about the problem of attributing specific weather events to the external drivers of climate change or, as he put it simply, "who to sue when the house price falls." A decade later, Richard Heede's work on identifying the 'Carbon Majors' (2014) identified 90 companies responsible for most of all carbon emissions produced by industry between 1880 and 2010. Heede's data was later updated (Ekwurzel et al. 2017) to describe the 20 fossil fuel companies directly linked to more than one-third of modern-era greenhouse gas emissions. The Paris Agreement, which was based on the climate science contained in the Fifth Assessment Report (AR5), initially described the science of attribution as "promising, but uncertain" (Berwyn 2021), but the IPCC's Sixth Assessment Report was less equivocal, stating that "human influence has likely increased the chance of compound extreme events since the 1950s" (IPCC 2023, 5). The work undertaken by Heede and others to identify the major greenhouse gas emitters, which informed the Paris Agreement, is now providing litigants the evidence needed to not only establish the causal relationships between the emission of greenhouse gases and extreme weather events but also to quantifiably connect emissions with the losses suffered by plaintiffs (Otto et al. 2022, 736). Of course, industry is watching these developments closely, especially the insurance industry which has long been on the front foot with climate modeling, or what the industry calls "catastrophe modeling." Heede's (2013) study determining how the mergers and acquisitions and other activities of 90 companies worldwide were responsible for emitting nearly two-thirds of the world's greenhouse gases particularly struck a chord with the industry quantifying the cost of catastrophe. For instance, in 2014, a transnational insurance workshop about the "new normal" warned if individual companies can be held responsible for climate change, "investors and insurers might want to brace themselves for massive payouts" (Reynolds 2019).

Communicating the Science of Attribution

One of the challenges for early attribution scientists, such as Heede and Stott, was the lag time between extreme weather events and the release of scientific research linking the disasters to climate change, which meant news and other media reporting of extreme weather rarely made the connection between extreme weather events and climate change. The challenge was how to make the connection with the full weight of empirical research.

Various efforts have been made to bridge the gap between scientific knowledge and public understanding of the links between extreme weather and climate change, such as Climate Central, an NGO established by scientists and journalists in 2008 to deliver localized climate information tailored for meteorologists, journalists, policymakers, and citizens. It aims to connect climate change to local events, including providing images, data visualization and local stories. In 2014, two climate scientists, Friedrieke Otto and Myles Allen, met with Climate Central's Heidi Cullen to discuss how to release scientific findings immediately after events (Mathiesen 2021). From that meeting the World Weather Attribution (WWA) service was established to provide public information attributing extreme weather events within days, rather than months, of the disaster, which is then followed by peer-reviewed studies translated into brief scientific summaries for policymakers and various agencies, and media releases (van Oldenborgh et al. 2021).

By preparing their data and publishing their findings in formats suited to news and other media and decision-makers, the WWA not only show a keen understanding of communication networks used by decision-makers, but their work also epitomizes the mediatization of science for the purposes of informing public understanding of climate policy, law and legal action. For Otto and her colleagues at WWA, attribution science is as much about the science of communication as it is about climate science. For instance, when writing about the importance of increasing public recognition of the link between greenhouse gas and climate change, they observe that framing climate change in terms of human rights and justice might be understood in policy and activist circles, but "has not yet reached the wider societal narrative in the same way that the existence of climate change and the need to cut emissions have" (Otto et al. 2022, 737). This observation raises many questions about the friction present in news and other media that is slowing down the narratives of human rights, social justice and, indeed, the attribution of blame, to wider audiences. Or, to put it another way, the gap between effective—even adequate—science communication and public understanding of science.

In an obituary for Geert van Oldenborgh, Otto (2021) describes the characteristics that apply broadly to successful science communicators. She recalls that van Oldenborgh was a scientist clearly aware of the power of media, who first created a website called Climate Explorer to make climate models and data available to anyone, before later developing the WWA service. Otto writes that van Oldenborgh "had the scientific experience, statistical skill and absolute drive to get the numbers right; I had the words to explain what the numbers say in simple terms," adding that van Oldenborgh's generosity ensured he was highly influential in turning a controversial idea into a field of science. Otto is herself a savvy media operator. In 2021, she was named one of *Time* magazine's 100 most influential people for her work and she has been likened to Dr Randall Mindy, Leonardo DiCaprio's character in the film *Don't Look Up* (Laville 2022). *Politico's* Karl Mathiesen (2021) describes Otto's work as shifting the conversation in many newsrooms from being cautious about linking any single event to climate change.

Other organizations are bridging the gap between scientists and decision-makers. For example, Uganda's African Centre for Rapid Evidence Synthesis (ACRES) at Makerere University is translating climate science to deliver timely and robust findings about local issues and encouraging connections between climate researchers and decision-makers (Nature 2022). According to its website, Carbon Brief has been building a map since 2017 "to track how the evidence on this fast-moving topic is stacking up" and claims to have mapped "every extreme-weather attribution study published to date." First developed by a visual data journalist, Rosamund Pearce in 2017 and updated by others since, the map has mostly drawn data from the American Meteorological Society and only uses studies published in English. The limitations of the map highlight how much of this work is being done by a handful of scientists who, like Otto and her colleagues at WWA, are mostly working voluntarily to perform a task of global proportions. That the map only includes studies written in English also indicates the limitations and northern orientation of this work in both scientific circles and more widely.

As a result of the communication work associated with attribution science, however, climate reporting is shifting from describing the tragedies of natural disasters as inexplicably apocalyptic to connecting "the dots" between the Carbon Majors and a heating planet. While climate scientists and websites ensure attribution science is being used as "a vehicle of interpretation" (Omoniyi 2022), local journalists play an important role in ensuring climate stories not only speak directly to their own audiences but in ways that foster debate and civic engagement about what is needed to change trajectories (Selva 2001). When scientific knowledge and claims, such as the attribution science informing the Paris Agreement, are drawn into debates about government and corporate responsibility we can also see the symbolic power of science transformed into material and political influence through the communicative process of green lawfare.

Attribution Science in the Courts

A few landmark cases are already showing the crucial role of attribution science in linking human activities to the damage caused by increasingly severe extreme weather events. The following cases, from Peru, Puerto Rico and the Netherlands provide a small sample of how attribution science is being used in courts worldwide.

Lliuya v. RWE

In 2015 Peruvian farmer, Saúl Luciano Lliuya, took legal action alleging RWE, Germany's largest electricity company, had contributed to the global heating that is melting the Palcaraju glacier and argued that RWE should bear some responsibility for the cost of mitigation efforts aimed at stopping a glacial lake from flooding the town of Huaraz (*Luciano Lliuya v. RWE*). Lliuya argued that as RWE, as a Carbon Major, was found to have contributed 0.47 percent of the total global industrial emissions of carbon and methane since the start of the Industrial Revolution, the company should contribute 0.47 percent of the expenses associated with flood mitigation efforts to protect the Huaraz community, which is costed at around US$20,000. While this sum may seem a trivial amount for one of the world's largest corporations, it carries substantial significance for a small community grappling with the costs of mitigation.

Lliuya could have chosen any company on Heede's list of Carbon Majors, but RWE was selected because the corporation is headquartered in Germany, a country with a court system that was likely to hear Lliuya's claim. The German NGO Germanwatch The first court rejected the claim, finding that a causal link between the greenhouse gas emissions of a single emitter and specific climate change impacts could not be proven. In 2017, on appeal, Germany's Higher Regional Court accepted the case had merit and could proceed to the evidence-gathering phase, marking the case as the first instance in which a European court declared a company's contribution to global warming could be attributed to the harms experienced by a specific community. While *Lliuya v. RWE* aims—it remains on appeal at the time of writing—to make a company pay for mitigation costs, the use of attribution science to argue for compensation for damages is also underway.

Municipalities of Puerto Rico v. Exxon Mobil Corp

In 2022, 16 Puerto Rican municipalities filed a suit in a Puerto Rican court arguing that several fossil fuel companies are liable for losses resulting from storms that struck North and Central America in 2017. In particular, *Municipalities of Puerto Rico v. Exxon Mobil Corp* focuses on the damage caused by Hurricane Maria that destroyed a third of Puerto Rico's homes and crippled the island's aging power grid and already struggling economy. The case is notable for being the first climate case to include the United States Racketeer Influenced and Corrupt Organizations Act (RICO), which allows plaintiffs to bring various disparate claims together as evidence of collusion and conspiracy. Such a move is seen as part of a broader climate litigation movement seeking damages from fossil fuel companies for damage done to cities and other communities (Silverman-Roati and Tigre 2022). Finally, the case is also notable for building on other cases, such as *Greenpeace v. TotalEnergies* and *ACCR v. Santos*, discussed in the previous chapter, in its allegations that the company's net-zero claims amount to misleading consumers and investors (Silverman-Roati and Tigre 2022).

Milieudefensie v. Royal Dutch Shell

Building from *Urgenda*, the Dutch environmental group Milieudefensie, as well as Friends of the Earth Netherlands and more than 17,000 Dutch citizens, filed a case in 2021 alleging Shell's contributions to climate change violated its duty of care under Dutch law. The plaintiffs sought a ruling from the court that Shell, one of the world's largest oil and gas companies, must reduce its CO_2 emissions in line with the Paris Agreement. In 2021, the court ruled in their favor, and ordered Shell to reduce its carbon emissions, including the emissions produced by the company and the emissions caused by Shell customers using its products. While the ruling in the *Urgenda* case found the Dutch Government's inadequate action on climate change violated a duty of care to its citizens, *Milieudefensie* is notable for being the first time a court found a private company to be violating its duty of care and human rights obligations by not taking enough action to curb contributions to climate change.

Following the win, Milieudefensie wrote to other large entities incorporated in the Netherlands, including BP, ExxonMobil and Unilever, advising that they too would be targeted by legal action. Two years after the ruling, Shell had moved its headquarters from the Netherlands to London, appealed the Dutch court's decision and announced that while the world still needed fossil fuel for energy, it would focus on carbon capture and storage. In turn, Milieudefensie launched a #BeatShell campaign that included calling on Shell's new chief executive to take responsibility for Shell's role in the climate crisis. The success of these cases is not necessarily in compensation but in the groundswell of cases with substantive and procedural decisions that are changing the wider narrative on corporate and government responsibility for climate change (Sato et al. 2023).

These three cases illustrate how attribution science is being used to not only inform policy and global governance initiatives, but to also litigate for losses and damages. While the use of attribution science in such matters is controversial, pressure from less materially affluent nations has led to calls for greater global commitments to "measuring, monitoring and assessing who is responsible and who will pay for losses and damages stemming from the effects of climate change" (Boyd et al. 2021, 1365). Increasingly, scientific attribution is accepted in courts around the world, leading to defense teams shifting from challenging the scientific evidence of climate change to what it means in terms of legal responsibilities (Buizza et al. 2021; Sato et al. 2023). A key challenge in this process is providing information in a form that is accessible to non-scientists, such as judges, in ways that not only serve to describe the catastrophe, but serve as "a catalyst for crucial mitigation and adaptation measures" (Spalding and Hales 2021, 6). A further challenge is ensuring that public understanding of climate change extends from accepting the scientific consensus on anthropogenic climate change to understanding that certain industries and activities can be held responsible for damage to homes, cultures and livelihoods.

The Media Logics of Attribution Science

Headlines, such as "What if polluters footed the climate bill?" (Gerretsen 2022), signal the salience of attribution science to journalists. After all, identifying a problem and its causes in ways that attribute blame is a well-established journalistic practice (Altheide 1997; Entman 1993) making attribution science a relatively good fit for media logics. Attribution science is also new, and therefore providing novel findings that make up the "new" of news. Despite two decades since Stott and company (2004) published their study of the 2003 European heatwave, scientists and journalists continue to spruik attribution study findings as "firsts", such as this lead from *The Conversation*: "Glaciers around the world are melting—and for the first time, we can now directly attribute annual ice loss to climate change" (Vargo 2020).

Attribution science is variously described by journalists as "connecting the dots" and "finding fingerprints." Metaphors alluding to forensic science abound especially analogies to the science that linked lung cancer to tobacco smoking. Writing about Saúl Luciano Lliuya's case in Peru, two journalists (Provant and Carey 2022) likened attribution science to doing an autopsy on a glacier. The translation of attribution science into news remains a rich field for inquiry. As James Painter and colleagues (2020) observe, despite a mountain of climate media research examining how media covers extreme weather events, those linking climate change to specific weather events, are sparse. As noted earlier, what is the friction that stops news and other media making these connections? How attribution science is being translated inside and outside of the courts, including by news and other media, is thus a rich ground for inquiry.

Critics of attribution science can be separated into two camps. The first are those arguing that climate change science is too complex, with too many variables, for any determination to be made. These challenges to attribution science are predictably coming from the usual pool of skeptics and what Mann (2021) calls "the inactivists." For instance, lawyers for the RWE, the energy company being sued by Saúl Luciano Lliuya, have argued that the link between greenhouse gas emissions and climate impacts is too complex for any single entity to be held responsible (Kaplan 2022). Unsurprisingly, the global fossil fuel lobby has launched a counter-narrative against attribution science by attempting to discredit scientists for a lack of objectivity. Again, the mediated networks involved in the circulation of such efforts to create doubt about attribution science remains fertile ground.

Those in the second "climate justice" camp, such as Lahsen and Ribot (2022), argue that the assumption that attribution can be followed by legal responsibility for damages overshadows the deeper, social causes of both the pollution and climate vulnerability. Such statements echo earlier criticisms of legal action against Union Carbide after Bhopal that focused on the corporation and enabled the Indian government to avoid accountability for the poor environmental or and industrial regulations that contributed to the disaster. Similarly, Lennart Olsson and colleagues (2022) challenge the use of attribution science in courts by arguing that its methodological choices can render findings "highly value-laden and political" and ethically problematic, especially when applied to loss and damage claims. In a list of quandaries that includes the question of who defines an "extreme event" and the problems associated with focusing on extreme events at the expense of the less spectacular, slower violence of myriad local problems, the authors also question the injustice of having gaps in the data that can render some problems invisible simply because there is no data to display. This second group of critics is largely constructive in their attempts to ensure climate justice is served, as intended, by attributive science. Then again, to criticize one area of action for not addressing an entire problem is to ignore that the wicked problem of climate change demands multiple courses of action from many actors (Lazarus 2009). While such criticisms may at times be constructive, such nuanced arguments also risk compounding confusion and playing into the hands of denialists in the same way as the consensus on the causes of anthropogenic climate change remained muddied for so long. As Norman Mailer observed, news is forever "munching nuances like peanuts" (in Ricketson 2004, 4), so attempts to downplay attribution may get lost in the wash of the 24/7 news cycle. Perhaps it is not only the spectacle of blame that attracts news and other media to use attribution science to join the dots. After years of the dirty politics of inaction on climate change, including the rhetorical absurdities of denial, it is not surprising that so many have embraced the ostensible certainty of attribution science.

Conclusion: Green Lawfare and the Communication of Science

Detection and attribution science have been presented here as distinct fields of study, but also as strategic partners in climate communication and climate litigation. These are, of course, just one area of science informing political and legal decision-making. As noted at the beginning of this chapter, a wide range of science is called on by the courts and the interactions between science, policy, government and law are not limited to action on climate change. Indeed, the prominence of science in many environmental issues suggests that science has a particular role in green lawfare that merits further attention. At the heart of this chapter is the exploration of how information and ideas flow from the arenas of scientific research, including universities and other scientific institutions, into the spaces occupied by law, policy and media, which is to say, into green lawfare. While other chapters have explored a range of contagious ideas informing the development of environmental law, this chapter focused on science, particularly attribution science, as a dynamic field of activity that is ensuring climate law remains "hot." Attribution science is poised to continue playing a crucial role in the formation of environmental and climate law by providing the scientific evidence to hold governments and corporations, especially the Carbon Majors, to account. Holding the powerful to account has, of course, long been a powerful narrative in environmental campaigns. In the discussion here, we have glimpsed at how powerful actors have countered accusations of responsibility with appeals and countersuits, but such responses barely describe the considerable efforts undertaken to control those calling for a more ecocentric and socially just world. As such, the next and penultimate chapter looks at the logics and strategies of green lawfare being used by powerful interests with deep pockets who also understand the material, symbolic and political power of legal ideas and legal action and the role of media and communication in contemporary networks of power and influence.

References

ABC News. 2019. "Greta Thunberg Declines Environmental Award Calling for Fewer Awards and More Action." *ABC News*, October 30. https://www.abc.net.au/news/2019-10-30/greta-thunberg-declines-environmental-award/11654092 (Accessed May 5, 2023).

Akin, Heather. 2017. "Overview of the Science of Science Communication." In *The Oxford Handbook of the Science of Science Communication*, edited by Kathleen Hall Jamieson, Dan M. Kahan, and Dietram A. Scheufele, 1:24–33. Oxford: Oxford University Press.

Allen, Myles. 2023. "Liability for Climate Change." *Nature* 421: 891–892.

Altheide, David L. 1997. "'The News Media, the Problem Frame, and the Production of Fear.'" *The Sociological Quarterly* 38 (4): 647–668.

Angelo, Mary Jane. 2008. "Harnessing the Power of Science in Environmental Law: Why We Should, Why We Don't, and How We Can." *Texas Law Review* 86 (7): 1527–1574.

Baker, Zeke. 2017. "Climate State: Science-State Struggles and the Formation of Climate Science in the US from the 1930s to 1960s." *Social Studies of Science* 47 (6): 861–887.

Berwyn, Bob. 2021. "Feature: How Climate Attribution Science Went Mainstream, and What It Means." *Society of Environmental Journalists* (blog). October 6. https://www.sej.org/publications/features/how-climate-attribution-science-went-mainstream-and-what-it-means (Accessed August 22, 2023).

Black, C. F. 2011. *The Land Is the Source of the Law: A Dialogic Encounter with Indigenous Jurisprudence*. New York: Routledge.

Boyd, Emily, Brian C. Chaffin, Kelly Dorkenoo, Guy Jackson, Luke Harrington, Alicia N'Guetta, Emma L. Johansson, et al. 2021. "Loss and Damage from Climate Change: A New Climate Justice Agenda." *One Earth* 4 (10): 1365–1370.

Breyer, Stephen. 1998. "The Interdependence of Science and Law." *Science* 280 (5363): 537–538.

Buizza, Roberto, Christine Bakker, Ivano Alogna, Jean-Pierre Gauci, Alina Holzhausen, and Riccardo Luporini. 2021. "The Role of Science in Climate Change Litigation." British Institute of International and Comparative Law (blog). December 6. https://www.biicl.org/blog/29/the-role-of-science-in-climate-change-litigation (Accessed August 22, 2023).

Burger, Michael, Jessica Wentz, and Radley Horton. 2020. "The Law and Science of Climate Change Attribution." *Columbia Journal of Environmental Law* 45: 57–240.

Cook, Kate. 2018. "Judging 'Best Available Science': Emerging Issues and the Role of Experts." *Journal of International Dispute Settlement* 9 (3): 388–400.

Diamond, Shari Seidman, and Richard O. Lempert. 2018. "When Law Calls, Does Science Answer? A Survey of Distinguished Scientists & Engineers." *Daedalus* 147 (4): 41–60.

Doremus, Holly, and A. Dan Tarlock. 2005. "Science, Judgment, and Controversy in Natural Resource Regulation." *Public Land and Resources Law Review* 26: 1–37.

Ekwurzel, B., J. Boneham, M. W. Dalton, R. Heede, R. J. Mera, M. R. Allen, and P. C. Frumhoff. 2017. "The Rise in Global Atmospheric CO_2, Surface Temperature, and Sea Level from Emissions Traced to Major Carbon Producers." *Climatic Change* 144 (4): 579–590.

Entman, Robert M. 1993. "Framing: Toward Clarification of a Fractured Paradigm." *Journal of Communication* 43 (4): 51–58.

Feldman, Robin. 2009. *The Role of Science in Law*. Oxford University Press. https://doi.org/10.1093/acprof:oso/9780195368581.001.0001.

Fermeglia, Matteo. 2020. "Climate Science Before the Courts: Turning the Tide in Climate Change Litigation." In *Ecological Integrity in Science and Law*, edited by Laura Westra, Klaus Bosselmann, and Matteo Fermeglia, 23–36. Cham: Springer International.

Foxwell-Norton, Kerrie. 2018. *Environmental Communication and Critical Coastal Policy Communities, Culture and Nature*. Abingdon and New York: Routledge.

Gauchat, Gordon. 2012. "Politicization of Science in the Public Sphere: A Study of Public Trust in the United States, 1974 to 2010." *American Sociological Review* 77 (2): 167–187.

Gerrard, Michael B. 2015. "Legal Implications of the Paris Agreement for Fossil Fuels." *Climate Law* (blog). December 19 https://blogs.law.columbia.edu/climatechange/2015/12/19/legal-implications-of-the-paris-agreement-for-fossil-fuels/

Gerretsen, Isabelle. 2022. "What If Polluters Footed the Climate Bill?" *BBC Future*, October 27. https://www.bbc.com/future/article/20221026-what-if-polluters-paid-for-climate-change-loss-and-damage

Gies, Lieve. 2008. *Law and the Media: The Future of an Uneasy Relationship*. Abingdon and New York: Routledge-Cavendish.

Hamm, Bernd. 2005. "Science and Truth as Cultural Imperialism." In *Essays on the Political Economy of Cultural Domination*, edited by Bernd Hamm and Russell Smandych, 60–75. Toronto: University of Toronto Press.

Hanekamp, Jaap C., and Lucas Bergkamp. 2016. "The 'Best Available Science' and the Paris Agreement on Climate Change." *European Journal of Risk Regulation* 7 (1): 42–48.

Heede, Richard. 2014. "Tracing Anthropogenic Carbon Dioxide and Methane Emissions to Fossil Fuel and Cement Producers, 1854–2010." *Climatic Change* 122 (1–2): 229–241.

———. 2022. "The Evolution of Corporate Accountability for Climate Change." In *Litigating the Climate Emergency*, edited by César Rodríguez-Garavito, 239–254. Cambridge: Cambridge University Press.

Howarth, Candice, and Alison Anderson. 2019. "Increasing Local Salience of Climate Change: The Un-Tapped Impact of the Media-Science Interface." *Environmental Communication* 13 (6): 713–722.

Hutchins, Brett, and Libby Lester. 2015. "Theorizing the Enactment of Mediatized Environmental Conflict." *International Communication Gazette* 77 (4): 337–358.

IPCC. 2023. "Summary for Policymakers" In *Climate Change 2023: Synthesis Report. Contribution of Working Groups I, II and III to the Sixth Assessment Report of the Intergovernmental Panel on Climate Change*, edited by H. Lee and J. Romero. Geneva, Switzerland. https://www.ipcc.ch/report/ar6/syr/downloads/report/IPCC_AR6_SYR_SPM.pdf

Jamieson, Kathleen Hall, Dan M. Kahan, and Dietram A. Scheufele, eds. 2017. *The Oxford Handbook of the Science of Science Communication*. Vol. 1. Oxford: Oxford University Press.

Jasanoff, Sheila. 1992. "What Judges Should Know About the Sociology of Science." *Jurimetrics Journal* 345: 345–360.

Jasanoff, Sheila. 2008. "Representation and Re-Presentation in Litigation Science." *Environmental Health Perspectives* 116 (1): 123–129.

Kahan, Dan M. 2015. "What Is the 'Science of Science Communication'?" *Journal of Science Communication* 14 (3): 1–12.

Kaplan, Sarah. 2022. "Climate Lawsuit over Melting Peru Glacier Could Set Global Precedent." *Washington Post*, August 28. https://www.washingtonpost.com/climate-environment/interactive/2022/peru-climate-lawsuit-melting-glacier/ (Accessed August 22, 2023).

Khamsi, Roxanne. 2004. "Human Activity Implicated in Europe's 2003 Heat Wave." *Nature* (blog) December. https://www.nature.com/news/2004/041129/full/news041129-6.html (Accessed August 21, 2023).

Kim, Rakhyun E., Catherine Blanchard, and Louis J. Kotzé. 2022. "Law, Systems, and Planet Earth: Editorial." *Earth System Governance* 11 (January): https://doi.org/10.1016/j.esg.2021.100127

Kinchy, Abby J. 2010. "Anti-Genetic Engineering Activism and Scientized Politics in the Case of 'Contaminated' Mexican Maize." *Agriculture and Human Values* 27 (4): 505–517.

Lahsen, Myanna, and Jesse Ribot. 2022. "Politics of Attributing Extreme Events and Disasters to Climate Change." *WIREs Climate Change* 13 (1). https://doi.org/10.1002/wcc.750open_in_new

Latour, Bruno. 1987. *Science in Action: How to Follow Scientists and Engineers through Society.* Cambridge: Harvard University Press.

Lazarus, Richard. 2009. "Super Wicked Problems and Climate Change: Restraining the Present to Liberate the Future." *Cornell Law Review* 94 (5): 1153–1234.

Maeseele, Pieter. 2009. "NGOs and GMOs: A Case Study in *Alternative* Science Communication." *Javnost—The Public* 16 (4): 55–72.

Mann, Michael E. 2021. *The New Climate War: The Fight to Take Back Our Planet.* London: Scribe.

Marjanac, Sophie, and Lindene Patton. 2018. "Extreme Weather Event Attribution Science and Climate Change Litigation: An Essential Step in the Causal Chain?" *Journal of Energy & Natural Resources Law* 36 (3): 265–298.

Mathiesen, Karl. 2021. "The Climatologist Who Put Climate Science 'on the Offensive.'" *Politico*, August 9. https://www.politico.eu/article/friederike-otto-world-weather-attribution-climate-science-heat-waves-floods-droughts/ (Accessed August 22, 2023).

McGarity, Thomas, and Wendy Wagner. 2008. *Bending Science: How Special Interests Corrupt Public Health Research.* Cambridge, MA: Harvard University Press.

Nature. 2022. "Wanted: Better Systems for Turning Evidence into Action." *Nature* 603: 7–8.

Oldenborgh, Geert Jan van, Karin van der Wiel, Sarah Kew, Sjoukje Philip, Friederike Otto, Robert Vautard, Andrew King, et al. 2021. "Pathways and Pitfalls in Extreme Event Attribution." Climatic Change 166 (1–2): 13. https://doi.org/10.1007/s10584-021-03071-7.

Olsson, Lennart, Henrik Thorén, David Harnesk, and Johannes Persson. 2022. "Ethics of Probabilistic Extreme Event Attribution in Climate Change Science: A Critique." *Earth's Future* 10 (3). https://doi.org/10.1029/2021EF002258

Osaka, Shannon, and Rob Bellamy. 2020a. "Natural Variability or Climate Change? Stakeholder and Citizen Perceptions of Extreme Event Attribution." *Global Environmental Change* 62 (May): https://doi.org/10.1016/j.gloenvcha.2020.102070

———. 2020b. "Weather in the Anthropocene: Extreme Event Attribution and a Modelled Nature–Culture Divide." *Transactions of the Institute of British Geographers* 45 (4): 906–920.

Osaka, Shannon, James Painter, Peter Walton, and Abby Halperin. 2020. "Media Representation of Extreme Event Attribution: A Case Study of the 2011–2017 California Drought." *Weather, Climate, and Society* 12 (4): 847–862.

Otto, Friederike E. L. 2021. "Geert Jan van Oldenborgh 1961–2021." *Nature Climate Change* 11 (12): 1017–1017.

Otto, Friederike E. L., Petra Minnerop, Emmanuel Raju, Luke J. Harrington, Rupert F. Stuart-Smith, Emily Boyd, Rachel James, Richard Jones, and Kristian C. Lauta. 2022. "Causality and the Fate of Climate Litigation: The Role of the Social Superstructure Narrative." *Global Policy* 13 (5): 736–750.

Painter, James, Shannon Osaka, Joshua Ettinger, and Peter Walton. 2020. "Blaming Climate Change? How Indian Mainstream Media Covered Two Extreme Weather Events in 2015." *Global Environmental Change* 63 (July): https://doi.org/10.1016/j.gloenvcha.2020.102119

Peel, Jacqueline, and Hari M. Osofsky. 2017. *Climate Change Litigation: Regulatory Pathways to Cleaner Energy*. Cambridge: Cambridge University Press.

Peel, Jacqueline, Hari M. Osofsky, and Anita Foerster. 2020. "'Next Generation' Climate Change Litigation in Australia." In *Climate Change Litigation in the Asia Pacific*, edited by Jolene Lin and Douglas A. Kysar, 175–206. Cambridge: Cambridge University Press.

Peters, Glen P. 2016. "The 'best Available Science' to Inform 1.5 °C Policy Choices." *Nature Climate Change* 6 (7): 646–649.

Provant, Zachary, and Mark Carey. 2022. "Who Is Killing the Glaciers? From Glacier Funerals to Glacier Autopsies." *Edge Effects* (blog). November 3. https://edgeeffects.net/glacier-funerals/

Reynolds, Dan. 2019. "Attribution Science Is Empowering Lawyers to Turn Climate Change into the Next Asbestos Liability." Risk & Insurance (blog). October 30. https://riskandinsurance.com/attribution-science/ (Accessed August 21, 2022).

Roston, Eric. 2021. "Climate Scientists Created a SWAT Team for Weather Disasters." *Bloomberg*, October 7, 2021. https://www.bloomberg.com/news/features/2021-10-07/how-climate-scientists-do-extreme-weather-attribution (Accessed August 22, 2023).

Ruben, Emma. 2023. "Hearings for Landmark Australian Climate Case Begin …" *National Indigenous Times*, June 20, 2023. https://nit.com.au/06-06-2023/6251/hearings-for-australian-climate-case-begin-in-zenadth-kes (Accessed August 22, 2023).

Ryder, Darren S., Moya Tomlinson, Ben Gawne, and Gene E. Likens. 2010. "Defining and Using 'Best Available Science': A Policy Conundrum for the Management of Aquatic Ecosystems." *Marine and Freshwater Research* 61 (7): 821–828.

Sato M, Gostlow G, Higham C, Setzer J, Venmans F (2023) Impacts of climate litigation on firm value. Centre for Climate Change Economics and Policy Working Paper 421/ Grantham Research Institute on Climate Change and the Environment Working Paper 397. London: London School of Economics and Political Science.

Schiermeier, Quirin. 2021. "Climate Science Is Supporting Lawsuits That Could Help Save the World." *Nature* 597 (7875): 169–171.

Sclafane, Susanne. 2021. "'Attribution Science' May Help Plaintiffs Push Climate Suits Ahead." *Claims Journal*. September 27. https://www.claimsjournal.com/news/national/2021/09/27/306166.htm (Accessed August 22, 2023).

Selmi, Daniel P. 2022. *Dawn at Mineral King Valley: The Sierra Club, the Disney Company, and the Rise of Environmental Law*. Chicago: University of Chicago Press.

Selva, Meera. 2021. "Why We Need a New Local Language of Climate Change Reporting." *Reuters Institute*, April 22, 2021. https://reutersinstitute.politics.ox.ac.uk/news/why-we-need-new-local-language-climate-change-reporting (Accessed August 21, 2023).

Silverman-Roati, Korey, and Maria Antonia Tigre. 2022. "Municipalities of Puerto Rico v. Exxon: A Unique Class Action against Fossil Fuel Companies Presses for Climate Accountability in the United States." *Climate Law, Sabin Centre* (blog). December 2. https://blogs.law.columbia.edu/climatechange/2022/12/02/municipalities-of-puerto-rico-v-exxon-a-unique-class-action-against-fossil-fuel-companies-presses-for-climate-accountability-in-the-united-states/ (Accessed August 22, 2023).

Spalding, Joanne, and Daniel Hales. 2021. "The Uses of Climate Change Attribution Science: The NGO Practitioner's View." *Environmental Law Reporter* 51(8): 10654–10658.

Stehr, Nico. 2022. *Knowledge Capitalism*. New York: Routledge.

Stirling, Andy. 2008. "Science, Precaution, and the Politics of Technological Risk." *Annals of the New York Academy of Sciences* 1128 (1): 95–110.

Stott, Peter A., D. A. Stone, and M. R. Allen. 2004. "Human Contribution to the European Heatwave of 2003." *Nature* 432 (7017): 610–614.

Stuart-Smith, Rupert F., Friederike E. L. Otto, Aisha I. Saad, Gaia Lisi, Petra Minnerop, Kristian Cedervall Lauta, Kristin van Zwieten, and Thom Wetzer. 2021. "Filling the Evidentiary Gap in Climate Litigation." *Nature Climate Change* 11 (8): 651–655.

Stuart-Smith, Rupert, Aisha Saad, Friederike Otto, Gaia Lisi, Kristian Lauta, and Thom Wetzer. 2022. "Attribution Science and Litigation: Facilitating Effective Legal Arguments and Strategies to Manage Climate Change Damages." Summary report for FILE Foundation. https://www.teraz-srodowisko.pl/media/pdf/aktualnosci/10545-Climate-litigation-background-practioner-paper.pdf (Accessible August 22, 2023).

Suzuki, David, and Sabaa Khan. 2021. "IPCC Report Could Be a Legal Game-Changer for Climate." David Suzuki Foundation (blog). September 1. https://davidsuzuki.org/story/ipcc-report-could-be-a-legal-game-changer-for-climate/ (Accessible August 22, 2023).

Vanhala, Lisa. 2018. "Is Legal Mobilization for the Birds? Legal Opportunity Structures and Environmental Nongovernmental Organizations in the United Kingdom, France, Finland, and Italy." *Comparative Political Studies* 51 (3): 380–412.

Vargo, Lauren. 2020. "How Climate Change Made the Melting of New Zealand's Glaciers 10 Times More Likely." *The Conversation*, August 4. https://theconversation.com/how-climate-change-made-the-melting-of-new-zealands-glaciers-10-times-more-likely-143626

Wentz, Jessica, Delta Merner, Benjamin Franta, Alessandra Lehmen, and Peter C. Frumhoff. 2023. "Research Priorities for Climate Litigation." *Earth's Future* 11 (1). https://doi.org/10.1029/2022EF002928

Worster, Donald. 1994. *Nature's Economy: A History of Ecological Ideas*. 2nd ed. Studies in Environment and History. Cambridge and New York: Cambridge University Press.

Cases

Ashgar Leghari v. Federation of Pakistan. Case No: W.P. No. 25501/2015.

Pabai Pabai & Anor v. Commonwealth of Australia (Federal Court of Australia Proceedings VID622/2021).

Greenpeace Australia Ltd v. Redbank Power Co. [1994] 86 LGERA 143.

Greenpeace France, Amis de la Terre France, Notre Affaire à Tous v. TotalEnergies SE, TotalEnergies Electricité, Gaz France, Court of Paris, March 2, 2022 (France).

Lliuya v RWE AG (2015) Case No. 2 O 285/15 (Essen Oberlandesgericht).

Massachusetts v. EPA, 549 U.S. 497 (2007).

Milieudefensie and others v. Royal Dutch Shell plc ECLI:NL:RBDHA:2021:5339.

Municipalities of Puerto Rico v. Exxon Mobil Corp. et al., 3:22-cv-01550 (D.P.R.).

The State of the Netherlands v. Urgenda Foundation Supreme Court of the Netherlands (December 20, 2019).

· 7 ·

GREEN LAWFARE AND POWER

Visibility and voice are central to environmental communication scholarship: What is seen and whose voice is heard are key questions for those observing how power is enacted by and through mediated communication. For some, controlling visibility includes ensuring people, activities and consequences remain invisible and unheard (Lester and Hutchins 2012), but many understand that mediated visibility is a weapon to be used in their struggles (Thompson 2005). Political life is inextricably tied to mediated visibility (Thompson 1995), but with each new development in information technology, it is increasingly difficult to control revelations and disclosures (Thompson 2020). Similarly, corporate interests understand mediated visibility as a source of recognition, reputation, brand loyalty, and prestige that not only sells products but also ensures entry into financial partnerships and the political sphere (Thompson 2020). Visibility is also central to protest because "without being visible, resistance and opposition are just that—resistance and opposition" (Lester 2019, 24). With mediated visibility comes the chance to not only be seen and heard, but to gain recognition, acceptance, and support from a widening circle, which carries with it the power to influence (Alexander 2006). Money buys visibility and globalized capitalism has enriched a particular group of people with financial wealth, social capital, and wide networks. By asserting themselves as key agents in wide networks of influence, these individuals work to further their goals and the redistribution of resources to their advantage (Giddens 1984). Such a description does not ignore their efforts to maintain a hold on power; even the elite must fight to keep their place at the table. Power is always shifting, balanced precariously on unstable alliances and networks and subject to challenge, and lawyers are there to manage the visibility and voices of their critics. Indeed, while mediatization encapsulates the myriad logics and processes that inform contemporary mediated visibility, it also provides a way to examine the logics and strategies deployed to control communication and visibility. As such, examining green lawfare in mediatized environmental conflict must include the strategies used to resist changing our social, political, legal and financial systems in response to our growing awareness of how close we are to social and ecological collapse.

Green lawfare is not limited to the legal mobilization of environmental groups. This chapter is a clarion call for a green lawfare lens to be applied to the various ways law is used by powerful interests to suppress efforts to align human activity with what we know about Earth systems. It presents three separate forms of green lawfare united by aims to obfuscate and distract, to chill and harass, and ultimately to ensure that projects of hegemonic dominance remain unhindered by concern for the public good, which includes concern for the ecological as well as the social. The first is the use of strategic lawsuits against public participation (SLAPPs) to harass and intimidate critics; second is the rise in draconian anti-protest legislation around the world signaling a turn in the use of law to control activism; and, third is the strategies used to resist regulatory control, which is one of the major hurdles to meaningful action on climate change.

Each of these areas encompasses large and distinctive areas of law, so the focus here is not so much on environmental law, but on the various legal instruments that can be weaponized to disrupt efforts to protect ecosystems and biodiversity, tighten regulations on pollution and waste, and coordinate global action on climate change. While these strategic uses of law extend well beyond the boundaries of environmental matters, each is notable for having a long history with environmental issues, for being an example of how green lawfare is enacted by those with pockets deep enough to enlist the world's courts and legal systems and, finally, each has a "chilling effect" on those who fear legal action, such as the journalist who decides not to pursue a story, the student who worries about posting a message on her socials, and the prime minister who avoids stronger environmental policy.

It would be naive to suggest that activists never, wittingly or otherwise, spread misinformation or defame others, that police should not monitor large public gatherings, or that investors should not receive compensation for thwarted investments. Rather, this chapter regards these instances of green lawfare as moments when the reach of power and counter-power raises important questions for civil society. For instance, what are the tolerable incursions into privacy and reputation in the name of free speech—or public order? What are the tolerable limits of disruption during protests—or industrial activity? In what way is the strategic use of law implicated in the expansion and restraint of hegemonic power? These questions provide the tension in each of the three examples of green lawfare described here.

Strategic Lawsuits Against Public Participation

In 2016, thousands gathered near the Standing Rock Sioux Reservation to stop the construction of the Dakota Access Pipeline. A couple of years earlier, the Texas-based company Energy Transfer had applied to build a pipeline to carry crude oil from the Bakken shale oil field in northwest North Dakota, through North and South Dakota and Iowa, to an oil storage and transport facility in Illinois. By 2016, the Dakota Access Pipeline had attracted one of the biggest Indigenous-led protests in United States history. The Standing Rock protest was a mix of environmentalists and landholders, led by Native Americans who were concerned about the potential water contamination and damage to sacred tribal sites caused by the proposed gas pipeline. The blockade made international headlines and Energy Transfer turned to the courts to sue Greenpeace International, BankTrack, and EarthRights International for US$900 million, claiming these NGOs and those affiliated with them had designed the Standing Rock protest as a fundraising stunt. Tone-deaf to their racism, *Energy Transfer v. Greenpeace* was an attempt to undermine public confidence in the NGOs supporting the protests by presenting the company as an ally of the Standing Rock Sioux Tribe and, in contrast, Greenpeace and the other NGOs as attaching themselves "like a parasite" to the Tribe's cause (Braun 2020). A year earlier, the same law firm, Kasowitz Benson Torres, and the same lawyer, Michael Bowe, had undertaken similar action against Greenpeace and others on behalf of Canada's largest logging company, Resolute Forest Products, alleging that Greenpeace's true objectives were "maximizing donations, not saving the environment" (Brown 2022). Both lawsuits also sought to reframe lawful protest as an unlawful conspiracy under the Racketeer Influenced and Corrupt Organizations Act (RICO), which allows apparently unrelated crimes to be linked and attributed to a criminal "enterprise," such as those run by Mafia-style organized crime. The cases against Greenpeace and the other NGOs tied Greenpeace resources into a long, complex and expensive legal fight.

Such lawsuits are not new. They are widely referred to as SLAPPs, a catchy anagram for Strategic Lawsuits/Litigation Against Public Participation, coined by American academics Penelope Canan and George Pring (1988). Studying lawsuits that threatened the right to petition, protest and otherwise engage in participatory politics, Canan and Pring found a high rate of legal claims being used to harass and intimidate activists, journalists, academics and anyone else who might attend a protest, distribute pamphlets or write to their local representatives had emerged in the United States in the 1970s and which appeared to be particularly aimed at neutralizing the emerging environmental movement (Canan 1989; Canan and Pring 1988; Pring 1989; Pring and Canan 1992).

SLAPPs are rarely about compensation for damages, but always about controlling communication. Canan and Pring found those with "deep pockets" use SLAPPs in retaliation for successful opposition, to stop future opposition and to send a message that any opposition would be punished. SLAPPs work by demanding considerable time, finances, and other resources, which not only intimidate individuals but also weaken organizations by diverting energies from campaigns to defending legal challenges. SLAPPs place a lot of stress on targeted individuals who are typically high-profile activists at the center of campaigns (White 2005, 768) and are designed to intimidate and overwhelm individuals, exhaust financial resources and morale, and erode reputations. In terms of controlling communication, Pring and Canan (1992, 941) wrote that SLAPPs are

> filed by one side of a public, political dispute, to punish or prevent opposing points of view. They are an attempt to "privatize" public debate—a unilateral effort by one side to transform a public, political dispute into a private, legal adjudication, shifting both forum and issues.

SLAPPS do not need to win in court, or even make it to court to achieve their aim of having a "chilling effect" on public criticism. Instead, SLAPPS work by discouraging people from speaking out, which stifles campaigns. Even if a defendant is able to successfully defend themselves in court, they are likely to have expended a lot of money and other resources in mounting a defense inside, but also outside, the court.

There is no singular definition of a SLAPP and cases vary on the situation and context, but they can be identified by their legally meritless arguments, convoluted and disproportionate claims, use of tactics to delay proceedings, and their attack on the reputations of defendants. The following case studies—an early one from the United Kingdom and a more recent example from Australia—illustrate how media and communication are implicated in this form of green lawfare in sometimes surprising ways.

McLibel

Pring and Canan are rightfully acknowledged for identifying SLAPPs, but it was the infamous McLibel case that brought the dark legal art to international attention. In 1990, the US-based McDonald's Corporation sued five British activists for distributing leaflets criticizing the fast-food giant outside some of the company's London restaurants. Three of the activists apologized and were removed from the case, but Helen Steel and Dave Morris took on the company in the courts by challenging each of the claims against them. The resulting case, *McDonald's Corporation v. Steel & Morris*, remains one of the longest trials in British legal history and an iconic protest.

The case coincided with the arrival of the Internet, which a network of supporters then used to launch the "McSpotlight" website to publish information about the trial and to criticize the company more generally, which included reproducing the original "offending" leaflet to a wider global audience than ever originally intended. After almost 15 years, the court found largely in favor of McDonald's, but this victory was regarded by many as pyrrhic—whatever had been won in the courts was shadowed by the damning publicity around the case. As Douglas Vick and Kevin Campbell (2001, 235) point out, McDonald's appeared to have survived the bad publicity partly because, they suggest, the company's omnipresent "feel-good" advertising "may have drowned out" the negative media coverage, especially when its main customers, which are young people, may not have been influenced by news coverage of the long-running trial.

Gunns 20

The Gunns 20 case, *Gunns v. Marr*, is a more recent example of how SLAPPs are crafted to overwhelm defendants with meritless claims. The Gunns 20 were a group of Tasmanian environmentalists and environmental groups sued by Gunns, an Australian logging company with a monopoly on forestry operations in Tasmania in 2004. The SLAPP was widely regarded as an attempt by Gunns to control a successful national campaign that had led to Gunns' logging operations being a deciding issue in the 2004 Australian Federal election (Ogle 2010, 38).

One of the defendants was Bob Brown, a longtime environmental campaigner and leader of the Australian Greens who is particularly attuned to the symbolic power of protest and mediated visibility. Brown said that when he received the writ, he called a media conference before he called his lawyers and also organized a public vigil to show the attack on democracy implicated in the suit (Manning 2011).

The statement of claims against the Gunns 20 was notoriously complex and lengthy. In Victoria's Supreme Court, Justice Bernard Bongiorno rejected the first statement of claims, telling the court: "This is a case that has the potential to tie up this court for many, many months and, if it goes to trial, for God knows how long" (Sydney Morning Herald 2005). He threw out the second and third for being "vague, incoherent, and contradictory" before allowing the case to eventually proceed (Taylor 2007). By then, the Gunns 20 had assembled a legal team of six law firms, including four senior barristers, to fight what was Australia's most costly SLAPP. By including news and other media as part of their strategy, the Gunns 20 and their supporters ensured the egregious case against them would receive national and international media attention, and condemnation for being a corporate abuse of power. Eventually, the company lost its case and in January 2010 was ordered to pay costs and compensation for the six years of harassment (see Beresford 2015).

SLAPPS Around the World

Different approaches to SLAPPS are taken depending on local contexts and available legal instruments. In turn, the definition of SLAPPs has evolved. While SLAPPs in wealthier nations typically use libel and other defamation-related charges, SLAPPs in developing nations also include criminal proceedings initiated by government agencies (Dutta 2020). Charges relating to computer crime laws have been used in Thailand and anti-boycott laws are popular in Israel (Zuluaga and Dobson 2021, 13). Most recently, the European Union's General Data Protection Regulation (GDPR) has been used in lawsuits against journalists in Hungary and other parts of Europe (Rucz 2022). European law, like those of the United Kingdom, tends to privilege privacy and public order over freedom of political expression, so SLAPPs in these countries tend to focus on journalists who bring visibility to the actions of others (Diaz Crego and Del Monte 2022; Donson 2010). Around the world, SLAPPs are increasingly being used as part of wider campaigns to harass journalists and others. One study (Zuluaga and Dobson 2021) identified that out of more than 3,100 attacks against human rights and environmental defenders, nearly half involved judicial harassment, including criminal and civil lawsuits, arbitrary detention, and contrived charges by government and business actors. While most of the suits were issued by transnational companies headquartered in the United States and Europe, the authors noted that less affluent countries carried the brunt of more than 70 percent of these SLAPPs. Similarly, in a survey of 63 investigative reporters from 41 countries (Coughtrie and Ogier 2020), nearly three-quarters of respondents reported receiving threats of legal action because of information they had published.

South America is often cited for having the most cases, followed by countries in the Asia-Pacific (Noorlander 2022, 4). Despite domestic environmental laws throughout the region and many countries being parties to international and regional environmental treaties, Southeast Asia is also mired in environmental conflict, especially because of international investment in timber, mining and manufacturing (Lester 2019). While most of these countries also have constitutional protection for freedom of expression, association, and peaceful assembly, activists and journalists are frequently targeted with violence and harassment and, increasingly, SLAPPs are being to silence dissent especially in Thailand, India, the Philippines (Dutta 2020).

The use of SLAPPs is so pervasive that anti-SLAPP laws have been introduced in the United States, Canada and Australia. Recent calls to address the prevalence of SLAPP suits in the British system illustrate the task of addressing the rising tide of vexatious legal suits designed to silence criticism. The plaintiff-friendly nature of its libel laws makes Britain a popular destination for SLAPPs. As Donson (2010, 89) observed after the McLibel case, Britain, unlike the United States, tends to privilege privacy over free speech, which often results in favoring commercial interests over the public interest. Geoffrey Robertson (2023) is less circumspect, writing that the "thuggish barons" who long ago negotiated the terms of Magna Carta continue to ensure that England's defamation and privacy laws continue to shield the rich and powerful from public scrutiny. Journalist Oliver Bullough (2022) summed up the use of SLAPPs in Britain as:

> instead of journalists being told what to do, we are threatened with seven-figure legal fees, so we preemptively avoid any discussion of oligarchs known to be litigious. The result is the same as you would find in an authoritarian country—oligarchs are left in peace to enjoy their hard-stolen wealth, undisturbed by tiresome publicity—but the way Britain gets there is so much more … sophisticated.

Three high-profile SLAPP cases against journalists shone an unflattering light on how British defamation and data protection laws are being used "to suppress scrutiny on an industrial scale" (Bullough 2022). The first was the 2020 legal action taken against *Financial Times* journalist Catherine Belton and her publisher, HarperCollins, for her book *Putin's People*. Then the 2021 lawsuit brought by Kazakh mining company, Eurasian Natural Resources Corporation, against finance journalist Tom Burgis and his publisher, HarperCollins (again) for his book *Kleptopia: How Dirty Money is Conquering the World* (2021) that detailed the suspicious deaths of three ENRC contractors. The third followed revelations about the relationship between Russian oligarch Yevgeny Prigozhin's legal team and several law firms in Britain and the United States that led an aggressive SLAPP against Eliot Higgins, the founder of the investigative website Bellingcat. This wave of litigation against journalists led one British politician, Liam Byrne, to describe Britain as "the global capital of the lawfare industry" (House of Commons, January 20, 2022).

Of course, Britain is not the only country confronted by how its legal system provides impunity to the very rich. In 2022, the European Commission asked the European Council and Parliament to develop anti-SLAPP legislation to filter SLAPPs out of the European court system (Behrens 2023). This call also followed a number of egregious cases of intimidation against journalists, in particular the Maltese investigative journalist Daphne Caruana Galizia who, at the time of her assassination, had at least 47 lawsuits against her (Coughtrie and Ogier 2020).

The mood to address the problem of SLAPPs is global. In South Africa, the *Mineral Sands* case, which included three defamation suits, became a tipping point (Noorlander 2022). The case was initiated by Australian company, Mineral Commodities Limited, and its subsidiary, Mineral Sand Resources, against environmental lawyers and activists who had published criticisms of the companies' mining operations, including allegations that the catastrophic impacts on the environment from mining had led to violent conflict between the mine operators and the local communities. Drawing on US and Canadian anti-SLAPP laws, the six defendants argued the case against them was a classic example of a SLAPP and the case was an abuse of process. The South African High Court upheld their argument, drawing on common law from other jurisdictions, including a UK House of Lords judgment, in which one of the judges said:

> The power wielded by the major multi-national corporations is enormous and growing. The freedom to criticise them may be at least as important in a democratic society as the freedom to criticise the government. (Noorlander 2022, 8)

Indeed, we can see the prescience of this observation if we include other efforts, namely protest legislation and the mechanisms in the international finance system, as we will soon discuss.

Green Lawfare and SLAPPs

While SLAPPs stand out as being one of the oldest tricks in the book, they also remain an example of the strategic use of law to control the flow of information and, as such, are a form of green lawfare. SLAPPs are notable for showing the imbalance of power that allows those with the financial resources to inflict the economic and emotional burden of a complex and protracted lawsuit that has little or nothing to do with achieving justice. As Canan (1989, 24) observed, SLAPPs are

> [p]olitical legal phenomenon. This means that we must treat each SLAPP as a window on a much larger process. So each SLAPP is not just the story of a legal dispute between opposing hostile parties. Rather, each SLAPP is a window on the relationship between democratic structures and judicial rules. It is a window on the link between political tolerance and economic dominance, and a window on the tension between constitutionalism and capitalism.

Like other areas of green lawfare discussed so far, SLAPPs tell us about the relationship between law and politics, and the role of courts in our political system, especially in adjudicating issues of public interest (Sheldrick 2014). As a form of green lawfare, these cases present the familiar paradox of conflicting rights, including the right to free political expression versus private rights. SLAPPs are designed to silence dissent, but as the networks that supported the defendants in the *McLibel* and *Gunns 20* cases showed, fighting SLAPPs requires mediated visibility of the case and the cause to ensure environmental problems, and the harassment of public interest advocates, remains in the public mind rather than hidden in legal obscurity. As a legal strategy to control visibility and information during environmental conflict, SLAPPs are a key area of green lawfare.

Controlling Protest

In May 2023, German police raided the homes of Last Generation activists using a law originally meant to target organized crime and terrorist groups (McGuinness and Kirby 2023). In June 2023, French authorities de-legalized the environmental group, Les Soulevements de la Terre (Earth Uprising), after violent clashes with police later criticized for using control measures that were a "largely disproportionate" response to a rally (Guillot 2023). In Australia, climate activists are being jailed for blocking roads and mining operations. The Covid-19 pandemic, the gradual shift to far-right politics, the impacts of climate change, and the rise in protests calling for action on climate have presented police and other authorities with novel problems, with many responding by tightening laws around protests and giving police and prosecutors "immense discretion over which protesters to arrest and prosecute" (Pender 2022). Like SLAPPS, the new tide of anti-protest laws around the world suppresses activism (Donson 2010). This use of law to control the visibility and voice of dissent makes anti-protest measures another form of green lawfare.

Non-violent protest often involves disruption: sit-ins and blockades stop workers from working, and rallies and marches block traffic. Disruption is part of the symbolic power of protest and causing inconvenience is a non-violent means of gaining attention, but these actions also stir debate about the limit of acceptable disruption to "our way of life," a popular dog whistle used by politicians and shock jocks to ostracize any group that threatens the status quo. To explore this idea, we will look at the rise in anti-protest laws in Britain and elsewhere before looking at how private security firms are working with law-and-order regimes sympathetic to private interests to remove civilian oversight of policing and other security measures targeting public participation in civic life.

Anti-protest Laws in Britain

Hidden beneath their jackets, 18 activists wore trademark orange "Just Stop Oil" t-shirts. Their plan was to join the crowd gathered near Trafalgar Square to view the 2023 coronation of King Charles III. The plan was to unveil their t-shirts as the royal carriage and its entourage passed—they even had little orange flags in their pockets they planned to wave—but each was arrested before the carriage carrying the new king to Westminster Abbey had even arrived (Naldrett 2023). There were at least 52 arrests under Britain's anti-protest laws in relation to the coronation. For some, wearing a t-shirt to send a message about action on climate was enough to see them forcibly removed from a public space. Others marveled at how the limits of acceptable disruption shifted depending on who was blocking the traffic.

In the United Kingdom, new legislation is clearly being used to control protests. In particular, the *Police, Crime, Sentencing and Courts Act 2022* provides new definitions of disruption, and amendments to the *Public Order Act 2023* have introduced new offenses including criminalizing "locking on" and tunneling—two common techniques used by protesters—as well as interfering with infrastructure and obstruction. The intention of the government to control climate protest is clear from its communications about the new laws, which includes justifying them because "the government needs to act in preventing serious disruption" and protect the "rights and freedoms of others" (Public Order Bill Factsheet, Gov.UK). Describing the right to protest as something that must be balanced against the rights of the public positions protest as an individual choice rather than an action undertaken for the public good. The government website also criticizes protesters for costing the taxpayer money—such as listing the total cost of policing Just Stop Oil protests at over £14.5 million—which again positions protest as a costly and disruptive performance by individuals rather than acts of political speech.

In the case of Britain's new anti-protest laws, we can see a concerted effort to erase the shared history of resistance to the tyranny of overreaching authority by framing the protesters as selfish and anti-social individuals. The idea that protest is a democratic right is largely lost. Noting that the "common law right to peaceful assembly dates back to the Magna Carta," Michael Head (2023, 80) argues that the exercise of democratic rights by everyday people, more so than anything done in parliaments or the courts, is what defends and extends democracy. Britain's anti-protest laws are about controlling political participation and, like SLAPP suits, these laws have a chilling effect on public participation. As well removing the claims and actions of protest away from the public gaze to be dealt with in the courts, anti-protest laws also provide governments and other critics the legitimizing language that drives a wedge between protesters and the wider public, as the debate about climate protesters in Australia shows.

Anti-protest Laws in Australia

In April 2022, four activists from Fireproof Australia, a group formed after Australia's Black Summer bushfires of 2019/2020, parked a truck on the southbound lane of the Sydney Harbour Bridge. One of the protesters, Deanna (Violet) Coco, stood on top of the truck and lit an orange flare. When police arrived, Coco became the first person arrested and charged under new laws making the obstruction of any tunnel, road, port, or similar infrastructure punishable by up to two years imprisonment. When Coco was sentenced some months later, then New South Wales, Premier Dominic Perrottet, told reporters (Loomes 2022):

> If protesters want to put our way of life at risk, they should have the book thrown at them, and that's pleasing to see ... We want people to be able to protest but you should do it in a way that doesn't inconvenience people right across NSW ... Those protests literally started to grind our city to a halt ... Everyone has the right to protest. Do so in a way that doesn't inconvenience people around you.

His choice of words were astonishing in their irony. On that very day he was framing climate protest as undemocratic inconvenience, Sydney traffic was in chaos because Perottet's government had closed a section of the city's light rail to put on a "long table lunch" to attract people back into the city center after pandemic lockdowns. Asked about the disruption caused by the cancellation of public transport on a major route, Perrottet defended the lunch saying, "One day without the light rail—no problem" (Evans 2022). One tweet summed up the hypocrisy:

> A climate protester is sentenced to 15 months in jail for blocking one side lane of the Sydney Harbor Bridge for 25 (minutes) ... Meanwhile, the entirety of the George St light rail route is blocked off all day for some wanky "Open for Lunch" event. (Evans 2022)

The shift in Australia's political mood for protest, including media coverage of protest, is palpable. After the arrest of climate protester Andrew George in

2022 after he ran onto the field during a football match wearing a cape emblazoned with Fireproof Australia, a journalist noted:

> Back in the day, it was an Aussie tradition for streakers to run onto the footy field or the cricket pitch during a match. A police officer would then cover the naked person's nether regions with their hat, and they'd be taken away, to receive a slap on the wrist. And the crowd loved it. (Grégoire 2022)

Instead, George joined Violet and others on Australia's growing list of protesters jailed for trying to raise the alarm.

Protests in forests and other wild places, demonstrations and rallies, and spectacular banner drops have for decades been part of Australia's political fabric. So too have efforts to make protesters folk devils. In 2017, when well-known environmentalist Bob Brown challenged new anti-protest legislation, Australia's High Court described the *Workplaces (Protection from Protestors) Act 2014* as "Pythonesque" in its absurdity and ruled them to be unconstitutional (Killick 2017). Tasmania's more recent *Police Offences Amendment (Workplace Protection) Act 2022* saw Tasmanian activist and veterinarian, Colette Harmsen, jailed for protesting against forestry and mining in the state. As Australian lawyer Mark Davis observed, a shift in political mood seems to be allowing many of the rights that Australians take for granted to "rapidly being ripped away from us by a late-night sitting in parliament" (Grégoire 2023).

Anti-protest Laws and News Media

Enacting laws to deter peaceful, though disruptive, protest is a form of green lawfare. Using legislation and police powers to control dissent includes controlling the mediated visibility that has, for decades, provided the environmental movement with its symbolic power. The strategic use of law to control media includes targeting the social media and networking apps used to mobilize and support protest, such as when Indian activist Dishi Ravi was arrested for sharing a tweet sent from Greta Thunberg in solidarity with striking Indian farmers (Ellis-Petersen 2021). These measures include police arresting and harassing journalists who attend sites of protest, such as in Britain when reporter Charlotte Lynch was arrested alongside photographers Tom Bowles and Ben Cawthra and filmmaker Rich Felgate while covering a Just Stop Oil protest in 2022 (Cooban 2022). In Australia, the harassment of journalists includes the 2019 arrests of French environmental reporter Hugo Clément and three others who were detained and charged with trespass for filming a protest outside an Adani coal terminal for a French documentary. Civil rights lawyers described bail conditions banning the journalists from reporting near Adani sites as an "abuse of police power" designed to "shield the company" (Smee 2019).

Across Europe, reporting on climate and other environmental issues is increasingly difficult because journalists face legal and physical harassment from polluters and police (EFJ 2023). The rise of independent environmental news outlets, such as Climate Home, and the increasing use of freelancers by established news outlets puts journalists at risk of arrest while covering protests. For instance, freelance journalist Grégoire Souchay was the only journalist arrested among several who attended a raid on a warehouse by protesters looking for evidence of GMO seed and, in Germany, journalist Marco Brás dos Santos was found guilty of trespassing while attending a protest calling for the closure of coal mines in 2019 (Council of Europe 2023). We can include the harassment of filmmaker Joe Berlinger for his work in Ecuador in this list. The Committee to Protect Journalists has described environmental journalism as one of the most dangerous types of reporting after war reporting, with as many as 29 murders in the past decade the tip of the iceberg of those attacked for investigating the social and environmental impacts "of corporate and political interests scrambling to extract wealth from the earth's remaining natural resources" (Garside and Watts 2019).

So, what are we to make of the increasing intolerance to protest, especially laws aimed at controlling the visibility of environmental and climate activism that enables the harassment of journalists? The term "authoritarian neoliberalism" describes the practices of repression and control in neoliberal policies and objectives such as the "deployment of the state's apparatuses that deter any form of external resistance" (Regilme 2019, 161). Often credited to the work of Ian Bruff and Cemal Burak Tansel (2019; also Bruff 2014), "authoritarian neoliberalism" describes a change in how state power is wielded by dominant groups in order to maintain hegemony—specifically via a range of coercive and legal measures that aim to insulate the state from popular contestation (Bruff 2014, 116). Bruff and Tansel (2019) highlight how contemporary capitalism is governed in a way that tends to rely upon practices that seek to marginalize, discipline and control dissenting social groups and oppositional politics rather than strive for their consent or cooperation (Bruff and Tansel 2019, 234).

Observing the rise of anti-democratic measures in liberal democracies, including the United States, Australia, Brazil, Turkey, Israel, Britain, Poland, Hungary and India, Eve Darian-Smith (2022) argues that the politicization and weaponization of anti-environmental ideology and policy is part of a wider, global rise of anti-democracy activity. While these countries have notable local specificities, she writes, each shares political agendas that favor the fossil fuel industry over citizens' concerns about health, air pollution, rising oceans, water and food security and biodiversity loss. These agendas include "actively rolling back or stalling on environmental protection policy and legislation [and] liberal democratic principles and institutions such as the right to vote and publicly assemble, a free press, an independent judiciary, and public access to education and health" (Darian-Smith 2022, 1). Indeed, without media coverage, the chilling effect of legal action on protesters and other critics would go largely unnoticed. As well as causing harm to individuals, including activists and journalists, such agendas suppress the expression and extension of democratic participation. As such, environmental movements and politics remain critical for those resisting the perpetual authoritarian impulse (McCarthy 2019). While news organizations have long been understood as a key institution, or Fourth Estate, to hold power to account, other media actors are increasingly filling this role as newsrooms shrink around the world. Mediated networks of activists and independent media are using the affordances of digital media to provide visibility to issues that mainstream media are not covering. Just as the important role of visibility is being outsourced to NGOs and independent media makers, so too is the task of protecting the powerful from the glare of public accountability being outsourced to private actors.

Corporate Espionage

So far, we have considered the transparent, if under-reported, uses of law and legislative powers by governments to remove the disruptive spectacularisms of protest from public view. In such cases, mediated visibility of protests and efforts to control protest informs debate about the allowable limits of disruption caused by protest activity and, also, the limits of state control over those dissenting. Into this picture are the more secretive efforts to control protest activity. These efforts include corporate espionage, which describes the use of surveillance tactics and technologies to intimidate and hinder protesters, journalists and anyone holding corporate power to account (Jones and Evans

2017) and police surveillance of activists and protest groups to anticipate, and therefore control, their lawful activities. While police surveillance on environmental groups is documented in many countries—notably in the United Kingdom, where it was revealed undercover policing tactics included targeting environmental and social justice groups (Jones and Evans 2017), and the 2004 revelations that the United States was using its surveillance capacity to report on the activities of Americans (Stanley 2004)— the ongoing coordination between the fossil fuel industry, private security firms and state-run law enforcement warrants closer examination within the framework of green lawfare.

In 2023, it was revealed that when activists from the Green New Deal Rising campaign group tried to attend a "State of London Debate with Khan" event—where they intended to ask questions of the London mayor Sidiq Khan and drop a banner protesting a new tunnel—a plain-clothes security officer identified them by name before banning them entering (Corderoy 2023). As one activist told the independent news site *openDemocracy* (Corderoy 2023), she was not talking to a police officer or other official, but rather a private security officer who appeared to recognize them:

> I think it was very concerning how they had all our names, how they knew exactly our plans from the tiniest detail that you wouldn't know unless you were covertly trying to find that out, and also the fact that we couldn't find out his name, we didn't know what company he was working for, we had no idea who and how that information had been gained.

The relationship between private security firms and national and state law enforcement agencies to identify and monitor activists is a global issue. In the United States, the resistance to the Dakota Access Pipeline (Brown et al. 2017) provides an excellent case study.

In October 2020, *The Intercept's* Alleen Brown requested documents relating to the private security firm TigerSwan held by the North Dakota Private Investigative and Security Board, the government agency that regulates North Dakota's private investigation and security industry. The board initially denied the request, so *The Intercept* sued the board, arguing that the requested documents were public records and discovered TigerSwan had been paid at least $17 million to provide a "militaristic approach" to infiltrate the protesters by spying on activists using drone footage, intercepting communications, and infiltrating groups through striking up friendships within the blockade (Brown 2022). Alarmingly, TigerSwan regarded independent journalists as "basically an intelligence collection node for whatever movement they're a part of … and thus part of an insurgency that must be quelled." Earlier investigations into TigerSwan (Brown et al. 2017) revealed the private security firm was allegedly contracted to build a "web-like map of funding nodes" to identify the wealthy individuals financing protesters at Standing Rock that would later be used in lawsuits alleging protest groups were operating in criminal collusion under the Racketeer Influenced and Corrupt Organizations Act (RICO).

Private investigators are being used by private interests to harass activists, with information gathered going on to inform SLAPPs, such as the one instigated against Australian climate activist, Ben Pennings, by Gautam Adani, one of the wealthiest men in the world. Adani has no chance of recovering the millions he is demanding of Pennings. The SLAPP not only carries the threat of bankrupting Pennings but includes the intimidation and harassment of being the target of private investigators. The suit, originally for more than $600million and later dropped to $17million, has included Adani hiring a private investigator to go through his partner's social media accounts and photographing Pennings taking his daughter to school. Two applications by the company's lawyers to raid Pennings' house were rejected by a court, but Pennings was ordered to handover his mobile phone and laptop to allow a forensic IT specialist to search his data. In India, the Adani Group of companies also targets activists and journalists, most notably veteran investigative journalist and filmmaker Paranjoy Guha Thakurta whose articles alleging the Adani Group practiced tax evasion were central to an international expose of the Adani Group over allegations of tax fraud (Barrett 2023). Thakurta, who investigates India's most powerful businesses, has spoken about the chilling effect that illegal surveillance, including the use of spyware and malware, is having on himself and journalism in India (Balaji 2021).

Green Lawfare and Controlling Dissent

News and other media coverage of protest provides an important platform for public debate about the acceptable limits of disruption caused by protest and public participation, including interrupting worksites, public events and traffic, but also the acceptable limits of the official and unofficial efforts used to control dissent, including surveillance undertaken by state agencies and private firms. We can see the chilling effect of anti-protest laws that make it more difficult for movements to gather a critical mass, which has resulted in different tactics using fewer people, such as the loosely organized actions of protesters, often just two, who are blocking roads or throwing soup over priceless artworks to call attention to the climate crisis. Groups, such as Just Stop Oil, appear to be stepping away from the structural limitations of the larger NGOs to build loose alliances of dissent (Ismail and Kamat 2018).

The arrest and jailing of those calling attention to climate action and other environmental issues can be seen as acts of green lawfare where the material and symbolic power of law is used to send a powerful message of intolerance to criticism and challenge. News and other media are implicated in this process. If and how these cases are covered, including how activists are framed—as criminals and troublemakers or as messengers paying a high price for raising the alarm— is essential for maintaining public understanding of protest as acts of democratic engagement rather than individual selfishness.

Connecting corporate espionage as an instance of green lawfare may seem tenuous. However, surveillance of activists and their networks, including media networks, is undertaken to limit public participation and media coverage of environmental politics which, in many instances, is then used to initiate and support legal action. Surveillance of individuals through publicly available data, but also data that is assumed to be private, implicates media and media law, especially in relation to data protection and people's assumptions about digital privacy. Research into this area must go beyond representation and instead seek to untangle how our reliance on communicative media implicates all of us in the networks that influence public understanding of social and environmental issues. As Libby Lester (2019, 51–52) writes:

> Questions of control and strategy in contemporary environmental politics cannot be fully understood without paying serious attention to the idea of invisibility or the planned and coordinated avoidance of media communication, attention and representation in order to achieve political, social and/or environmental ends. Conditions that allow political actors and activists to stay out of the media spotlight, conceal their activities or to slow and block the distribution of information are changing to such an extent that the ability to strategically avoid appearing in the media is arguably a key resource.

Having described how the threat of legal action is used to silence and intimidate protesters and the journalists reporting on their activities, we now turn our attention to the way the international finance system challenges state power while ensuring the activities of some of the world's most powerful people remain largely invisible and unaccountable.

The International Finance System

In 2016, the Italian Government re-introduced a general ban on oil and gas exploration and production within a 12-mile limit of the Italian coastline. The role of sustained protest by a well-coordinated local network of environmental groups leading up to the Italian Government's decision cannot be overstated (Cernison 2018; Wu 2023). The ban on exploration interrupted the plans of London-based exploration company, Rockhopper, to build an oilfield off the Italian coast. Although construction was yet to start, the corporation had already invested millions of pounds into the project and Rockhopper sued the Italian Government for breaching its investment obligations under the Energy Charter Treaty, a multilateral energy treaty, and won: the Italian Government was ordered to pay the corporation €240 million, which included €185 million in lost profit, plus interest (Rockhopper v. Italy).

Rockhopper was not unprecedented. In the seven years since the signing of the Paris Agreement, the fossil fuel industry has lodged at least 192 claims against countries for changes to energy policies, with at least another 175 cases filed for changes to environmental policies (UNCTAD 2022). Unlike the *Rockhopper* case, most of these investor-state arbitration cases go unreported. When they do make news, the coverage tends to emphasize the undemocratic, exploitative and clandestine nature of investor-state arbitration (Puig and Strezhnev 2017), so it is unsurprising that efforts are made to control the visibility of these actions. This section discusses investor-state arbitration (also called investor-state dispute settlement or ISDS) as an area of environmental conflict that warrants closer attention by those researching the transnational activities of activists and industry in global environmental conflict. As the discussion below outlines, the legal frameworks of the international investment system, especially investor-state arbitration, are hindering government efforts to respond to climate change and other environmental and human rights issues.

The international investment system is a complex network of treaties and other instruments, including over 3,000 international trade agreements. For instance, the Energy Charter Treaty (ECT), which was largely designed to protect international companies investing in energy projects in the former Soviet Union countries in the post-Cold War era, has been the basis of at least 150 arbitrations since 1998, including the *Rockhopper* case (Belyi 2021). Most of these agreements have provisions for investor-state arbitration that serve as "a form of political risk insurance" to protect foreign investors from changes in government policy (Tienhaara et al. 2022, 2). The system is governed by the International Centre for Settlement of Investment Disputes (ICSID) that was established to facilitate arbitration, manage conciliation and risk, and promote investment flows. While protecting investors and their investments from political vicissitude, including expropriation in countries with weak rule of law and institutions, investor-state arbitration is also criticized for enshrining the exploitation of poorer nations in law (Puig and Strezhnev 2017) and is considered the biggest challenge to global action on climate (Tienhaara et al. 2022). For this reason, arbitration within the international finance system is discussed here as the third area of green lawfare. In particular, this section looks at how investor-state arbitration binds countries to fossil fuel extraction and other environmentally harmful activities by making it economically and politically costly to change environmental policies without invoking the wrath of legal action (Chriki 2020; Tienhaara 2011, 2018). The resulting "regulatory chill" has led some (in particular, Chriki 2020) to compare investor-state arbitration to SLAPPs.

When disagreements arise, international arbitration provides a process of mediation and settlement. Under investor-state arbitration rules, when an investor (such as Rockhopper) and a country (in this case, Italy) have a disagreement, each party chooses a legal representative and together, they agree on a third arbitrator from a small pool of specialist lawyers. Investor-state arbitration notoriously favors corporations over nation-states for a number of reasons. Firstly, only investors, not states, can initiate legal proceedings and investors are not obliged to acknowledge the existence of a case, let alone reveal the compensation they are seeking, and the arbitration process is conducted outside a country's national laws and with little media oversight or scrutiny. Adding further mystery to the process, those involved in investor-state arbitration do not have to follow precedents established by previous decisions, making it difficult for any party to predict outcomes and there are few opportunities to appeal or review a decision. Compensation usually amounts to billions because it is calculated using the initial investment costs plus the expected future profits had the project gone ahead. Finally, if a country does not want to pay costs, the plaintiffs can seize assets owned by the country as payment. As the *Economist* (2014) neatly summed up:

> If you wanted to convince the public that international trade agreements are a way to let multinational companies get rich at the expense of ordinary people, this is what you would do: give foreign firms a special right to apply to a secretive tribunal of highly paid corporate lawyers for compensation whenever a government passes a law to, say,

> discourage smoking, protect the environment or prevent a nuclear catastrophe. Yet that is precisely what thousands of trade and investment treaties over the past half century have done, through a process known as "investor-state dispute settlement."

The lack of transparency, and therefore accountability, in the investor-state arbitration process contributes to a perceived lack of legitimacy of these processes, especially when tribunals debate matters of public interest behind closed doors (Howard 2017).

Media coverage of such cases matters, but empirical studies on the correlation of media coverage and public sentiment about international trade and investment agreements are few. One study (Brutger and Strezhnev 2022) analyzed Canadian and United States media coverage of international trade agreements and found domestic audiences judge the merit of agreements based on whether they perceive the agreement to be beneficial or harmful to their own or national interests. The authors also found news media disproportionately covered stories where international law was used against the home country which, they argue, fuels public skepticism about investor-state arbitration and decreases support for international trade agreements, especially for individuals susceptible to nationalist rhetoric. Findings such as these explain, in part at least, why arbitration tribunals tend to exclude interest groups, news media and the public generally, from the process. The secrecy around the tribunals is regarded favorably by most parties because it protects the business secrets and public image of the corporations initiating legal action and it also protects governments from public scrutiny of decisionmaking (Zhao 2019). While staying behind closed doors ensures the dispute does not become politicized, the secrecy around the system supports the "corporate architecture of impunity" (Guamán 2020) and raises serious questions about whether avoiding matters of public interest is ever healthy for democracy.

The long-running dispute between United States oil companies and the Indigenous people living in the Ecuadorian Amazon forests serves as a good example here of the tensions of publicity and secrecy around proceedings under international trade agreements. As discussed in previous chapters, Ecuador has for decades been the site of intense conflict over its petroleum resources, most of which lie under some of the world's most biodiverse forests. One of the many lawsuits in this long-running conflict involved Chevron suing Ecuador for breaching its obligations under the United States-Ecuador Bilateral Investment Treaty (BIT). During that case, *Chevron v. Ecuador*, the tribunal did not allow two non-governmental organization petitioners—the International Institute for Sustainable Development and Fundación Pachamama—to present their concerns to the tribunal. As Natalie Bernasconi-Osterwalder (2011) noted, the refusal to admit local people to provide testimony about the impact of oil drilling is an example of how these tribunals "are resolving matters of significant public interest, but doing so without giving those affected an opportunity to access all relevant information or provide relevant input regarding the disputes." The reluctance to allow local organizations into the tribunal to "speak" for the forests echoes the efforts of others, such as Michael Black in the *Tasmanian Dams* case (*Commonwealth v. Tasmania)* (see Chapter Four), to ensure courts and tribunals forums engage with all the perspectives and stakeholders informing the conflict.

In another case, *Eco Oro v. Colombia*, the Canadian mining company Eco Oro Minerals Corporation drew on the Canada–Colombia Free Trade Agreement (CCFTA) to sue the Colombian Government for nearly US$700 million for not being allowed to mine for gold in the country's *páramos*, the high altitude Andean ecosystems that supply the country's freshwater. The arbitration followed a Colombian Constitutional Court ruling against a legal loophole that permitted mining operations into the *páramos*. That case was the result of a long-running campaign by local and national officials, environmentalists, and residents— organized by the Committee for the Defense of Water and the Santurbán Páramo— that used mass protests in the city of Bucaramanga and appeals for greater regulation of the wetlands. At the heart of the *Eco Oro v. Colombia* was whether the company could mine for gold in a fragile ecosystem, whether the company should have anticipated in its due diligence that regulation of the *páramos* was shifting and, finally, whether the decision to not allow Eco Oro to mine the concession was an example of expropriation if the mining ban did not discriminate between foreign and local investors (Trew 2021). In the tribunal, a number of groups were not permitted to provide testimony, notably the Committee for the Defense of Water and the Santurbán Páramo, whose application to provide a testimony was rejected because, the tribunal claimed, their claim to have "important knowledge of the Santurban paramo and the associated social and environmental problems" would not help resolve the case (Harris 2019). In its final decision, the tribunal was divided: while it found no expropriation of investment had taken place, the tribunal also found the company's rights to "fair and equitable treatment" had been violated. In short: the tribunal found that while Colombia had the right to respond to public appeals for greater environmental protection, it was also liable for not providing a stable and predictable regulatory environment (Trew 2021). Such a finding raises questions about the right of financial entities to expect security in a world made unstable and unpredictable by climate change and other crises. While perhaps being a matter of international law, such questions engage more broadly in the question of the role of law in responding to public calls for action, for defining the responsibility for social and environmental stability and, finally, defining the cost and who pays (Cotula 2023). Research into these broad questions, especially those relating to how we define and understand responsibility and cost, occurs at the intersection of activism, media and communication, government and private interests. In other words, green lawfare.

The International Finance System and Globalization

The number of investor-state arbitration cases has increased from just six known cases in 1995 to 1332 in 2023, with most cases launched by investors in Europe and North America suing less affluent nations (Müller and Olivet 2019). As such, it is difficult to ignore the relationship between the international finance system and globalization. As Arjun Appadurai (2000, 3) succinctly describes

> [g]lobalization is inextricably linked to the current workings of capital on a global basis; in this regard it extends the earlier logics of empire, trade, and political dominion in many parts of the world. Its most striking feature is the runaway quality of global finance, which appears remarkably independent of traditional constraints of information transfer, national regulation, industrial productivity, or "real" wealth in any particular society, country, or region.

A snapshot of the extent of investor-state arbitration and related cases targeting countries provides a grim picture of how foreign investment programs influence domestic policy. Seventy percent of lawsuits against African countries were initiated by European countries, with the total claims against African countries since 1993 amounting to more than US$55 billion which, as Müller and Olivet (2020, 6) note, "have the potential to bring the public budgets of most African countries to breaking point". A similarly grim picture emerges in Latin America, where the majority of 282 known claims made by investors against Latin America and Caribbean countries up until 2020 were settled in favor of investors, which amounted to more than US$31 billion (Guamán 2020). Adoración Guamán (2020) notes that Latin American countries that spent the first 15 years of this century trying to reform their economies, notably Argentina, Venezuela, Mexico and Ecuador, were subjected to a total of

267 claims, which represented more than a quarter of worldwide claims in that period.

The International Finance System and Climate Change

Rockhopper and *Eco Oro* provide just two examples of how investor-state arbitration is used to stop national legislation aimed at curtailing their activities. The use of investor-state arbitration by the fossil fuel industry to protect its assets and activities puts investor protection ahead of climate action (IPCC 2022). In the years since the signing of the Paris Agreement, the fossil fuel industry has emerged as the "pioneer of the ISDS system" and "the most litigious industry in the ISDS" with a particular appetite for exploiting the opportunities of arbitration (Di Salvatore 2021, iii). More than a third of public fossil fuel arbitration decisions involve environmental aspects, with a rising trend in cases challenging specific climate actions, like fossil fuel phase-outs. In most of these cases, the investors win and the sums awarded in these cases, averaging over US$600 million, are up to five times that of non-fossil fuel cases (Di Salvatore 2021, iv). In other words, countries are finding themselves faced with the impossible task of meeting their obligations under the Paris Agreement and their legal obligations under international trade agreements (Tienhaara et al. 2022). The question of who determines the price for action on climate change should not, as it is now, be occurring behind the closed doors of investor-state arbitration tribunals.

While the Paris Agreement compels countries to act, many are frustrated with the apparent intransigence of national governments to respond and are turning to the courts. Untangling the relationships and networks of vested interests actively delaying action on climate change requires the inclusion of the international finance system, especially investor-state arbitration yet, as noted earlier, research in this area is limited. If we are to understand the reasons behind humanity's apparent unwillingness to respond swiftly to climate change, then we must look closely at how the Carbon Majors use law to hinder climate action. A good place to start would be the Energy Charter Treaty (ECT), which is the most frequently used treaty in matters relating to energy (Di Salvatore 2021). For instance, when the Dutch parliament passed a law banning coal burning for power generation, Germany's two largest energy companies, RWE and Uniper, sued the Dutch Government for the pending closure of two of their power plants (Taylor 2021). The Dutch Government responded to the case in the German courts and as part of a settlement, the German government agreed to take over 99 percent of Uniper in exchange for the company agreeing to withdraw its claim against the Netherlands. International media coverage of the announcement generally framed Germany's bailout of Uniper as a rescue package to avert energy shortages caused by Russia's invasion of Ukraine, with little or no mention of the company's stranded assets left by changes in Dutch policy or the use of the courts to resist action on climate and, failing that, making the Dutch people pay (Setzer and Higham 2022, 24). As noted earlier, controlling the narrative around investor-state arbitration includes managing public perception of international trade law and public attitudes to domestic policy and decision-making. Here, too, we find news and other media playing an important role in ensuring the transparency of decision-making informing the decarbonisation of economies.

As well as a focus on official announcements and news media coverage, much more can be learned by examining the extensive global exchange of ideas and approaches among the networks influencing government decisions. Here we can learn more about the communication strategies that enable powerful interests to avoid media scrutiny while they stall the momentum of public participation and good governance and decision making away from the public eye.

Conclusion: Green Lawfare as Retaliation

More than half a century of environmental protest has led to a global movement with complex mediated networks that are rising to meet the complex and transnational challenge of climate change and other global crises. In *Rockhopper,* the Italian Government's decision to ban gas and oil drilling was in response to a well-organized campaign that "inherited connections and strategies" from previous campaigns and was regarded by some as a "last step in a continuous history of local resistance" (Cernison 2018). In the case of *Eco Oro*, local organizers were assisted by transnational organizations and NGOS, including the Centre for International Environmental Law and MiningWatch Canada. Examining the communication networks and legal strategies of this growing area of activity can bring insights to the contemporary formation of social movements and legal mobilization, but which must include the efforts to control mediated visibility and the flow of information by those resisting change, described here as "retaliation". Such instances, can be found in defamation and other litigation aimed at silencing critics; the increased, and often draconian, policing of protest and other campaign activity; the surveillance of protesters, campaigners and journalists, which includes harassment and breaches of privacy; and, finally, the use of the international finance system to protect the vested interests of a few at the expense, literal and otherwise, of the common good. In each of these instances, law can be seen as a tool used to assert and maintain the hegemonic power of nation-states and corporate interests. While each example and case study here carries its own particularities, each illustrates how law can be used to "chill" the actions of individuals, organizations, and governments seeking to shape a better world for all.

It would be easy to feel defeated by the extent to which law can be used to quash dissent and the imaginaries of more sustainable futures, so it is worth pausing here to look at an example of a long-running campaign, which was the long fight against the Keystone XL pipeline in the United States, in which campaigners withstood the full gamut of green lawfare described in this chapter to achieve their goals.

Keystone XL Pipeline

The proposed Keystone XL pipeline was designed to pump oil sands and some crude oil from Alberta, Canada across the United States to refineries on the Texas Gulf Coast. The green lawfare enacted during the battle over the pipeline included SLAPPs and criminal charges against protesters, changes to public participation laws, surveillance of activists, an investor-state dispute settlement, and plenty of media attention. The fight over the pipeline drew protests from Native Americans, environmentalists, climate activists, ranchers and many others who gathered along the route and in the cities to show their disapproval of the pipeline. Rolling protests and mass arrests became a key motif in this long-running fight until eventually the company, TransCanada, announced it would abandon plans in 2021. But let's start at the beginning.

In January 2013, TransCanada initiated a SLAPP against a group of activists and organizations from the Tar Sands Blockade claiming that protests blockading the building of the Keystone XL pipeline had resulted in a financial loss of $5 million for TransCanada. In an out-of-court settlement, the eight Texans faced with losing their homes for speaking out agreed to stop and the costs against them were dropped. While eight were silenced, news media coverage of the case and ongoing protests carried the voices of many others who said they would not be deterred (Terry 2013) and the campaign continued until the Obama administration vetoed its construction in 2015.

In 2016, TransCanada Corporation launched an investor-state arbitration case for compensation in response, which was reported by some to be a decision based as much on politics as it was on policy (Cryderman and McCarthy 2016). In its claim, *TransCanada v. United States*, TransCanada argued for $15 billion, which was five times more than the $3.1 billion that TransCanada said it already had invested in the pipeline project. Up until this time, the United States had never lost a NAFTA lawsuit, but the Keystone XL pipeline debate coincided with negotiations on the Paris Agreement in which both the United States and Canada were pressing for stricter temperature limits, which put more media attention on TransCanada's case against the United States than might normally be expected (Goldenberg 2016). The result was a national debate over the merits of the international finance system, with Republican voices warning that American taxpayers would have to foot the bill for "potentially billions of dollars in fines and legal costs" that contrasted with the likes of environmental campaigner Bill McKibben, who said: "The idea that some trade agreement should force us to overheat the planet's atmosphere is, quite simply, insane" (Goldenberg 2016).

As the debate raged, there was political pressure to control protesters, which included the introduction of anti-protest laws. It was later revealed that between November 2012 and June 2014, the FBI had closely monitored anti-pipeline activists and "collated inside knowledge about forthcoming protests, documented the identities of individuals photographing oil-related infrastructure, scrutinized police intelligence and cultivated at least one informant" (Lewis and Federman 2015). In 2017 President Donald Trump announced he would permit the completion of the Keystone XL pipeline and construction resumed, as did protests against the pipeline. In 2021, President Joe Biden revoked the permit and TransCanada, rebranded as TC Energy, announced it would abandon its plans.

The Keystone XL protest was notable for the combination of old-school protests and newer forms of digital activism that used media to maintain political pressure until the project was neither financially nor politically viable (Hamilton 2016; Hodges and Stocking 2016). The Keystone XL battle also showed the extent to which the "climate periphery," that is action not directly related to reducing greenhouse gas emissions but rather contributing to the legal, political, or economic changes necessary to climate action, play an important role in the ongoing struggle to reduce global emissions. As

Hamilton (2016, 27) writes, the movement to stop the pipeline had to take a "diffuse and multifaceted" path that included finding legal opportunities relating to private property rights, challenges to collusion between industry players and administrative decision-makers and defending anti-pipeline activists in court over criminal charges. He writes that while:

> These efforts shifted judicial attention away from climate-change harms and toward various supports, effects, and causes of the fossil fuel economy [and] the success of these legal actions was measured less by individual courtroom victories than by contributions to the lengthy delay and the ultimate, decidedly political rejection of the pipeline. (Hamilton 2016, 27)

Beyond the courts, Hamilton (2016, 36) adds that the success of the Keystone XL protest can be measured in how the protest activities kept that the battle against the fossil fuel industry shaped media coverage and public opinion for years, including drawing legal attention to corporate and federal malfeasance and reframing the battle as a "political confrontation rather than as a scientific or administrative issue" (Hamilton 2016, 277). Seen in this light, the battle over the Keystone XL reminds us of Lazarus's (2023) observation that the legal cases that build environmental and climate law are built on moments when openings are found in small ways to contribute towards a bigger picture. While it can be said that the pipeline found some reprieve with the election of Donald Trump, overall the power of public attention and action prevailed. While the story on some days may have been a local court trying a bunch of protesters for trespass, it is difficult to determine the ripple effects of that story on the momentum built over nearly a decade that ultimately defeated the pipeline.

Comprehending the often unseen or poorly understood pressures that limit our responses toward a better future, this chapter examined three legal areas used to control efforts to address climate change and other environmental crises. In each area, questions of balance—between free speech and false information; between the right to petition and the need to maintain public order; between securing investor confidence and protecting sovereign interests—were tested in courts and tribunals, but also in the court of public opinion. Mediated networks and news and other media are part of this momentum. Mediated visibility of SLAPPs, increased and forceful policing, state and corporate surveillance, and the privileging of corporate profits over the public interest, provide the scrutiny needed for citizens to debate the acceptable levels of government oversight of the transnational finance system and corporate activity. Invisibility provides immunity to the powerful. Without publicity about the tactics described in this chapter, the ongoing inaction by some governments on climate change and other environmental issues will remain bewildering, even testament to humanity's inability to prevent its own extinction. In contrast, wide publicity about the use of SLAPPs, increased policing and laws limiting public participation, collusion between state and private interests in surveillance, and the use of investments to resist efforts to act, shines a light on the individuals, organizations and social structures, at local, national and international levels, that are actively resisting efforts to respond to the global ecological and social crises the world faces. Understanding and communicating the systems of this resistance is part of telling the story of how we can act to protect the environment, and therefore ourselves, from the tyranny of greed.

References

Alexander, Jeffrey C. 2006. *The Civil Sphere*. Oxford and New York: Oxford University Press.

Appadurai, Arjun. 2000. "Grassroots Globalization and the Research Imagination." *Public Culture* 12 (1): 1–19.

Balaji, R. 2021. "Pegasus: Paranjoy Guhathakurta Moves Sc Against Snooping Scandal." *The Telegraph*, August 3. https://www.telegraphindia.com/india/pegasus-paranjoy-guha-thakurta-moves-sc-against-snooping-scandal/cid/1825006 (Accessed May 5, 2023).

Barrett, Jonathan. 2023. "US Activist Investor Who Accused Adani of 'Biggest Con in Corporate History' Dares Indian Group to Sue." *The Guardian*, January 27. https://www.theguardian.com/business/2023/jan/27/hindenburg-research-dares-adani-group-to-sue (Accessed May 5, 2023).

Behrens, Eva. 2023. "The European Commission's Anti-SLAPP Directive Is a Step in the Right Direction, But Member States Need to Pass Anti-SLAPP Laws Too." Center for Data Innovation (blog). February 24. https://datainnovation.org/2023/02/the-european-commissions-anti-slapp-directive-is-a-step-in-the-right-direction-but-member-states-need-to-pass-anti-slapp-laws-too/ (Accessed May 5, 2023).

Beresford, Quentin. 2015. *The Rise and Fall of Gunns Ltd.* Sydney: NewSouth.

Bernasconi-Osterwalder, Nathalie. 2011. "Chevron v. Ecuador." International Institute for Sustainable Development (blog). https://www.iisd.org/projects/chevron-v-ecuador (Accessed August 22, 2023).

Brown. Alleen. 2020. "In the Mercenaries' Own Words: Documents Detail TigerSwan Infiltration of Standing Rock." *The Intercept*, November 15. https://theintercept.com/2020/11/15/standing-rock-tigerswan-infiltrator-documents/ (Accessed May 5, 2023).

Brown, Alleen. 2022. "New Federal Anti-SLAPP Legislation Would Protect Activists and Whistleblowers from Abusive Lawsuits." Inside Climate News (blog). September 23, 2022.

https://insideclimatenews.org/news/23092022/new-federal-anti-slapp-legislation-would-protect-activists-and-whistleblowers-from-abusive-lawsuits (Accessed May 5, 2023).

Brown, Alleen, Will Parrish, and Alice Speri. 2017. "Dakota Access Pipeline Company Paid Mercenaries to Build Conspiracy Lawsuit Against Environmentalists." *The Intercept*, November 16. https://theintercept.com/2017/11/15/dakota-access-pipeline-dapl-tigerswan-energy-transfer-partners-rico-lawsuit/ (Accessed May 5, 2023).

Bruff, Ian. 2014. "The Rise of Authoritarian Neoliberalism." *Rethinking Marxism* 26 (1): 113–129.

Bruff, Ian, and Cemal Burak Tansel. 2019. "Authoritarian Neoliberalism: Trajectories of Knowledge Production and Praxis." *Globalizations* 16 (3): 233–244.

Brutger, Ryan, and Anton Strezhnev. 2022. "International Investment Disputes, Media Coverage, and Backlash Against International Law." *Journal of Conflict Resolution* 66 (6): 983–1009.

Bullough, Oliver. 2022. "SLAPP: How UK Libel Law Helps Oligarchs Silence Journalists." *openDemocracy* (blog). September 22. https://www.opendemocracy.net/en/oliver-bullough-oligarchs-libel-journalism-slapp/ (Accessed May 5, 2023).

Burgis, Tom. 2021. *Kleptopia: How Dirty Money Is Conquering the World.* London: William Collins.

Business and Human Rights Resource Centre. 2022. "Slapps in Latin America: Strategic Lawsuits Against Public Participation in the Context of Business and Human Rights." Business and Human Rights Resource Centre (blog). https://www.business-humanrights.org/en/from-us/briefings/slapps-in-latin-america/ (Accessed August 22, 2023).

Canan, Penelope. 1989. "The SLAPP from a Sociological Perspective." *Pace Environmental Law Review* 7 (1): 23–32.

Canan, Penelope, and George W. Pring. 1988. "Strategic Lawsuits Against Public Participation." *Social Problems* 35(5): 506–519.

Castells, Manuel. 2009. *Communication Power*. Oxford: Oxford University Press.

Cernison, Matteo. 2016. The No Ombrina/No Triv protests in Abruzzo: Organisational models and scales of action. *Cosmos–Centre on Social Movement Studies*, European University Institute. Available: https://cosmos.sns.it/wp-content/uploads/2018/01/Cernison_No_Oil_Abruzzo.pdf. (Accessed August 22, 2023).

Chriki, David. 2020. "Strapping Down Regulatory Space with Investment Arbitration: A New Breed Of International SLAPPs." *Georgetown Journal of International Law* 51: 415–447.

Cooban, Anna. 2022. "UK Police Arrest Journalists Covering a Climate Protest." *CNN*, November 10, 2022. https://edition.cnn.com/2022/11/10/media/uk-journalist-arrests-climate-protest/index.html (Accessed August 22, 2023).

Corderoy, Jenna. 2023. "Exclusive: Environmental Campaigners 'Spied on' Ahead of Sadiq Khan Event." openDemocracy (blog). February 2, 2023. https://www.opendemocracy.net/en/environmental-campaigners-spied-on-mayor-london-sadiq-khan-o2/ (Accessed August 22, 2023).

Cotula, Lorenzo. 2023. "International Investment Law and Climate Change: Reframing the ISDS Reform Agenda." *The Journal of World Investment & Trade* 24 (4–5): 766–91. https://doi.org/10.1163/22119000-12340310.

Coughtrie, Susan, and Poppy Ogier. 2020. "Unsafe for Scrutiny: Examining the Pressures Faced by Journalists Uncovering Financial Crime and Corruption around the World." The Foreign Policy Centre. https://fpc.org.uk/wp-content/uploads/2020/11/Unsafe-for-Scrutiny-November-2020.pdf (Accessed August 22, 2023).

Council of Europe. 2023. "War in Europe and the Fight for the Right to Report." Council of Europe. https://cpj.org/wp-content/uploads/2023/03/CoE_report_03-07-2023.pdf.

Cryderman, Kelly, and Shawn McCarthy. 2016. "Anti-Pipeline Accord Could Deepen Divide in Indigenous Communities." *Globe and Mail*, September 23, 2016. https://www.theglobeandmail.com/report-on-business/industry-news/energy-and-resources/anti-pipeline-accord-could-deepen-divide-in-indigenous-communities/article32032426/ (Accessed August 22, 2023).

Darian-Smith, Eve. 2022. *Global Burning: Rising Antidemocracy and the Climate Crisis*. Stanford University Press.

Diaz Crego, Maria, and Micaela Del Del Monte. 2022. "Strategic Lawsuits against Public Participation (SLAPPs)." European Parliamentary Research Service. https://www.europarl.europa.eu/RegData/etudes/BRIE/2022/733668/EPRS_BRI(2022)733668_EN.pdf (Accessed August 22, 2023).

Di Salvatore, Lea. 2021. *Investor-State Disputes in the Fossil Fuel Industry*. Winnipeg: International Institute for Sustainable Development.

Donson, Fiona. 2010. "Libel Cases and Public Debate—Some Reflections on Whether Europe Should Be Concerned about SLAPPs: Should Europe Be Concerned About SLAPPs?" *Review of European Community & International Environmental Law* 19 (1): 83–94.

Dutta, Nikhil. 2020. "SLAPPs in the Global South: Features and Policy Responses." International Center for Not-for-Profit Law (ICNL). https://www.icnl.org/wp-content/uploads/SLAPPs-in-the-Global-South-vf.pdf (Available August 22, 2023).

Ellis-Petersen, Hannah. 2021. "India: Activist Arrested over Protest 'toolkit' Shared by Greta Thunberg." *The Guardian*, February 15, 2021. https://www.theguardian.com/world/2021/feb/15/india-activist-arrested-over-protest-toolkit-shared-by-greta-thunberg

European Federation of Journalists (EFJ). 2023. "Climate Journalists in Europe Face Harassment and Threats." Ifex (blog). January 9, 2023. https://ifex.org/climate-journalists-in-europe-face-harassment-and-threats/#:~:text=In%202022%2C%20several%20journalists%20reporting,central%20Serbia%20received%20death%20threats (Available August 22, 2023).

Evans, Jack. 2022. "Rage over Government-Run Sydney Food Event Which Blocked the Light Rail," *news.com.au*, December 3, 2022. https://www.news.com.au/national/nsw-act/news/rage-over-governmentrun-sydney-food-event-which-blocked-the-light-rail/news-story/f9991969a694b06c8df6fbca9ae88a37 (Available August 22, 2023).

Fabry, Adam, and Sune Sandbeck. 2019. "Introduction to Special Issue on 'Authoritarian Neoliberalism.'" *Competition & Change* 23 (2): 109–115.

Garside, Juliette, and Jonathan Watts. 2019. "Environment Reporters Facing Harassment and Murder, Study Finds." *The Guardian*, June 18. https://www.theguardian.com/environment/2019/jun/17/environment-reporters-facing-harassment-murder-study (Accessed August 22, 2023).

Giddens, Anthony. 1984. *The Constitution of Society: Outline of the Theory of Structuration*. Berkeley: University of California Press.

Gijs, Camille, Federica Di Sario, and Karl Mathiesen. 2023. "Brussels Backtracks: EU Prepares to Quit Dirty Energy Club." *Politico*. https://www.politico.eu/article/european-union-quit-dirty-energy-treaty-commission-climate-goals/ (Accessed August 22, 2023).

Goldenberg, Suzanne. 2016. "Keystone XL Company Takes Legal Action after Obama 'Overstepped Authority.'" *The Guardian*. https://www.theguardian.com/environment/2016/jan/06/keystone-xl-transcanada-lawsuit-obama-nafta (Accessed August 22, 2023).

Gov.UK. 2023. "Public Order Bill Factsheet." (website) https://www.gov.uk/government/publications/public-order-bill-overarching-documents/public-order-bill-factsheet#background (Accessed August 22, 2023).

Gregoire, Paul. 2022. "The Death of Protest in NSW: An Interview with Greens MLC Abigail Boyd." Sydney Criminal Lawyers (blog). April 6, 2022. https://www.sydneycriminallawyers.com.au/blog/the-death-of-protest-in-nsw-an-interview-with-greens-mlc-abigail-boyd/ (Accessed August 22, 2023).

Guamán, Adoración. 2020. "Lex Mercatoria, Market Authoritarianism and Popular Resistance." The Transnational Institute Longreads (blog). January 18. https://longreads.tni.org/stateofpower/architecture-of-impunity (Accessed August 22, 2023).

Guillot, Louise. 2023. "France Disbands Climate Movement over 'Eco-Terrorism' Allegations." *Politico*, June. https://www.politico.eu/article/france-emmanuel-macron-disbands-climate-movement-eco-terrorism-allegations-soulevement-de-la-terre/ (Accessed August 22, 2023).

Hamilton, Ted. 2016. "The Virtues of Uncertainty: Lessons from the Legal Battles Over the Keystone Xl Pipeline." *Vermont Journal of Environmental Law* 8 (2): 222–286.

Harris, Paul. 2019. "Arbitration Court Rejects NGOs in Eco Oro Case." *Mining Journal*, February 22, 2019. https://www.mining-journal.com/gold-and-silver-news/news/1357181/arbitration-court-rejects-ngos-in-eco-oro-case (Accessed August 22, 2023).

Head, Michael. 2023. "Defending the Right to Protest." *Griffith Journal of Law & Human Dignity* 11 (1): 70–91.

Hodges, Heather E., and Galen Stocking. 2016. "A Pipeline of Tweets: Environmental Movements' Use of Twitter in Response to the Keystone XL Pipeline." *Environmental Politics* 25 (2): 223–247.

IPCC. 2022. "Climate Change 2022: Impacts, Adaptation and Vulnerability. Contribution of Working Group II to the Sixth Assessment Report of the Intergovernmental Panel on Climate Change." https://www.ipcc.ch/report/ar6/wg2/ (Accessed August 22, 2023).

Ismail, Feyzi, and Sangeeta Kamat. 2018. "NGOs, Social Movements and the Neoliberal State: Incorporation, Reinvention, Critique." *Critical Sociology* 44 (4–5): 569–577.

Lester, Libby. 2019. *Global Trade and Mediatised Environmental Protest: The View from Here*. Cham: Springer International Publishing.

Lester, Libby, and Brett Hutchins. 2012. "The Power of the Unseen: Environmental Conflict, the Media and Invisibility." *Media, Culture & Society* 34 (7): 847–863.

Lewis, Paul, and Adam Federman. 2015. "Revealed: FBI Violated Its Own Rules While Spying on Keystone XL Opponents." *The Guardian*, May 12. https://www.theguardian.

com/us-news/2015/may/12/revealed-fbi-spied-keystone-xl-opponents (Accessed August 21, 2023).

Loomes, Phoebe. 2022. "Throw Book at Climate Activists: Perrottet." *The West Australian*, December 5. https://thewest.com.au/news/environment/throw-book-at-climate-activists-perrottet-c-9065239 (Accessed August 21, 2023).

Manning, Paddy. 2011. "The Felling of Gunns." *Sydney Morning Herald*, March 12. https://www.smh.com.au/national/the-felling-of-gunns-20110311-1br9d.html (Accessed August 21, 2023).

McCarthy, James. 2019. "Authoritarianism, Populism, and the Environment: Comparative Experiences, Insights, and Perspectives." *Annals of the American Association of Geographers* 109 (2): 301–313.

McGuinness, Damien, and Paul Kirby. 2011. "Bbc.Com-German Police Raid Climate Activists Who Blocked Traffic.Pdf." *BBC*, March 12. https://www.bbc.com/news/world-europe-65693412 (Accessed August 22, 2023).

Müller, Bettina, and Cecilia Olivet. 2019. *ISDS In Numbers: Impacts of Investment Arbitration Against African States*. Amsterdam: Transnational Institute.

Naldrett, Chloe. 2023. "Arrested for Wearing a T-Shirt? The Coronation Heralded a Frightening Slide towards Authoritarianism." *The Guardian*, May 7, 2023. https://www.theguardian.com/commentisfree/2023/may/07/coronation-just-stop-oil-republic-activists-peaceful-protests (Accessed August 22, 2023).

Noorlander, Peter. 2022. "Fighting SLAPPs: What Can Media, Lawyers, and Funders Do?" Washington, DC: The Center for International Media Assistance.

Ogle, Greg. 2010. "Anti-SLAPP Law Reform in Australia." *Review of European Community & International Environmental Law* 19 (1): 35–44.

Nosek, Grace. 2020. "The Fossil Fuel Industry's Push to Target Climate Protesters in the U.S." *Pace Environmental Law Review* 38 (1): 53–108.

Pender, Kieran. 2022. "In the Sharma Decision the Federal Court Says: We See the Climate Risk but Cannot Act." *The Guardian*, March 16, 2022 (Accessed August 22, 2023).

Pring, George W. 1989. "SLAPPs: Strategic Lawsuits against Public Participation." *Pace Environmental Law Review* 7 (1): 3–22.

Pring, George W., and Penelope Canan. 1992. "Strategic Lawsuits against Public Participation (SLAPPs): An Introduction for Bench, Bar and Bystanders." *University of Bridgeport Law Review* 12 (4): 937–962.

Puig, Sergio, and Anton Strezhnev. 2017. "The David Effect and ISDS." *European Journal of International Law* 28 (3): 731–761.

Regilme, Salvador Santino F. 2019. "The Decline of American Power and Donald Trump: Reflections on Human Rights, Neoliberalism, and the World Order." *Geoforum* 102 (June): 157–166.

Robertson, Geoffrey. 2023. *Lawfare: How Russians, the Rich and the Government Try to Prevent Free Speech and How to Stop Them*. London: TLS Books.

Rucz, Melinda. 2022. "SLAPPed by the GDPR: Protecting Public Interest Journalism in the Face of GDPR-Based Strategic Litigation against Public Participation." *Journal of Media Law* 14 (2): 378–405.

Setzer, Joana, and Catherine Higham. 2022. "Global Trends in Climate Change Litigation: 2022 Snapshot." London: Grantham Research Institute on Climate Change and the Environment and Centre for Climate Change Economics and Policy, London School of Economics and Political Science.

Sheldrick, Byron M. 2014. *Blocking Public Participation: The Use of Strategic Litigation to Silence Political Expression*. Waterloo: Wilfrid Laurier University Press.

Smee, Ben. 2019. "Adani Protest: French Journalists Arrested While Filming Anti-Coal Activities." *The Guardian*, July 4. https://www.theguardian.com/business/2019/jul/22/adani-protest-french-journalists-arrested-while-filming-anti-coal-activities (Accessed August 22, 2023).

Stanley, Jay. 2004. "The Surveillance Industrial Complex: How the American Government Is Conscripting Businesses and Individuals in the Construction of a Surveillance Society." American Civil Liberties Union. https://www.aclu.org/files/FilesPDFs/surveillance_report.pdf (Accessed August 22, 2023).

Stoddart, Mark C. J., D. B. Tindall, and Riley E. Dunlap. 2022. "The Contours of Anti-Environmentalism: An Introduction to the Handbook of Anti-Environmentalism." In *Handbook of Anti-Environmentalism*, edited by D. B. Tindall, Mark C. J. Stoddart, and Riley E. Dunlap. Cheltenham and Northampton: Edward Elgar Publishing.

Sydney Morning Herald. "Gunns Logging Case to Be Lengthy: Judge." *Sydney Morning Herald*. https://www.smh.com.au/business/gunns-logging-case-to-be-lengthy-judge-20050617-gdlj5o.html (Accessed August 22, 2023).

Taylor, Gordon. 2007. "Abc.Net.Au-Gunns Decision.Pdf." *ABC RN*, April 4, 2007. https://www.abc.net.au/listen/programs/radionational-breakfast/gunns-decision/3396322 (Accessed August 22, 2023).

Terry, Bobbie. 2013. "Activists Settle Lawsuit against Keystone XL Pipeline, TransCanada Claimed $5 Million in Damages." https://www.cbs19.tv/article/news/activists-settle-lawsuit-against-keystone-xl-pipeline-transcanada-claimed-5-million-in-damages/501-266419693 (Accessed August 22, 2023).

Thompson, John B. 1995. *The Media and Modernity: A Social Theory of the Media*. Stanford: Stanford University Press.

———. 2005. "The New Visibility." *Theory, Culture & Society* 22 (6): 31–51.

———. 2020. "Mediated Interaction in the Digital Age." *Theory, Culture & Society* 37 (1): 3–28.

Tienhaara, Kyla. 2011. "Regulatory Chill and the Threat of Arbitration: A View from Political Science." In *Evolution in Investment Treaty Law and Arbitration*, edited by Chester Brown and Kate Miles, 1st ed., 606–628. Cambridge: Cambridge University Press.

Tienhaara, Kyla. 2018. "Regulatory Chill in a Warming World: The Threat to Climate Policy Posed by Investor-State Dispute Settlement." *Transnational Environmental Law* 7 (2): 229–250.

Tienhaara, Kyla, Rachel Thrasher, B. Alexander Simmons, and Kevin P. Gallagher. 2022. "Investor-State Disputes Threaten the Global Green Energy Transition." *Science* 376 (6594): 701–703.

UNCTAD. 2022. "Treaty-Based Investor-State Dispute Settlement Cases and Climate Action." United Nations Conference on Trade and Development. https://unctad.org/system/files/official-document/diaepcbinf2022d7_en.pdf (Accessed May 5, 2023).

Vick, Douglas W., and Kevin Campbell. 2001. "Public Protests, Private Lawsuits, and the Market: The Investor Response to the McLibel Case." *Journal of Law and Society* 28 (2): 204–241.

Council of Europe. 2023. "War in Europe and the Fight for the Right to Report." Council of Europe, March 7. https://www.coe.int/en/web/portal/-/safety-of-journalists-platform-2023-report-a-war-on-journalism-in-parts-of-europe (Accessed May 5, 2023).

White, Rob. 2005. "Stifling Environmental Dissent: On SLAPPS and Gunns." *Alternative Law Journal* 30 (6): 268–273.

Wu, Dihu. 2023. ICSID tribunal finds that Italy committed an unlawful expropriation under ECT's Art. 13(1). The International Institute for Sustainable Development (IISD) April 2, 2023. Available: https://www.iisd.org/itn/en/2023/04/02/icsid-tribunal-finds-that-italy-committed-an-unlawful-expropriation-under-ects-art-131/#_ftn2. (Accessed August 22, 2023).

Zhao, Mary. 2019. "Transparency in International Commercial Arbitration: Adopting a Balanced Approach." *Virginia Journal of International Law* 175: 175–219.

Zuluaga, Lady Nancy, and Christen Dobson. 2021. "Slapped but Not Silenced: Defending Human Rights in the Face of Legal Risks." https://media.business-humanrights.org/media/documents/2021_SLAPPs_Briefing_EN_v657.pdf (Accessed August 22, 2023).

Cases

Chevron Corporation and Texaco Petroleum Corporation v. Ecuador (II), PCA Case No. 2009-23.

Commonwealth v. Tasmania (1983) 158 CLR 1 (July 1, 1983).

Eco Oro Minerals Corp. v. Republic of Colombia (ICSID Case No. ARB/16/41).

Energy Transfer Equity, L.P. v. Greenpeace International, 1:17-cv-00173.

Greenpeace, Inc. v. The Dow Chemical Co., Case No. 13-CV-685 (D.C. C.A., August 21, 2014).

Gunns Ltd v. Marr [2005] VSC 251.

McDonald's Corporation v. Steel & Morris [1997] EWHC 366 (QB).

Mineral Sands Resources (Pty) Ltd and Others v. Reddell and Others (CCT 66/21) [2022] ZACC 37 (November 14, 2022).

Rockhopper Exploration Plc, Rockhopper Italia S.p.A. and Rockhopper Mediterranean Ltd v. Italian Republic, ICSID Case No. ARB/17/14.

TransCanada Corporation and TransCanada PipeLines Limited v. United States of America (I) (ICSID Case No. ARB/16/21).

· 8 ·

COMMUNICATING COMMON GROUND

This book set out to describe and better understand the strategic use of law during mediatized environmental conflict. It is an interdisciplinary bridge-building project using key concepts and approaches across a range of disciplines to conceptualize how networks of actors engage with law—including legal systems, concepts and principles—to achieve political, social, and economic objectives. In doing so, the discussion throughout this work located the deliberate strategies using the material and symbolic power of law and the symbolic power of media by a range of actors, including grass roots activists and transnational corporations, to influence political decision-making and governance.

This book is about connections rather than differences and it reaches far and wide to make these connections. Indeed, bridges can be precarious and can tell us as much about differences as they can connections. Scoping the terrain of any subject at a global level risks choosing breadth over depth. This book responds to Simon Cottle's (2023, 11–12) call for a "panoramic planetary vision" that risks the uncertainty of interdisciplinarity, which skates "on thin academic ice" beyond the certainties that are "ring-fenced in national contexts," to find the connective tissue of mediatized environmental conflict at local and transnational levels. Such a theoretical approach needs to be both universally recognizable, but also adaptable to local contexts and it needs to emphasize the "contagious ideas" informing developments in environmental law, including legal principles, understandings about humanity's relationship to the natural world, and communication strategies that circulate through global networks like seeds to be planted in different contexts. By continually returning to the interlocking activities of actors engaged in the strategic use of law, green lawfare is envisaged as part of a much wider struggle to bring visibility to environmental harm by observing the "bottom-up" pressure of protest and grassroots campaigns, the "top-down" influences of the international community, and the horizontal exchange of ideas and strategies across the mediated networks of grassroots activism, mainstream environmental politics and corporate interests that constitute contemporary environmental conflict.

As a bridge-building exercise, the theorization of green lawfare had to establish some "common ground" by locating media and communication in the early environmental movement and following the evolution of environmental communication. From the signing of Magna Carta and its lesser-known companion text, the Charter of the Forest, to more recent discussions around the Anthropocene, a common thread of struggle—against the occupation and enclosure of shared resources, the devasting forces of colonialization, and more recently, the economic logic and actors driving globalization—emerged as an enduring tension. This tension between greed and the common good is entwined throughout history and, to stretch the metaphor of the double helix even further, central to and replicated throughout the moments of resistance and retaliation described here. By identifying the tension between exploitation and conservation, self-interest and altruism, greed and temperance, individualism and collectivism as a historical basis for much of our ideas about law and justice, the lose "catch-all" of tyranny was adopted to describe the social force against which social movements resist, which echoes Jeffrey Alexander's (2006) notion of a greater project for solidarity:

> With this understanding of protest as an act of hope in mind, tyranny describes not only the injustices of theft and dispossession, discrimination, and marginalization but also the arrogance, willful ignorance and impunity, and other displays of hegemonic power that motivate resistance.

The ways in which the tension between solidarity and tyranny inform green lawfare can be understood as running parallel to Elizabeth Fisher's (2013) idea of environmental law being "hot law" that invites investigations into the non-legal influences on environmental law. By observing the changing social norms and political contexts influencing environmental law, we found networks of communication among activists, lawyers and others sharing "contagious" ideas, including new ideas and old principles, emerging and dominant discourses, and examples and strategies, being transplanted into various contexts and scenarios. The communication of these ideas can be found in news and other media; whether buried in a small news story, mentioned on the blogs and websites of interest groups, or lauded internationally as a landmark win, these ideas are the "green shoots" of hope planted amid dismal critiques of tyranny and the grim warnings of ecological catastrophe. The earliest buds of hope are found in sites, both real and virtual, where people gather to resist tyranny and put forward other imaginaries for society and the future.

The discussion drew on some early landmarks in environmental law, such as *Sierra Club v. Morton* and the *Tasmanian Dams* case, and several case studies showed the different ways law, media and politics are interlocked in action against industrial pollution (*Mehta v. Union of India*) and water catchments (*Eco Oro v. Colombia*). These cases all drew on legal mechanisms particular to their local contexts but also used legal principles and other contagious ideas from further afield to build a case for action to protect the environment and those who depend on it. Other cases were more explicitly transnational, such as Peruvian farmer Saúl Luciano Lliuya, who used a range of international principles and laws to challenge the assumed impunity of major carbon polluters. The discussions and case studies increasingly turned to examples of climate change. As a rapidly developing area of "hot law," the international work and principles informing climate law, such as the Paris Agreement, were noted for providing states with weak environmental provisions with access to legal principles that they could apply. Here news and other media form a communicative space for these ideas to be translated and tested in terms of public acceptance and political salience, making green lawfare an example of the extent to which the distinction between law and politics and principle and policy has blurred (Kennedy 2016, 238). We might consider then, that the pejorative view of green lawfare, especially by Australian conservatives, is not so much about the turn to litigation and other legal action to achieve environmental goals, but rather an unease with a communication environment that uses the legal system, not as a safe harbor for those avoiding the visibility of environmental politics, but as an arena of contest used to challenge the powerful.

Rather than treat the evolution of environmental and climate law as a linear trajectory, from small actions against individual projects to more complex cases targeting major polluters at an international level, the discussion presented the evolution of environmental law as a circular process that continually draws on the local and the global, the proven and the abstract, and the uncontested and the aspirational as a response to our shifting understanding of the nature of the environment and the remedies to its problems. In this sense, environmental law echoes the adaptive nature of Earth systems. In terms of early efforts to bring local environmental issues into the courts, more work is yet to be done on how green lawfare is informing the development of environmental law in specific locations. To observe the dynamics of green lawfare in local contexts, research might begin to find traces of efforts in the small news stories about local "eclectic" efforts to use what is at hand, such as planning laws, while also looking at the way government and private actors are using media and legal methods to quell these efforts. In countries with active judiciaries, news stories about questionable environmental practices might also prompt an inquiry into what constitutes an opening for action; in other places, news coverage of legal action may reveal the connections between discourses about law and policy.

As a communicative process, environmental law is understood to run parallel to the wider discourses and activities of the environmental movement, that long-running, global project that is both amorphous in its organization but distinctive in its aims. In particular, the environmental movement, especially the climate movement, is increasingly turning its attention to the structural affordances of globalization as the source of the problems it is trying to address. In doing so, it has adapted to the growing networks of news and other media which points to the opportunities and limitations of an increasingly fragmented and polarized mediascape. While the environmental movement may seem "old news" to some, the intersections of media, politics, activism and industry in the forming and reforming of environmental law make green lawfare a rich field from which to engage with questions about the flow of power in the real and virtual spaces where information and ideas are shared and visible, or controlled and silenced.

The interplay of science and scientists in the enactment of green lawfare, especially the communication of risk and the translation of science, remained parallel to much of the discussion. While the environmental movement as a project has moved well beyond the scientific discourses of the early ecologists, science continues to be carried into environmental discourses as evidence to support claims, for instance in the current turn to attribution science. While the discussion briefly alluded to debates about whether science can be regarded as a sphere of action, much like that of activism and media, whether science is a sphere of action in its own right, or a set of information and discourse used by other spheres remains unresolved. Certainly, when scientists, such as Friederike Otto, are outspoken about their goals to produce scientific knowledge to support legal action, the assumptions we make about science and scientists as objective arbiters of truth are challenged. Or given more nuance. Focusing on the emerging field of attribution science as an example of how science communication is being used strategically to progress climate action inside and outside of the courtroom is a rich area for further exploration. The interaction of scientists and lawyers, and science and law, also warrants closer inspection. Both science and law are characterized by particular knowledge, expertise and practices, yet their boundaries are porous and both scientists and lawyers clearly have various masters, including industry, that determine the nature of their work. Oreskes and Conway (2010) found parallels in the weaponization of science to confuse public debates about tobacco smoking and the hole in the ozone layer and similar work can be done to explore the role of law and lawyers, especially among the networks of private corporations, conservative think tanks and media, to spread confusion and doubt about action on climate.

Overall, several areas of green lawfare were described, including the use of protest in the early developments of environmental law; litigation and other legal action that draws on these laws; and the emerging efforts to attribute harm to specific actors. Critics may argue that law has long been the preferred instrument of the powerful, including the tyrants who ignore the rule of law in preference of arbitrary decrees, and that the conceptualization of green lawfare described here is too optimistically weighted in favor of the transformative potential of law. As a remedy, the penultimate chapter looked at how media and law are deployed strategically to control and silence those working toward a more sustainable future. Several seemingly disparate areas of green lawfare were examined, including strategic lawsuits against public participation (SLAPPs) and other legal action that is used to harass and intimidate critics; the rise in draconian anti-protest laws and the weaponization of police and private security; and, the use of the international finance system. Each of these areas encompasses large and distinctive areas of law, but all shared the hallmarks of deliberate efforts to silence the voices of dissent and chill public participation and democratic practices and confirmed that while law and media can be weaponized by all actors, the powerful tend to have bigger budgets. Some might also criticize attempts to translate environmental jurisprudence and other legal topics for wider audiences. However, these topics are important and while ideas of justice and fairness are universal, there is limited research into how law is understood as essential to healthy societies and environments. While much can be left to legal expertise, a lack of understanding of law leaves a huge gap between our frustration with the problems we face and an appreciation of some of the tools available to regulate human activities, including extractive industries, agriculture and urban development. In the absence of public understanding of rights and responsibilities, of the potential for brighter futures built on collective responsibility, are the voices of politicians and their friends in industry deriding efforts to protect our environment with fear campaigns about extremism and the burden of regulation.

There may be something to be learned from science communication when considering this void in the public understanding of law. Law and science are two siblings in the family of civil institutions that inform the institutions of governance. Compared to the public understanding of science, which is a well-established field of research, there is less effort applied to the public understanding of law, and even less to the public understanding of environmental law. Perhaps the argument would be that law is too diversely spread across various jurisdictions, or too specialized or too arcane to inspire much interest. But surely too, those deeply involved in their niches of microbiology and astrophysics might equally say there is little in their field of expertise that the public might grasp. Nevertheless, scientists are increasingly called on to engage with their wider community in order to improve public understanding of science and therefore, the legitimacy and authority of science—and attendant funding. A similar argument for law might be warranted. Perhaps the reliance on public funding provides a greater impetus for science than law to seek public approval but there are reasons beyond funding to engage with people. We might be challenged to find a parallel with the aims of science communication to encourage people to find the pleasure, enjoyment and attractiveness of science, but then again, we might find that increasing public understanding of law, like science, includes increasing awareness of the influence of that enterprise on society. Here we might take the justification for the communication of science, such as this excerpt borrowed from Miriam Solomon (2021), where "science" is substituted with "legal" to come up with a statement:

> In a democratic society … it is important for the public, as well as legislators, to be able to understand the legal background to environmental policy questions. This is

> because the public vote, they take political action, and—in a strong democracy—they participate in deliberation.

Beyond the obvious advantages of informed public participation, we can also think about public understanding of environmental law in terms of enforcement. Governments and their agencies rely on non-governmental bodies (and the wider public overall) to identify potential breaches of environmental law, so it makes sense that these agencies provide resources, such as informational materials on agencies' websites explaining policies and laws and directing concerned citizens to external resources. As well as enhancing the quality of complaints and saving agency time and resources, including public understanding of environmental law in agency strategies would facilitate effective public involvement in all environmental protection, not just the enforcement of laws. But we have digressed and should return to the areas presented by this initial foray into green lawfare that might warrant further investigation.

Future Directions for Green Lawfare Research

This work is both speculative and hypothetical and written to encourage further inquiry. As well as some of the suggestions noted above, we might look more closely at the environmental challenges of our increasingly mediated social life. For instance, what are the intersections of media, law and policy relating to the impacts of manufacturing, operating and disposing of digital technologies, such as the ubiquitous smartphone? Or the environmental impact of the energies and materials spent on storing big data in "the cloud," which remains mostly fossil fuel dependent, and blockchain technology which is a major contributor to greenhouse gas emissions (Truby 2018) and the associated harms of any technology reliant on mining and manufacture.

As the demand for digital technologies continues to grow, there will be increasing calls for regulation on environmental grounds. For now, environmental impact assessments are the main tool in managing the impact of mining, manufacture, and disposal of e-waste, a term that points to the social and environmental problem of disposing the tons of toxic plastic and rare earth metals associated with our communication technologies. To date, the built-in redundancy in media and communication technology (as with most other products) contributes to the problem, so too does the prioritizing of economic opportunities over environmental and social gains. How, then, can news media producers and users—which includes most of us—navigate the environmental damage caused by the technologies we use to communicate change?

Throughout the cases discussed here, "big data" emerges as a source of information for scientists but also police and security agencies, suggesting more work is to be done to better understand how the large datasets are used to interpret the natural and human worlds to various ends. While much of this book acknowledged the ways in which environmentalists are early adopters of communication technology, their opponents have also shown similar enthusiasm. For instance, while global digital networks enable the flow of information between activists, such channels are also vulnerable to surveillance by governments and private interests. What do developments, including facial recognition technology, mean for public participation in protests and demonstrations? And what happens to public participation when recognition technologies force people online leaving artificial intelligence to scour the Internet for their conversations (Schneir 2015, 31)? In the realm of attribution science, big data is already providing new analytical tools and methodologies to produce the scientific knowledge used to guide action on climate, but much of the work on attribution science is being undertaken by small groups of mostly Anglophone scientists. As such, the communication of attribution science is potentially a distorted picture, and such a distortion invites questions as to the practices and processes that contribute to the misrepresentation (Lajaunie et al. 2019).

The twin and entwined ecological crises of climate change and ecological collapse demand action, perhaps even a "new story", but we need more than stories. If we are going to draw from the well of media and communication theory, we can find more than the idea of storytelling. Instead, further work into green lawfare might consider the dialogue made possible by the networks that are sharing contagious ideas and strategies. In that sense, some of the most interesting voices being heard are those coming from the peripheries, not the centers of global hegemony. But who is listening to these voices? If we return to the early debates about green lawfare in 2015—when Australia's national environment laws led to a little-known lizard and snake providing the best legal grounds for stopping a massive coal mine—we saw the emergence of a particularly articulate contempt for the use of law to protect our natural environments and those trying to protect them. That contempt for the democratic possibilities of law continues to grow in Australia and elsewhere, evidenced by efforts to wind back the protections already in place to support the natural world and its defenders. All the while, efforts to install a global framework for climate governance continue, mixed as that project is with the hopes for global solidarity and the colonializing tendencies of universalism. The struggle to use the authority of law to protect and exploit is an old story. The question is who is speaking for law as a democratizing force that can be used to keep the tyrannies of greed at bay?

References

Alexander, Jeffrey C. 2006. *The Civil Sphere*. Oxford and New York: Oxford University Press.

Burns, Terry, John O'Connor, and Susan Stocklmayer. 2003. "Science Communication: A Contemporary Definition." *Public Understanding of Science* 12 (2): 183–202.

Cottle, Simon. 2023. "Reporting Civilizational Collapse Research Notes from a World-in-Crisis." *Global Media and Communication* 19 (2): 269–288.

Fisher, Elizabeth. 2013. "Environmental Law as 'Hot' Law." *Journal of Environmental Law* 25 (3): 347–358.

Hutchins, Brett, and Libby Lester. 2015. "Theorizing the Enactment of Mediatized Environmental Conflict." *International Communication Gazette* 77 (4): 337–358.

Kennedy, David. 2016. A *World of Struggle: How Power, Law, and Expertise Shape Global Political Economy*. Princeton: Princeton University Press.

Lajaunie, Claire, Burkhard Schafer, and Pierre Mazzega. 2019. "Big Data Enters Environmental Law." *Transnational Environmental Law* 8 (3): 523–545.

Oreskes, Naomi, and Erik M. Conway. 2010. *Merchants of Doubt: How a Handful of Scientists Obscured the Truth on Issues from Tobacco Smoke to Global Warming*. Bloomsbury Press.

Schneier, Bruce. 2015. *Secrets and Lies: Digital Security in a Networked World*. 15th anniversary ed. Indianapolis: John Wiley & Sons.

Solomon, Miriam. 2021. "Trust: *The Need for Public Understanding of How Science Works*." *Hastings Center Report* 51. https://doi.org/10.1002/hast.1227

Truby, Jon. 2018. "Decarbonizing Bitcoin: Law and Policy Choices for Reducing the Energy Consumption of Blockchain Technologies and Digital Currencies." *Energy Research & Social Science* 44 (October): 399–410. https://doi.org/10.1016/j.erss.2018.06.009.

INDEX

A

B

C

F

G

H

J

K

L

M

R

S

T

U

V

W

Simon Cottle, *General Editor*

From climate change to the war on terror, financial meltdowns to forced migrations, pandemics to world poverty, and humanitarian disasters to the denial of human rights, these and other crises represent the dark side of our globalized planet. They are endemic to the contemporary global world and so too are they highly dependent on the world's media.

Each of the specially commissioned books in the *Global Crises and the Media* series examines the media's role, representation, and responsibility in covering major global crises. They show how the media can enter into their constitution, enacting them on the public stage and thereby helping to shape their future trajectory around the world. Each book provides a sophisticated and empirically engaged understanding of the topic in order to invigorate the wider academic study and public debate about the most pressing and historically unprecedented global crises of our time.

For further information about the series and submitting manuscripts, please contact:

Dr. Simon Cottle
Cardiff School of Journalism
Cardiff University, Room 1.28
The Bute Building, King Edward VII Ave.
Cardiff CF10 3NB
United Kingdom
CottleS@cardiff.ac.uk

To order other books in this series, please contact our Customer Service Department at:

peterlang@presswarehouse.com (within the U.S.)
order@peterlang.com (outside the U.S.)

Or browse online by series:

www.peterlang.com

www.ingramcontent.com/pod-product-compliance
Ingram Content Group UK Ltd.
Pitfield, Milton Keynes, MK11 3LW, UK
UKHW021058130926
8556IPUK00046B/1168

9 781433 19644